Women and Mental Health

We know that gender traits and mental disorders are based on social, cultural, personal and physiological background. In order to formulate the best management plan for the patient, the mental health practitioner needs to incorporate all available information.

Women and Mental Health provides a comprehensive overview of the most prominent mental health problems in women today. Examining the physiological, social and psychological factors of mental illness, and providing an up-to-date perspective on the etiology of different disorders, the book will help mental health professionals formulate the best management plan for the individual.

Covering issues including **perinatal psychiatric disorders**, **depression**, **eating disorders**, **schizophrenia**, and **alcohol and drug abuse** – from a female perspective – *Women and Mental Health* will prove a valuable tool for all those working in the fields of mental health.

Dora Kohen is a Consultant Psychiatrist and an Honorary Senior Lecturer. She runs an acute psychiatric service for women.

Women and Mental Health

2
6

Edited by Dora Kohen

London and Philadelphia

First published 2000 by Routledge
11 New Fetter Lane, London EC4P 4EE

Simultaneously published in the USA and Canada
by Taylor & Francis Inc., 325 Chestnut Street, Philadelphia, PA 19106

Routledge is an imprint of the Taylor & Francis Group

© 2000 Dora Kohen, editorial matter and selection; individual chapters,
the contributors

Typeset in Times by Mayhew Typesetting
Printed and bound in Great Britain by Biddles Ltd, www.biddles.co.uk

British Library Cataloguing in Publication Data
A catalogue record for this book is available from the British Library

Library of Congress Cataloging in Publication Data
Women and mental health / edited by Dora Kohen
    p. cm.
  Includes bibliographical references and index.
    ISBN 0-415-18884-9 (hbk) — ISBN 0-415-18885-7 (bbk)
    1. Women—Mental health. 2. Women—Psychology. I. Kohen, Dora,
1946–
    RC451.4.W6 W642 2000
    616.89'0082—dc21   99-056760

ISBN 0–415–18884–9 (hbk)
ISBN 0–415–18885–7 (pbk)

Contents

Tables

Contributors

Catherine Haw, Ph.D is employed by the City and Hackney Community Services NHS Trust as a Clinical Psychologist and works in a women's inpatient unit and mother and baby unit. She has carried out research in the area of women's employment and wellbeing and has a long-standing interest in gender issues and mental health. She is training as a family therapist at the Tavistock Clinic and her current research interests include family attachments and their relation to women's mental health in the post-natal period.

Sheila Hillier, BSc, MSc, Ph.D is Professor of Medical Sociology and Head of the Division of Community Sciences at St Bartholomew's and The Royal London School of Medicine and Dentistry, Queen Mary Westfield College, University of London. She has conducted research into women's health for many years. Her current research interests include the mental health of women from minority ethnic groups and the effect of migration on women's health.

Janet Holmshaw, RMN, RGN, BSc, MSc is a Research Fellow at The Sainsbury Centre for Mental Health, 134–138 Borough High Street, London SE1 1LB and tutor at St Bartholomew's and The Royal London School of Medicine and Dentistry. Previous research experience has been mainly in the area of child and adult mental health. Current research interests include mental health service provision, training/staff development issues for mental health professionals, including obstacles to implementation of newly acquired skills/ knowledge, and sociological factors relating to severe mental illness.

Dr Dora Kohen, MD, FRCPsych is a Consultant in Adult and Liaison Psychiatry in London. She works on different aspects of women and mental health. Her research interests are in psychopharmacological treatment of mental illness in women, side effects of psychotropic medication and neuroleptic malignant syndrome. Her publications include issues on psychiatric services for women, psychopharmacological treatment of women and neuroleptic malignant syndrome.

Dr Jane Marshall, MRCPI, MRCPsych is a Senior Lecturer/ Consultant in Addictions in the National Addiction Centre at the Institute of Psychiatry, London. Her current research interests are in the area of dual diagnosis, alcohol and drug abuse, homelessness and mental illness, and services for women with substance misuse.

Dr Eleni Palazidou, MD, Ph.D, MRCP, MRCPsych is a Consultant/Honorary Senior Lecturer at The Royal London Hospital (St Clement's). She is an Honorary Senior Lecturer at MRC Psychopharmacology Unit, Institute of Psychiatry, and St Bartholomew's and The Royal London Hospital Medical and Dental College. She has a special interest in the assessment and treatment of mood disorders and, in particular, treatment-resistant depression. She has been involved in research into the biology of depression and the pharmacology of antidepressant treatments.

Ulrike Schmidt, Ph.D, MRCPsych is a Consultant Psychiatrist in the Eating Disorders Unit at the South London and Maudsley NHS Trust. Her interests include research into the childhood antecedents of eating disorders, and into brief psychological treatments of eating disorders and self-harm. With colleagues she has developed manual-based treatments for bulimia nervosa and para-suicide.

Dr Lucinda Scott, Ph.D MRCPsych is a Lecturer in Clinical Psychiatry at Trinity College Medical School, St James's Hospital in Dublin. Her main interests are in the neurophysiology of the central nervous system and neurotransmitter changes in affective disorders. She has been involved in basic sciences research with the Departments of Endocrinology and Psychiatry. She has a long list of publications including several chapters on the neurobiology of psychiatric disorders especially depression.

Dr Gabriella Zolese, MD, MRCPsych is a Consultant/Honorary Senior Lecturer at St George's Hospital Medical School. She has worked as part of a community and hospital team to establish appropriate psychiatric services for the mentally ill in the community. She has been involved in research and publications on schizophrenia.

Preface

Psychiatric disorders in women have been the basis for centuries of discussion and speculations.

The aim of this book is to underline several aspects of the debate on psychiatric problems in women bringing a number of disciplines together to establish the state of knowledge in psychiatry today and to highlight the data on mental health issues and gender differences.

The introductory chapter sets the pace on epidemiology and gives an overview of the psychiatric diagnoses that are more common in women, psychiatric disorders that may have different implications in women and gender specific psychiatric disorders. There are three chapters on the basic sciences that contribute to the understanding of mental health problems in women. The biological, social and psychological determinants of mental health are discussed in detail. It is hoped that they receive the acknowledgement they deserve.

Affective disorders are commoner in women. The population with eating disorders is up to 90–95 per cent female. The background, the present state of information, treatment and management are of interest to all involved in gender issues in psychiatry. Schizophrenia is a universal disorder seen across the board in all cultures and both genders. Clinical differences in females have been documented but the new data in the last decades sets the scene for this disorder that causes incredible human suffering and takes a lot of resources from the health service and mental health professionals.

Perinatal psychiatric disorders are gender specific and have not received the attention they warrant. It is important to have a clear understanding of the extent of the suffering and unresolved problems on the subject and have a wider discussion on the problems generated for the mother, the development of the child and the family in general.

Alcohol and drug abuse are on the increase in the female population. They will probably emerge as even greater problems and part of dual diagnosis in the future.

The modest summary of the state of the specific psychiatric services for women must open the way for wider and more comprehensive discussion. The differences between gender in various psychiatric disorders need medical and scientific attention. That will lead to better understanding, wider acceptance and action to change.

This book is not a comprehensive account of all the available information on this complex subject but I hope that it will serve the purpose of contributing to the debate on gender differences in psychiatric disorders and hence improve their management.

Dr Dora Kohen
March 1999

Chapter 1

Introduction

Dora Kohen

Although women as a gender do live longer than men, they have more mental health problems. The individual's risk of encountering health problems is influenced by biological, political, economic, social and psychological adversities. In women the biological basis of mental health problems is concentrated mainly around the menses, childbirth and the menopause. Studies of social trends and epidemiological issues have established that women beset by a lifetime of social and psychological disadvantage, coupled with long years of childbearing and neglect, often end up experiencing poverty, isolation and chronic psychological disability. Because of a preference for male children, in many parts of the world female children may receive less care, nutrition and emotional support. Poverty, discrimination and possible violence towards the female child have long-lasting, debilitating and other adverse effects on the woman's physical as well as mental health (Craft, 1997a,b,c). In adults long-term unemployment, and/or income inequalities can lead to psychological problems and women who face disparities may become more vulnerable. Adverse social trends in childhood and adulthood may accumulate as risk factors over subsequent decades.

The history of psychiatric disorders and psychological differences between men and women are long standing. Madness in women has been recognized in all cultures and mad behaviour has been attributed to different causes including divinity, passion and alcohol. Hippocrates in the fourth century BC described madness in women as related to the womb or 'hysteron' in Greek and hence the term 'hysteria'. According to this belief all madness in women stemmed from the womb and womb-related functions. The idea that the womb increased women's vulnerability to mental disfunction and mental weakness continued for centuries. In the middle ages and later women were either deemed psychologically lesser and weaker creatures and therefore not deserving equal rights or, if they diverted from the narrow norm, they were seen as dangerous and burnt as witches. Their childbearing functions made them special but still not equal to men. The menopause was especially thought to be a period of great irritability and distress. In 1890 Kraepelin coined the term 'Involutional Melancholia' for a syndrome describing agitated depression, hypochondriasis and delusion in menopausal women. This was a diagnostic category in DSM-I and DSM-II until it was excluded from DSM-III in the 1970s due to lack of evidence as a specific psychiatric diagnosis.

On one hand, women may be seen as fragile, irritable, over-sensitive and fluctuating in mood and therefore be given diagnoses such as hysteria and involutional melancholia. On the other hand, real issues such as socio-cultural and personal inequalities that may make a difference to the mental health and quality of life of women have not received the recognition and attention they deserve. In the last decades social psychiatry, clinical psychology, sociology and social sciences in general have contributed to an in-depth under-standing of the social determinants of mental illness. Modern methodological data and validated and reliable computerized clinical instruments have brought better understanding and more powerful definitions which in turn have led to better clinical classi-fication. In most instances, it is possible to differentiate between crisis situation, disease states and personal traits and there are established reliable criteria for caseness. Special instruments and statistical tools to differentiate social variables from psychological components have been widely accepted. Accumulation of data on social and psychological determinants of mental disorders have been sufficient to make valid generalizations and draw conclusions. But the recommendations drawn from this reliable data have not yet been fully implemented.

EPIDEMIOLOGY AND MENTAL HEALTH IN WOMEN

Gender differences in the prevalence of psychiatric disorders have been known for several centuries. With the modern understanding of epidemiology it is well established that women have a higher prevalence of depression, dysthymia, deliberate self-harm, seasonal affective disorder, generalized anxiety disorder, panic attacks, social phobias and eating disorders, including anorexia nervosa, bulimia and obesity, than men.

The OPCS (Office of Population Censuses and Surveys) for psychiatric morbidity in Great Britain, commissioned by the Department of Health, the Scottish Home and Health Department and Welsh Office, provided information on the prevalence of psychiatric problems among the adult population, their associated social disabilities and the use of services (Meltzer et al., 1995). The survey revealed that women were more likely to have neurotic psychopathology as compared to men. Women were around twice as likely to have somatic symptoms and phobias and more likely to have fatigue, obsessions, poor concentration, forgetfulness, compulsions, panic attacks and depressive ideas. Also statistically, the odds of the disorders were increased by being female. The odds of generalized anxiety disorder were increased by about two thirds and the odds of mixed anxiety and depressive disorder were increased by more than two thirds in females.

When considering epidemiological issues in women with mental health problems, one needs to take into account that some psychiatric problems and diagnoses are more common in women, some psychiatric diagnoses deserve attention because of their differing clinical implications in women and some psychiatric diagnoses are exclusive to women.

Some psychiatric disorders are more common in women

All neurotic disorders, including generalized anxiety disorder, panic disorder, obsessive compulsive disorders, agoraphobia and other phobias, have higher prevalence rates in women. There is a marked sex difference in all studies in which both sexes have been examined. Females exceed males in a ratio of 3:2 to 2:1. Studies assessing specific populations give an insight into the extent of the issue and the needs of the female population. Hagnell (1966) studying a Swedish population found a lifetime expectancy for neurosis of 7.5 per cent for men and 17 per cent for women. The epidemiological catchment area studies (ECA) in the US has shown that both at 6 months prevalence and at lifetime prevalence, the rates show that women have three times more phobias and at least twice as much obsessive compulsive disorder as men (Myers *et al.*, 1984; Robins *et al.*, 1984). Women with obsessive compulsive disorders are more likely to suffer from comorbid anorexia and food and weight-related obsessions.

Studies have shown that life events, social class, housing and employment have a complex interaction and are associated with the mental health of women as much as with that of men.

Depression

All estimates of the prevalence of depression show that it is twice as common in women as in men. The difference is maximal in young adults and decreases with age. Women have a high incidence of depression in their reproductive years while men do not. Also social class differences in the prevalence of depression, which showed higher rates of affective disorder in working class women, has been confirmed by Brown and Harris (1978). Social roles, biological, hormonal and genetic characteristics have all been implicated in the origins of higher prevalence rates of depression. Chapter 2 and Chapter 5 contain detailed information on the biological basis, and treatment and management issues in depression.

Anxiety disorders and panic attacks

Generalized anxiety disorder (GAD) is the commonest psychiatric disorder in the population and is more prevalent in women. Women with GAD are more likely to experience depression, panic attacks and post-traumatic stress disorder which are frequent in all women (Robins *et al.*, 1984). The biological reasons of this increased frequency of GAD in women needs further elucidation. Heritability for anxiety disorders and panic attacks has only a specific influence on the emergence of clinical symptoms. Environmental factors such as increased demands on the person, lack of reward systems, low self confidence and past history of various forms of abuse play a considerable role in increasing the rates of women with anxiety disorders.

The risk of panic disorder is twice as high in females as in males. The sex difference can be difficult to interpret but it is now well established that the sex ratio is characteristic of the disorder and not a selection bias. The diagnosis of panic disorder with agoraphobia is three times more common in women (Bourdan *et al.*, 1988).

Eating disorders

Eating disorders such as anorexia nervosa, bulimia nervosa and obesity are predominantly seen in women. Estimates of the incidence of anorexia nervosa, which are mainly derived from case registers, show a range of 0.24 to 14.6 per 100,000 of the female population per annum. The majority of studies show that the incidence has increased in recent years (Lucas et al., 1991). The syndrome seems to be uncommon in men and only a maximum of 10 per cent of the cases are male. The incidence of bulimia nervosa among young women in Britain and North America is generally between 1 per cent and 2 per cent but male cases are rare. This syndrome has become more common over the past three decades. Chapter 8 contains detailed information and discussion on treatment and management issues in patients with eating disorders.

Deliberate self-harm

Deliberate self-harm (DSH) is an indicator of social deprivation and a marker of long-term social and psychiatric problems. It is closely associated with unemployment, overcrowding, substance abuse, previous child sex abuse and physical abuse. It has been a major health problem in the UK in the last three to four decades. There are 150,000 documented acts of DSH per year in the UK. The majority of these cases are women. It is more prevalent in the lower social classes and is seen in association with juvenile delinquency, cruelty to children, and single parenthood. Most attempts of DSH occur in an interpersonal context and can be better understood from a socio-cultural point of view.

DSH is commonly encountered among adolescents and young adults aged between 15 and 25. It has a higher prevalence in women at all ages, although after the age of 50 years the gender difference is not statistically significant. There has been a general decline in the rate in the 1970s in older teenage girls (Sellar et al., 1990). But there has been an upward trend in the late 1980s especially in older adolescent women (Hawton and Fagg, 1992). Hawton et al. (1997) have shown a substantial increase in DSH rates during the last decade. There has been an increase of 62 per cent in males and 42 per cent in females and an increased rate of repetition in both genders, particularly in females.

Women tend to use drug overdose, the majority being paracetamol with or without antidepressants, while men who DSH may use more violent and dangerous methods. The increase of paracetamol abuse has been most marked in females in whom the paracetamol overdose increased from 29.6 per cent in 1985 to 52.6 per cent in 1995. Among the population admitted to general hospital following DSH, male patients took their own discharge more often than females.

An average of 10.2 per cent of all DSH patients each year are admitted to inpatient psychiatric care. This proportion is on the increase and the change is more marked in females than males (Hawton et al., 1997). The increased rate of DSH and demographic characteristics of the patient population should be taken into consideration in planning future services.

Women and psychiatric consequences of child sex abuse

Childhood Sex Abuse (CSA) and rape of adult females are both associated with severe psychological and psychiatric problems. One in 6 women and 1 in 10 men in the general population have been victims of child sex abuse (Baker and Duncan, 1985; Finkelhor et al., 1990). When psychiatric patients are assessed for CSA the rates show that around 30 per cent of female patients report CSA (Chu and Dill, 1990).

CSA may have an irreversible effect on the child's development. Even if victims do not fulfil the criteria of psychiatric caseness they are found to have long-lasting personal difficulties such as distrust, low self-esteem, insecurity, sleeping difficulties and isolation. Sexual dysfunction has been seen in a majority of sexually abused women. Psychosexual development is usually arrested and there is a wide range of sexual problems.

A past history of CSA may be associated with physical and medical complaints often in the form of gastrointestinal distress, chronic headaches, recurrent abdominal pain, obesity and higher rates of surgery (Felliti, 1991). It is now documented that abuse is associated with the psychiatric diagnosis of depression, anxiety and panic attacks, dysthymia, agoraphobia, interpersonal problems, personality disorder, paranoid and psychotic symptomatology, somatization, eating disorders and post-traumatic stress disorder (Bryer et al., 1987).

CSA has also an impact on personality problems and recurrent suicide attempts, self-destructive acts and different forms of impulsive self-injurious behaviour. Davidson et al (1996) concluded that a history of sexual trauma before the age of 16 strongly correlated with attempted suicide.

Women who have been sexually abused during childhood tend to have a higher prevalence of alcohol abuse. In a study, over half of the women with drinking problems identified themselves as victims of sex abuse (Moncrieff et al., 1996). Ogata et al. (1990) studied prevalence of CSA and physical abuse in female psychiatric inpatients with the diagnosis of borderline personality disorder and two out of three of the patients reported some form of CSA.

Victims of CSA have an increased risk of victimization in their adult lives. Almost half of CSA victims report domestic violence and brutal partners. This in turn may lead to further psychiatric and psychological problems. Victims of CSA are at an increased risk of prostitution, and other risk behaviour such as working as models in pornography. Victims of CSA have a higher incidence of social problems often resulting in an increased involvement in the criminal justice system.

The psychological problems and mental health problems involved in the transition from being a victim to growing into a perpetrator have been established in females (Welldon, 1988; De Zulueta, 1993; Welldon, 1996). Female abusers and other women who show deeply ingrained maladaptive behaviour may have a past history of sexual, physical and psychological abuse themselves.

Scott (1992) studied the association between CSA and the mental health status of the community and estimated that almost 4 per cent of all psychiatric cases within the population were associated with CSA.

Sleep disorders

Insomnia is one of the most common complaints in general practice, affecting psychological wellbeing and day-to-day functioning. It is a symptom that in time may escalate to a full disorder but more often it may not come to the attention of professionals for many years. It is known that there is a large population suffering silently, therefore it would be difficult to estimate prevalence rates. But it is also known that twice as many women as men seek treatment for insomnia in general practice. Since insomnia is one of the symptoms of affective disorders that in turn are more commonly seen in women, one could extrapolate that insomnia is more common in women.

It has been noted that REM (rapid eye movement) sleep is affected by the menstrual cycle (Driver, 1996). In perimenopausal women complaining of insomnia, oestrogen replacement therapy has been found to reduce wakefulness (Thomson and Oswald, 1977). Also peri- and postmenopausal women experiencing hot flushes tend to have less effective sleep and longer REM latencies than those not experiencing hot flushes (Shaver *et al.*, 1991).

With the growing evidence that sleep is affected by the reproductive status in women, more attention should be directed to its hormonal and perimenopausal components (Driver, 1996).

SOME PSYCHIATRIC DIAGNOSES HAVE DIFFERENT IMPLICATIONS IN FEMALE PATIENTS

Major psychiatric morbidity such as schizophrenia, bipolar affective disorder and other psychoses of a different nature may not show significant differences in prevalence between male and female patients, but differences in clinical symptomatology, side effect profile and long-term management issues need to be taken into consideration. Schizophrenia is a markedly biological disorder but the well-established social and interpersonal components associated with relapse and several other variables that are notably different in women will be discussed in Chapter 6.

In bipolar affective disorder gender ratio between men and women is equal but a review of the literature shows that there are some significant differences in various aspects of the illness (Leibenluft, 1996). There is a greater prevalence of rapid cycling in female patients. Females have more episodes of depression while men have more episodes of mania. The female reproductive system has a possible significant effect on the bipolar cases with postpartum episodes, the longer course of the treatment and the greater use of antidepressants.

Gender differences in the clinical expression of bipolar illness and the effect of the female reproductive system, gonadal steroids and thyroid dysfunction on the course of and response to treatment of the illness need to be studied longitudinally.

Gender-specific psychiatric disorders

Premenstrual dysphoric disorder (PMDD)

This DSM-IV diagnosis describes recurrent emotional and physical symptoms that occur in the last week of premenstrual cycle and remit in the first two days following the onset of menstruation. The diagnosis is made prospectively over two consecutive cycles. Five per cent of the female population have symptoms severe enough to meet criteria for PMDD.

The biological changes during the menstrual cycle are now thought to play a significant role because these symptoms are absent in puberty or after menopause. In DSM-IV, PMDD is characterized by depressed mood, marked anxiety and affective lability, persistent anger, irritability or increased interpersonal conflicts, lethargy, lack of energy and motivation, easy fatigability, increased appetite and specific food cravings, hypersomnia or insomnia and physical symptoms such as tenderness, swelling and headaches. Abnormal levels of oestrogen, progesterone, FSH (follicle stimulating hormone), LH (luteinizing hormone), cortisol, thyroid hormones and serotonin have been suggested as etiological factors, however, no specific etiology has been identified (Rubinow, Hoban, Grover et al., 1988). Chapter 2 establishes the physiological basis of gender-specific psychiatric disorders and gives a biological perspective of PMDD.

The menopause

The menopause or the cessation of the period is when a woman has ceased menstruating. The menopause was thought to be a period of distress and irritability and the syndrome of involutional melancholia was accepted until the 1970s when it was excluded from classifications due to lack of distinguishing evidence.

The perimenopause is regarded as the period starting five years before the menopause and is characterized by irregular ovulatory cycles. The climacterium describes the years of decreasing ovulatory periods. During the perimenopausal period with its hormonal changes the woman may experience various physical and some associated mood changes. Although it is now well established that the menopause by definition does not increase the risk for depression, the hormonal and physical changes and additional life events coupled with psychosocial stressors may increase the risk of affective symptomatology (Kaufert *et al.*, 1992; Avis and McKinlay, 1995).

It is also accepted that mood disorders prior to the menopause, such as PMDD, contraceptive related dysphoria or postnatal depression, all predispose women to affective changes and even depression in the menopausal period.

Abortion and infertility in women

Today, the act of abortion is often the result of social, personal and psychological deprivation in couples and especially in women who may be socially and psychologically disadvantaged to the point where they cannot access contraception. Before and after the act of abortion, women usually go through a period of insurmountable personal difficulties and vulnerability. Abortion may be associated with feelings of guilt that can escalate to generalized anxiety, different fears and phobias and a diagnosis of depression (Zolese and Blacker, 1992).

Infertility in women is the inability to achieve pregnancy. Historically, solely women were held responsible for the inability to conceive and have been punished for failure to become pregnant. In many cultures social degradation, loss of status and authority and loss of social gains associated with womanhood have accompanied infertility. Loss of the partner's attention and a second wife in the family have led to despair and even suicide among women. Even today infertility is still a great source of distress and anxiety. Women exhibit psychological reactions to infertility and to its different forms of treatment (Burt and Hendrick, 1997).

Miscarriage is a traumatic event and the experience may lead to consequences such as depression and anxiety (Friedman and Gath, 1989). The psychological effects of early miscarriages are viewed as perinatal bereavement and may need very similar input provided in bereavement and even post-traumatic stress. The trauma associated with miscarriage has never received the attention it deserves. Moulder (1994) comments that despite the increased recognition of the distressing effects of miscarriage, training and organizations for dealing with the woman's emotional care have not reached the same prominence.

Perinatal psychiatric problems are distinctive. Chapter 7 gives an overview on the complexities of the psychiatric problems encountered in pregnancy and following delivery.

Gender-specific research and pharmacological treatment

There is a growing perception that medical research has focused more on the health problems of men than women, with lower rates of women participating in clinical studies (Mastroianni et al., 1994). The findings of such studies may not have the validity to be generalized to women. Gender differences continue to be insufficiently studied with respect to the effects of contextual and bio-medical variables on the etiology and treatment of the diseases (Stewart, 1996). In women, body size, composition, metabolism and sex hormones should receive specific consideration. Exclusion of women from clinical trials grew from understandable concerns for the foetus. While this is an important consideration future research should make use of more participatory models.

Gender issues in pharmacological treatment are important. In prescribing psychotropic drugs attention should be paid to differences in absorption, distribution and metabolism between men and women. Gender differences in the pharmacokinetics of psychotropic agents have important clinical implications. It is important to determine and provide the appropriate dose for female patients so that side effects are minimized (Yonkers et al., 1992 and 1996). Although gender-related pharmacokinetic parameters do exist they still have not been translated into clinical practice.

MENTAL HEALTH ISSUES IN WOMEN DESERVE SPECIAL ATTENTION

Women's health issues are in the forefront of many gender-related discussions today (Seager, 1997). But at the same time it does not appear to be easy to implement the necessary changes even if there is acknowledgement of the differences. Taking action on the subject has not come naturally.

Women's health issues have been the centre of controversy in the European Union and in other parts of the world. The European Parliament now has an agenda item to raise the profile of women's health issues. Legalisation of abortion, and physical illnesses such as osteoporosis, hormonal treatment, breast and cervical cancer, depression and eating disorders are all accepted health issues that need attention.

It is generally accepted that all psychiatric disorders have biological, social and psychological determinants that contribute to the clinical picture in differing degrees. They contribute to the differences in prevalence, social context, lifestyle, risk factors, symptoms, course and outcome. Concentrating on diverse factors such as hormonal responses, sexual behaviour, coping strategies, psychosocial factors, psychological adjustment, multiple social roles, illness behaviour and psychiatric morbidity in women will give a clearer picture. This should also lead to strategies to improve both recognition and amelioration of the condition.

THE BOOK

The aim of this book is to summarize the prominent determinants of psychiatric morbidity and to give factual data on psychiatric disorders in women. Some disorders have been included because the higher prevalence in women brings a new perspective into the etiology and treatment. Some have been included because of different factors that impact on the future understanding and management of the disorder and their various biological, social and psychological precipitants.

The book starts with three chapters which bring basic insight into psychopathology in women. The physiological perspective by Dr Scott introduces research data on basic biological factors that are known to influence different aspects of mental state in women. The sociological perspective by Janet Holmshaw and Professor Hillier reviews the literature on social concomitants of psychopathology in women.

There are many psychological problems viewed as unique to women. Dr Haw reviews basic psychological theories and their input into psychological understanding of mental health problems in women.

Dr Palazidou has written about one of the commonest conditions in psychiatry today, depression.

Dr Zolese has summarized a wealth of literature on women and schizophrenia. Although the epidemiology of schizophrenia may not be different in the genders it is well established that the demographic and clinical data can make the treatment and management quite different.

Eating disorder is a condition where 95 per cent of all patients are female. Dr Schmidt has given an understanding of the clinical problems, treatment and management of this increasingly frequent and potentially lethal female disorder.

There is an increase in the recognition and sensitivity of drug and alcohol abuse in women and problems in management. Dr Marshall presents the female perspective in the management of these very complex situations.

I have summarized perinatal psychiatric disorders with the hope that it will gain prominence and receive the attention it deserves in the field of women and mental health.

This is the era of services discussions. I know that there are different approaches and experimentation on different services for women at various localities in the UK and all around the world. The last chapter in the book, on mental health services for women, will contribute to more specific and more sensitive services for women. The increase in novel views and the accumulation of reliable data will improve recognition, treatment and management of psychiatric conditions and hence the quality of life of female patients.

I hope that this book will help to raise sensitivity to and awareness of gender differences in psychiatric conditions and the specific needs of female patients. I also hope the book will contribute to debates on the subject by different mental health professionals.

REFERENCES

Avis, N.E. and McKinlay, S.M. (1995) 'The Massachusetts Women's Health Study; an epidemiologic investigation of the menopause', *Journal of American Medical Women Association* 50: 45–9.

Baker, A.W. and Duncan, S.P. (1985) 'Child sex abuse: a study of prevalence in Great Britain', *Child Abuse and Neglect* 9: 457–67.

Bourdan, K.H., Boyd, J.H. and Rae, D.S. *et al.* (1988) 'Gender differences in phobias: results of the ECA community survey', *Journal of Anxiety Disorders* 2: 227–41.

Brown, G.W. and Harris, T. (1978) *The Social Origins of Depression*, London: Tavistock.

Bryer, J.B., Nelson, B.A., Miller, J.B. and Krol, B.A. (1987) 'Childhood sexual and physical abuse as factors in adult psychiatric illness', *American Journal of Psychiatry* 44: 1426–30.

Burt, V.K. and Hendrick, V.C. (1997) *Women's Mental Health*, Washington DC: American Psychiatric Press Inc.

Chu, J.A. and Dill, D.L. (1990) 'Dissociative symptoms in relation to childhood physical and sexual abuse', *American Journal of Psychiatry* 144: 1474–6.

Craft, N. (1997) Women's Health, *British Medical Journal*, a. 'Women's health is a global issue' 315: 1154–7; b. 'Life span: conception to adolescence' 315: 1227–30; c. 'The childbearing years and after' 315: 1301–4.

Davidson, J.R.T., Hughes, D.C., George, L.K. and Blazer, D.G. (1996) 'The association between sexual assault and suicide attempt in the community', *Archives of General Psychiatry* 53: 550–5.

De Zulueta, F. (1993) *From Pain to Violence: the Traumatic Roots of Destructiveness*, London: Whurr Publications.

Driver, H.S. (1996) 'Sleep in women', *Journal of Psychosomatic Research* 40: 227–30.

Felliti, V.J. (1991) 'Long term medical consequences of incest, rape, and molestation', *Southern Medical Journal* 84: 328–31.

Finkelhor, D., Hotaling, G. and Lewis, I.A. *et al.* (1990) 'Sexual abuse in a national survey of adult men and women: prevalence, characteristics and risk factors', *Child Abuse and Neglect* 14: 19–28.

Friedman, T. and Gath, D. (1989) 'The psychiatric consequences of spontaneous abortion', *British Journal of Psychiatry* 155: 810–13.

Hagnell, O. (1966) 'Incidence and duration of episodes of mental illness in a total population', in E.M. Hare and J.K. Wing (eds) *Psychiatric Epidemiology*, Oxford: Oxford University Press.

Hawton, K., Fagg, J., Simkin, S., Bale, E. and Bond, A. (1997) 'Trends in deliberate self harm in Oxford, 1985–1995', *British Journal of Psychiatry* 171: 556–60.

Hawton, K. and Fagg, J. (1992) 'Trends in deliberate self poisoning and self injury in Oxford, 1976–1990', *British Medical Journal* 304: 1409–11.

Kaufert, P.A., Gilbert, P. and Tate, R. (1992) 'The Manitoba Project: a reexamination of the link between menopause and depression', *Mayuritas* 14: 143–55.

Leibenluft, E. (1996) 'Women with bipolar illness: clinical and research issues', *American Journal of Psychiatry* 153: 163–73.

Lucas, A.R., Beard, C.M., O'Fallon, W.M. and Kurland, L.T. (1991) '50 year trends in the incidence of anorexia nervosa in Rochester, Minnesota: a population based study', *American Journal of Psychiatry* 148: 917–28.

Mastroianni, A.C., Faden, R. and Federman, D. (eds) (1994) *Women and Health Research*, vols 1 and 2, Washington DC: National Academic Press.

Meltzer, H., Gill, B., Petticrew, M. and Hinds, K. (1995) *The prevalence of psychiatric morbidity among adults living in private households*, OPCS (Office of population censuses and surveys) of psychiatric morbidity in Great Britain, Report 1, London: HMSO.

Moncrieff, J., Drummond, D.C. and Candy, B. *et al.* (1996) 'Sexual abuse in people with alcohol problems: a study of prevalence of sexual abuse and its relationship to drinking behaviour', *British Journal of Psychiatry* 169: 355–60.

Moulder, C. (1994) 'Towards a preliminary framework for understanding pregnancy loss', *Journal of Reproductive and Infant Psychology* 12: 65–7.

Myers, J.K., Weisman, M.M. and Tischler, G.L. *et al.* (1984) 'Six months' prevalence of psychiatric disorders in three communities', *Archives of General Psychiatry* 41: 959–67.

Ogata, S.N., Silk, K.R. and Goodrich, S. (1990) 'Childhood sexual and physical abuse in adult patients with borderline personality disorder', *American Journal of Psychiatry* 147: 1008–13.

Robins, L.N., Helzer, J.E. and Weissman, M.M. *et al.* (1984) 'Lifetime prevalence of specific psychiatric disorders in three sites', *Archives of General Psychiatry* 41: 949–58.

Rubinow, D.R., Hoban, M.C. and Grover, G.N. *et al.* (1988) 'Changes in plasma hormones across the menstrual cycle in patients with menstrually related mood disorders and control subjects', *American Journal of Obstetrics and Gynaecology* 158: 5–11.

Scott, K.D. (1992) 'Childhood sexual abuse; impact on a community mental health status', *Child Abuse and Neglect* 16: 285–95.

Seager, J. (1997) *The State of Women in the World*, London: Penguin Books Ltd.

Sellar, C., Hawton, K. and Goldacre, M.J. (1990) 'Self-poisoning in adolescents: hospital admissions and deaths in the Oxford region 1980–1985', *British Journal of Psychiatry* 56: 866–70.

Shaver, J.L.F., Giblin, E. and Paulsen, V. (1991) 'Sleep quality subtypes in midlife women', *Sleep* 14: 18–23.

Stewart, D. (1996) 'Women's health and psychosomatic medicine', *Journal of Psychosomatic Research* 40: 221–6.

Thomson, J. and Oswald, I. (1977) 'Effect of oestrogen on the sleep, mood, anxiety of menopausal women', *British Medical Journal* 2: 1327–9.

Welldon, E.V. (1988) *Mother, Madonna, Whore: The Idealization and Denigration of Motherhood*, London: Free Association Books.

Welldon, E. (1996) 'Women as abusers', ch. 13: 176–189, in K. Abel, M. Buszewicz, S. Davison, S. Johnson and E. Staples *Planning Community Services for Women*, London: Routledge.

Yonkers, K.A., Kando, J.C., Cole, J.O. and Blumenthal, S. (1992) 'Gender differences in pharmacokinetics and pharmacodynamics of psychotropic medication', *American Journal of Psychiatry* 149: 587–95.

Yonkers, K.A., Kando, J. and Hamilton, J. (1996) 'Gender issues in psychopharmacological treatment', *Essential Psychopharmacology* 1: 54–69.

Zolese, G. and Blacker, R.C.V. (1992) 'The psychological complications of therapeutic abortion', *British Journal of Psychiatry* 160: 742–9.

Chapter 2

A physiological perspective

Lucinda V. Scott

The study of psychobiology of gender is in its infancy, but already there are emerging findings of interest to clinicians and researchers. The aim of this chapter is to examine the manner in which female biology may influence mental health. Women are disadvantaged with respect to certain psychiatric disorders such as depression; whilst environmental, psychological and social factors may be contributory, the impact of female hormones on the brain may explain more parsimoniously this apparent gender effect. In support of this possibility is the observation that prior to puberty psychological/psychiatric difficulties are more common in boys (Earls, 1987); with the onset of the reproductive years, prior to which the brain's hormonal environment in males and females is similar, differences in psychopathology between men and women emerge (Finegan *et al.*, 1988).

The influence of female hormones is most readily apparent in disorders specific to women such as premenstrual dysphoric disorder or premenstrual syndrome (PMS), psychological problems occurring perimenopausally and most notably the disorders associated with the postpartum period; the 'blues', postnatal depression and postpartum psychosis. Female hormones are known to influence certain neurotransmitter systems that have been implicated in psychiatric disorders and also to impact on the hypothalamic-pituitary-adrenal (HPA) axis, the core endocrine stress axis in man (Selye, 1974); the sex differences in stress system responsivity may be partly explained on this basis. The relevance of this to anxiety disorders and depressive illness will be explored. At a cellular level, that oestrogens are neuroprotective with respect to neuronal degeneration and growth has led to their implication in the sex differences in rates and course of illnesses such as Alzheimer's Disease and possibly schizophrenia.

Prior to discussing these in more detail a brief outline of normal female physiology is warranted.

NORMAL FEMALE PHYSIOLOGY

Until the sixth week of gestation males and females are undifferentiated, at which time testes develop in males and produce androgens. Follicular stimulating hormone (FSH) is present in the pituitary gland of both sexes but increases dramatically in females between weeks 12 and 20 and it is thought to play a role in foetal ovarian development. From this time, however, until puberty, the central or brain hormonal environment of females is similar to males. With the onset of menstruation in females hormone levels of women fluctuate to a much larger range than do men's.

Dramatic alterations occur during the menstrual cycle initially to induce ovulation and then prepare the uterus for a possible pregnancy. Gonadotropin-releasing hormone (GnRH) produced from the hypothalamus brings about the release of FSH and luteinizing hormone (LH) from the anterior pituitary, FSH and LH binding to cell surface receptors in the ovary. FSH acts primarily to promote ovulation during the follicular phase, whilst LH is indispensable for the maintenance of the corpus luteum in the luteal phase. The gonadal steroids released, oestrogens, progesterone and testosterone, exert a long-loop negative feedback effect at a hypothalamic level acting to stabilize endocrine homeostasis and restrain hypothalamic-pituitary stimulation of target tissues.

Several classic neurotransmitters including the endogenous opioid peptides, serotonin, dopamine and gaba-amino butyric acid (GABA) are believed to have direct synaptic contacts on GnRH neurons. This relationship has been examined by conducting neuroendocrine challenge paradigms of several neurotransmitters at various phases of the menstrual cycle. Steroid hormones have been implicated in the regulation of many central neurotransmitters including serotonin and the endogenous opioids. The LH response to opioidergic blockade is greatest during the late follicular and early luteal phase of the cycle suggesting a priming effect of oestrogens on opioidergic functioning (Grossman, 1983). O'Keane and co-workers (1991) demonstrated a similar effect of oestrogens on the prolactin response to the serotonin agonist d-fenfluramine, this test affording an indication of central serotonergic activity. This group also showed a strong relationship between oestrogen and progesterone levels and the growth hormone (GH) response to pyridostigmine, this challenge paradigm reflecting cholinergic neurotransmission (O'Keane et al., 1992).

This apparent impact of circulating sex steroid levels on central neurotransmitter functioning is relevant for a number of reasons. First, for example, in relation to depressive illness, a modulating effect of the sex steroids on monoaminergic functioning may be pertinent to the monoamine hypothesis of depression (Janowsky et al., 1972). Second, and importantly, these studies indicate the necessity of controlling for phase of menstrual cycle when conducting neuroendocrinological tests in women of reproductive age both in a research and clinical setting. In addition, dysregulation of the hypothalamic-pituitary-adrenal (HPA) axis has been implicated in a range of psychiatric disorders, including depression, anorexia nervosa and post-traumatic stress disorder. Serotonin has a positive regulatory effect on HPA activity (Dinan, 1996). As stated gonadal steroids can modulate central serotonergic functioning but have also been shown to have a direct impact on HPA regulation. Thus, gonadal steroids can influence HPA activity at a suprahypothalamic neurotransmitter (NT) level and also at the level of the hypothalamus.

MOOD DISORDERS

While the lifetime prevalence of bipolar or manic-depressive illness is approximately 1 per cent for both sexes, unipolar depressions are twice as common in women than in men (Kessler et al., 1993). These differences between prevalence do not emerge until adolescence (Buchanan et al., 1992). It is suggested that at this time young women, now they are old enough to do so independently, seek treatment for psychological problems more frequently than young men. Social role, birth cohort effects and access to health care have all been implicated in the determinations of sex differences in depression in different population samples (Harris, 1991; Paykel, 1991; Seeman, 1997). It is notable that studies in developing countries such as India and New Guinea have not shown the doubling of rates of depression in women relative to men (Shaw, Kennedy and Joffe, 1995).

Some researchers have attempted to explain differences in personality factors and coping styles associated with sex role as intrinsic to the female vulnerability to depression (Boyce *et al.*, 1991; Seeman, 1997). Specifically, women are found to have a more passive, ruminative style of coping, whereas men adopt a more distraction-orientated approach which is considered in some way to be protective (Nelen-Hoeksema, 1990).

Biological aspects of depression

The HPA axis is the core stress axis in man. Corticotropin-releasing hormone (CRH) is released from the parvicellular neurons of the paraventricular nucleus, which impacts at the corticotropes of the anterior pituitary to release adrenocorticotropic (ACTH) hormone, this in turn stimulating cortisol release from the anterior pituitary. Both physical and psychological stressors activate the HPA and set in motion central and peripheral responses designed to preserve homeostasis. These responses, designated 'general adaptational responses' by Selye in 1936, are mediated primarily by the HPA and sympathetic nervous system. Chrousos and Gold (1992), in a seminal article overviewing stress and stress system disorders, have implicated a disruption in HPA activity and the ensuing compromised homeostasis as pivotal to a range of both psychiatric and non-psychiatric disorders.

Dysregulation of the HPA in major depression is one of the consistently documented biological abnormalities in any psychiatric disorder. It is characterized by elevated plasma cortisol levels, dexamethasone non-suppression, a blunted ACTH response to stimulation with exogenous CRH, enlarged adrenal glands and raised central CSF CRH levels. This evidence has led to a theory of depression based on overactivity of the HPA/stress system (Nemeroff, 1996).

Several groups have looked at the possibility that HPA responses to stress vary with gender, contributing to gender differences in the prevalence of depression. Dorn and colleagues (1996) looked at a cohort of depressed and non-depressed adolescents. They found a pattern of ACTH and cortisol responses to oCRH which was normal in adolescents with depression and postulated that this reflected normal negative feedback at this age, the latter being the mechanism whereby cortisol feedback can terminate HPA activation and the stress response. Gender differences in hormone responses were attributed to differences in peripheral metabolism of ACTH. On examining non-depressed young men and women, the latter were found to have diminished basal concentrations of ACTH indicating an enhanced adrenal sensitivity to ACTH in these subjects (Born, 1995). However, responses to hCRH/vasopressin (VP) were stronger in young females suggesting an enhanced pituitary-responsiveness to the augmenting effect of VP on ACTH release in this group. An enhanced pituitary-adrenal responsiveness has also been shown to oCRH alone in healthy women (Gallucci et al., 1993; Akil et al., 1993). It has not, however, been consistently demonstrated, for example, that CRH/ACTH blunting is greater in female than in male depressives. Vasopressin, the core companion HPA regulator, with CRH, has of late been implicated in the pathophysiology of depression. It is possible that the increased sensitivity of women to the augmenting effect of VP masks a greater blunting to CRH alone in this group. Although exploration of gender differences in HPA sensitivity has not provided a simple explanation of gender differences in depression rates it remains an intuitively reasonable avenue for further examination. This is particularily the case in the light of recent studies detailing the effects of gonadal steroids on HPA regulation. In rat studies increased circulating corticosterone levels induced by oestrogen mediate the inhibitory effects of oestrogens on CRH expression centrally (Paulymer-Lacroix et al., 1996). This observation may explain the gender-related differences in basal and stress-induced HPA activity.

Higher rates of sexual abuse of girls during childhood and adolescence have also been considered as possible explanations for high rates of depression in women. In an intriguing study De Bellis and colleagues (1994) conducted a comprehensive assessment of HPA activity in a cohort of young girls who were sexual abuse victims but not considered to be clinically depressed. The attenuated plasma ACTH and normal cortisol responses to CRH stimulation and normal 24-hour urinary free cortisol output in the sexually abused compared to a non-abused control group suggested a dysregulation of the HPA. Whilst this was not directly comparable to the demonstrated hyperactivity of the HPA axis described in major depression in adulthood, it does suggest a fragility of HPA activity which these victims carry with them to their adult years. The dysregulation of the stress system may render them more vulnerable to the development not only of major depression but to other psychiatric disorders such as eating disorders, somatization disorders and post-traumatic stress disorders, all of which occur with more frequency in women with a history of abuse than in women without such a background (Mullen et al., 1988; Morrison, 1989).

Serotonergic hypofunctioning has also been implicated in the pathophysiological basis of major depression; both 5HT-mediated prolactin release (O'Keane and Dinan, 1991) and 5HT-mediated ACTH release (Lesch et al., 1990) have been studied employing fenfluramine (5HT2a/2c agonist) and ipsapirone (5HT1a agonist) as the respective challenge agents in subjects with major depressive disorder. A blunted release of prolactin and ACTH respectively were found in the depressed cohort compared to a healthy volunteer group. No gender effect was observed, that is, depressed females were not found to have a greater impairment of response compared to their depressed male counterparts, undermining a defect in serotonergic functioning specific to women as a satisfactory explanation for the excess of depression in this group. Healthy subject studies have similarly not established an effect of gender on serotonergic function (Lesch, 1989). Although human cytochemical studies on 5HT1a receptors in the hippocampus and neocortex suggest an absence of gender effect (Palego et al., 1997), binding of 5HT2 receptor in the frontal and cingulate cortices is significantly higher in men than in women (Biver et al., 1996). This is hypothesized to account for the differing liability of men and women to suffer from psychiatric disorders responsive to serotonergic agents such as eating disorders and aggressivity.

NEUROTIC/ANXIETY DISORDERS

For almost all anxiety disorders ranging from simple phobia to agoraphobia with panic attacks there is an overrepresentation of women compared to men. Seeman (1997) in a review of psychopathology in women and men examines the evidence that this gender difference may be hormonally based. It is suggested that the cyclic withdrawal of oestrogens and progesterone that occurs with each menstrual cycle may have a 'kindling' effect on neuronal systems and promote anxiety states by mechanisms similar to those which have been implicated in the perimenstrual exacerbation of epilepsy (Narbone et al., 1990). This theory is based on the observation that oestrogens upregulate the GABA(A)/benzodiazepine receptor complex, and that progesterone metabolites have agonist properties at this complex and thereby act as anxiolytics (Maggi and Perez, 1986).

Although HPA dysregulation and in particular CRH activity have been associated with a range of anxiety disorders, including panic disorder and post-traumatic stress disorder (PTSD), the implications of such a pathophysiology for the apparent gender specificity of anxiety has not received much attention. CRH is an arousal-producing peptide, the central administration of which in rodents increases the range and extent of anxiety-related behaviours including decreased sleeping, enhanced fear responses, suppressed sexual behaviour and decreased food consumption (Butler *et al.*, 1990). As in depressive illness, elevated CRH levels may explain the insomnia and motor agitation intrinsic to an anxiety state.

HPA activity in women who developed PTSD following abuse has been recently explored. It is pertinent to this that women more commonly develop PTSD after traumatic experiences than do men (Yonkers and Ellison, 1996). Stein and co-workers (1997) demonstrated in adult women traumatized by sexual abuse an enhanced suppression of plasma cortisol following dexamethasone. This HPA disturbance is distinct from that found in major depression. Although women with PTSD have been shown to have greater responsivity to the dexamethasone-suppression test, a similar finding in male combat veterans suggests that it is an alteration mediated by PTSD as opposed to a gender effect (Yehuda *et al.*, 1993).

An abnormality of serotonin neurotransmission in obsessive-compulsive disorder (OCD) is suggested by the apparent benefit from drugs that enhance serotonergic activity. A recent study in which d-fenfluramine-mediated cortisol responses were significantly altered in female OCD subjects compared to male OCD subjects, and male and female healthy controls, suggests a gender specific abnormality of 5HT transmission in this disorder (Monteleone *et al.*, 1997). Given that there is an equal male : female ratio of OCD sufferers and that no gender specificity exists with regard to response vs non-response to pharmacological intervention, the significance of this biological gender difference is not readily apparent.

SCHIZOPHRENIA

Though the incidence of schizophrenia in men and women is more or less equal, the onset of symptoms in women occurs later (Hafner *et al.*, 1997). This age disparity disappears when one studies familial schizophrenia, suggesting that genetic influences in familial schizophrenia may overshadow the protective effects of oestrogens considered by some to play a protective role and account for the late onset of symptoms in this group (Gorwood *et al.*, 1995; Seeman, 1997). The recent demonstration of an equal frequency of obstetric complications in the maternal histories of preschizophrenic men and women undermines this as a non-hormonal explanation of the age disparity observed (Hultman *et al.*, 1997).

The neurodevelopmental hypothesis of schizophrenia links disruption at critical phases of embryonic life resulting in a disorganization of neuronal migration and growth with a subsequent vulnerability to the illness. Oestrogens, which are known to stimulate nerve growth factors and promote nerve survival, spanning the life cycle from foetal development to old age, may exert some protective effect during early life and influence the sex differences in schizophrenia (Toran-Allerand, 1996). This theory is, however, putative and difficult to explore further.

Seeman (1997), in reviewing the possible role of hormones in schizophrenia, reports that women, in particular when they are young, have been shown to respond better to antipsychotic medication. A possible explanation for this is the antidopaminergic actions of oestrogen hormones, such as their effect in reducing the rate of tyrosine hydroxylase gene transcription and thereby increasing the bioavailability of catecholamines (Blum *et al.*, 1987). Extrapolating from this oestrogen effect one could hypothesize that late-onset schizophrenia, which is more common in women, may reflect an oestrogen withdrawal effect. No correlation has been shown between a deterioration of symptoms in schizophrenic women and a declining oestrogen level. Contrary to previous reports a recent study has not confirmed any menstrually related symptom changes in women with schizophrenia (Harris, 1997).

PREMENSTRUAL SYNDROME/LATE LUTEAL PHASE DYSPHORIC DISORDER

The term 'pre-menstrual tension' was first introduced by Frank in 1931 to describe a group of women in whom typical cyclical symptoms appeared in the second half of the menstrual cycle which were relieved by menstruation. In common parlance 'premenstrual syndrome' (PMS) has become the most widely used term. The intrinsic role of cyclical ovarian activity in its pathogenesis has more recently been indicated by the term 'late luteal phase dysphoric disorder' introduced in the USA as a classification within the third edition of the *Diagnostic and Statistical Manual of Mental Disorders* published by the American Psychiatric Association (APA, 1984). It has been found to be a stable syndrome that may best be viewed as part of the spectrum of recurrent mood disorders (Bloch, 1997).

The most common and severe physical symptoms include mastalgia and breast swelling, abdominal bloating and weight gain; less frequently headaches and altered bowel habit are described (Faratian 1984). The psychological symptoms of irritability, tension, tiredness, mood swings and depression can be the most debilitating aspects of the disorder. Most women are found to have a mix of complaints with only 10.3 per cent being affected by purely physical and 3.5 per cent by only psychological/behavioural premenstrual symptoms.

Despite the introduction of operational criteria by DSM-III, daily prospective symptom recordings are considered a vital part of the diagnostic work-up in these patients (Rubinow, 1984). In summarizing the available data Reid (1985) has proposed that 5–10 per cent of women suffer from severe premenstrual distress, with 30 per cent having moderate premenstrual symptoms and only 10–15 per cent of women being relatively asymptomatic. Genetic studies suggest a significant genetic component to the disorder. Condon (1993) examined PMS scores in two groups of twins, 157 pairs of monozygotic (MZ) twins and 143 pairs of dizygotic (DZ) twins. The concordance rates in the monozygotic twins were significantly higher than in the dizygotic twins. Clearly, the fact that MZ twins may share greater environmental similarities than DZ twins needs to be considered. A similar twin study employing factor analysis showed that the menstrual and premenstrual symptoms were relatively independent of one another and baseline neurotic symptoms (Kendler, 1992). This study suggests that the genes which predispose to the development of premenstrual symptoms are largely distinct from those that predispose to neurotic symptoms.

Exploration of the genesis of LLPDD has focused largely on the likelihood of an aberrant neuroendocrinology, but a precise pathophysiological basis remains elusive. Recent work has implicated a dysregulation of serotonergic neurotransmission. In the luteal phase women with PMS have decreased uptake of serotonin by platelets and whole blood compared to a control group (Ashby, 1988). Cerebrospinal fluid samples of women with LLPDD reveal an abnormality of serotonin and monoamine metabolites in the luteal phase compared to a healthy female cohort (Eriksson, 1994). This abnormality of serotonergic functioning has been supported by a neuroendocrine challenge test employing dl-fenfluramine, a serotonergic agonist, which following administration releases prolactin, levels of the latter providing an index of serotonergic functioning (Fitzgerald, 1997). Fenfluramine-mediated prolactin responses have been shown previously to alter significantly throughout the menstrual cycle with greatest responses at mid-cycle, these diminishing premenstrually to a nadir in the early follicular phase (O'Keane, 1991). One possible explanation is a priming effect of oestrogen on the lactotrophs of the anterior pituitary, from where prolactin is released. Women with LLPDD were found to have blunted output of PRL to fenfluramine challenge compared to healthy female subjects, suggestive of a serotonergic deficiency. The administration of m-chlorophenylpiperazine (m-CPP), also a serotonergic challenge drug, to women with LLPDD again implicated the 5HT system, but proposed that the abnormality was not phase specific and that the 5HT system had a modulatory but not causal role in this disorder (Su, 1997). It is of interest that the acute administration of m-CPP resulted in significant symptomatic improvement. A dysregulation of the GABA(A)/benzodiazepine receptor complex in patients with PMS has recently been reported (Sundstrom, 1997).

The demonstration of this altered 5HT neuroendocrine profile in LLPDD led to a number of studies examining the impact of the SSRIs (selective-serotonin re-uptake inhibitors), most commonly used as antidepressant agents, on its symptomatology. Paroxetine (Sunblad, 1997), sertraline (Yonkers, 1997) and fluoxetine (Su, 1997) have all produced beneficial effects. To date fluoxetine has been the most widely studied of these. Two hundred women with LLPDD completed a recent study of sertraline; the daily record of severity of problems, Hamilton Depression Rating scale, Clinical Global Impression scale and Social Adjustment scale were all used in the assessment of outcome. Compared to placebo, active treatment had a significant impact on depression ratings and functional impairment (Yonkers, 1997). Intermittent treatment (luteal phase) has been suggested to be sufficient (Halbreich, 1997). D-fenfluramine itself has been shown to reduce menstrual depression scores by 60 per cent as opposed to 30 per cent in placebo-treated patients. It was also found to suppress significantly the premenstrual rise in calorie uptake and carbohydrate and fat intake (Brezezinski, 1990).

Gonadotrophin releasing hormone agonists such as leuprolide have also been shown to reduce symptoms of premenstrual syndrome as have oestrogen therapy and danazol (Freeman, 1997). Their impact and therapeutic efficacy is wrought by the inhibition of cyclical ovarian activity. On the basis of a treatment study of leuprolide in PMS, Schmidt and colleagues (1998) concluded that the occurrence of symptoms in women with PMS represented an abnormal response to normal hormonal changes. Although evidence has accumulated that the combined contraceptive pill may ameliorate premenstrual complaints, a proper placebo-controlled trial is outstanding.

The range of other suggested treatments for PMS/LLPDD mirrors the numerous theories relating to aetiology. Other than an impact on isolated symptoms few have been supported by well conducted placebo-controlled trials; diuretics, vitamin B6 and progesterone would fall into this category. This plethora of therapeutic strategies reflects in part the likelihood that a single aetiological factor is not responsible for the diverse range of symptoms associated with the disorder. Social and psychological factors, in addition to biological factors, are pertinent to its presentation.

It is notable that an assessment of pituitary-adrenal hormones across the menstrual cycle in women with premenstrual syndrome and controls did not support previous reports of abnormalities in plasma levels of either ACTH or beta-endorphin, undermining the likelihood of a primary HPA/stress response dysregulation in PMS (Bloch, 1998).

MENOPAUSE

A strict definition of the menopause is the cessation of menstruation, but amennorrhoea is often preceded by years of oestrogen-dependent symptoms; the characteristic symptoms of oestrogen deficiency include hot flushes, night sweats, palpitations, headaches and dizziness. It is suggested that the flushes are caused either by the pulsatile discharge of hypothalamic GnRH and/or the noradrenergic pathways controlling the hypothalamus (Casper, 1979). Psychological symptoms associated with the menopause include mood swings, irritability, loss of self esteem, concentration difficulties, poor energy and depression. Twenty per cent of women in a general outpatient clinic report these symptoms compared to 86 per cent in a menopause clinic. Two major health problems associated with the menopause include osteoporosis and cardio-vascular disease.

Episodes of change in oestrogen levels, whether increasing or decreasing, are 'high-risk periods' for the emergence of psychological symptoms in some women. Brace and McCauley (1997) have suggested that this may be due to a 'kindling effect' for women with previous psychological disturbance, an effect on circadian rhythm activity and therefore altered neurovegetative functions, or an effect on central rhythmic functioning between the hypothalamus and cerebral cortex, all mediated by effects on neurotransmitter systems. A role for oestrogen in maintaining psychological wellbeing has been implicated on this basis. The evidence regarding the effects of hormone replacement therapy (HRT) with oestrogens on psychological and psychiatric symptoms of menopause have been examined in a recent study. Women attending a menopause clinic for continuing HRT by oestrogen implants were studied in a randomized, double-blind, placebo-controlled manner with oestrogen reimplantatation vs implantation with a placebo preparation. No significant difference was found between the groups two months after entry into the study. The only physical effect of HRT was a non-significant reduction in hot flushes. Psychiatric morbidity of the study population was high with nearly half being 'psychiatric cases' according to the Present State Examination at both initial assessment and follow-up. The authors concluded that non-hormonal factors, psychosocial and psychological in nature, may influence a woman's request for repeated implantation and should be regularily assessed at clinics in addition to hormonal status.

Aside from the influence of HRT, Pearlstein and colleagues (1997) in reviewing mood disorders and the menopause state that studies of depressive symptoms in menopausal women do not support an increased rate of depression at this time, although mild mood and anxiety symptoms do occur in the few years prior to the menopause. Sleep disruption may mediate the mood changes experienced by menopausal women (Baker, 1997). Overall it is accepted that there is little scientific backing for hormonal treatment of psychological problems on their own around the time of the menopause. It is important that the examining clinician be aware of the possibility of discrete psychiatric conditions such as major depression, anxiety states and alcohol abuse anteceding or appearing concurrently with menopausal symptoms, and that a presentation with menopausal symptoms may mask a background of psychological distress. In these cases other appropriate interventions such as antidepressants, supportive psychotherapy etc. may be introduced. A caveat to this is, that after surgical menopause, oestrogens have shown superiority over placebo in the treatment of low mood (Backstrom, 1995).

The sexual dysfunction that can accompany the menopause can cause significant psychological distress; symptoms related to oestrogen-deficiency such as vaginal dryness, dysparuenia, reduction in libido and delayed orgasm can, however, be substantially ameliorated by HRT and is one of the clearer indications, in addition to incapacitating hot flushes, for its use (Pearce, 1996). Non-menopausal aspects of the sexual relationship must also be considered.

It is relevant to this article that hormone replacement therapy (HRT) not only impacts on the common initial symptoms, notably hot flushes, mentioned above, but it can also exert a cardioprotective effect and a risk reduction, through its impact on the vascular system, of developing a vascular dementia. HRT has been found to reduce the relative risk of Alzheimer's Disease (Funk, 1991). Henderson (1994), moreover, found that oestrogen could enhance the cognitive performance of women affected by the illness. A large observational study found that the age of onset of Alzheimer's Disease was significantly later in women who had taken oestrogen than those who did not.

POSTPARTUM DEPRESSION/PSYCHOSIS

That the postpartum period is characterized by a marked vulnerability to affective disorders is without question. Approximately, 40–60 per cent of postpartum women develop a mild form of clinical depression, called the 'blues'; as stated above about 13 per cent develop frank postpartum depression, and, rarely, probably 0.1–0.2 per cent of women may develop a severe form of postpartum psychosis.

Recent neuroendocrinological work has focused on the possible implication of HPA dysregulation for the increase in psychiatric manifestations in the postpartum period (Magiakou, 1996). The last trimester of human pregnancy is characterized by mild hypercortisolism and 24-hour urinary free cortisol increased to those levels seen in mild Cushing's Disease (Abou-Samra, 1984; Goland, 1986). The observed hypercortisolism appears secondary to the increased CRH levels secreted by the placenta (Goland, 1994). Exogenous administration of glucocorticoids, for even a two-week period, have been associated with adrenal suppression, the HPA taking weeks or years to normalize following their withdrawal (Graber, 1965; Streck, 1979). Magiakou and colleagues (1996) have postulated that the hypercortisolism in pregnancy is of sufficient magnitude and duration to cause adrenal suppression in the postpartum. They supported this with the observation that the depression which occurs postpartum has many atypical features, and other states associated with similar symptomatology including seasonal depression, chronic fatigue syndrome and fibromyalgia syndromes, have all been characterized by mild central hypocortisolism. In exploring this possible pathophysiology the psychological status and HPA axis of euthymic pregnant women were prospectively evaluated during the latter half of pregnancy and in the postpartum. In euthymic women, following oCRH a blunted release of ACTH was observed, this normalizing by the twelfth week postpartum. The cortisol responses were within the normal range suggesting that the adrenal cortices retained some hypertrophy from the last trimester and explaining the dexamethasone non-suppression previously documented in the immediate postpartum period (Smith, 1987; Scott, 1990). The women with the 'blues' or depression had more severe and prolonged blunting of CRH-mediated ACTH release than those of the euthymic women. No differences in cortisol response were established, consistent with other studies showing no difference in morning plasma cortisol or 24-hour urinary free cortisol between women with or without the 'blues' or depression 6 weeks postpartum (O'Hara, 1991; Pedersen, 1993). This is at odds with the elevated free cortisol secretion found in women with non-puerperal depression. Overall the data support an association between hypothalamic CRH suppression and negative affect in the postpartum period. These findings point to a number of therapeutic possibilities none of which has of yet been systematically explored; pharmacological methods such as CRH agonists which would raise CRH levels could be employed, as could a 'prescription' of exercise which would raise CRH levels in a physiological, non-pharmacological manner (Luger, 1987).

The implication of gonadal hormones in the genesis of puerperal psychosis has focused largely on oestrogens, these, when circulating in elevated quantities during pregnancy impacting on central neurotransmitters. It is postulated that the sudden reduction in oestrogen levels postpartum can, in a vulnerable population in which the receptors adapt less quickly, lead to a receptor over-sensitivity and the emergence of a psychotic process. Dopamine in particular has been implicated. In a prospective study of those with previous psychotic episodes it was demonstrated that those with the greatest growth hormone response to challenge with apomorphine, a DA agonist, predicted non-psychotic relapse in subjects with a history of both bipolar and unipolar mood disorder.

SUMMARY

The mental health of women differs from that of men not only in terms of the greater incidence of specific illnesses, such as depressive illness in women; the chronology and course of an illness such as the later onset of schizophrenia in women; but also in terms of the exclusivity to women, because of their biology, of disorders associated with menstruation and the postpartum period. Recent original research and reviews have focused on the role of female hormones – oestrogens in particular – as central to the differing psychopathological profile of men and women across the lifespan. Specifically, oestrogens may have a protective effect on neuronal systems; they may influence central (suprahypothalamic neuro-transmitter systems) but perhaps most importantly there is an emerging body of evidence to suggest an impact on HPA or stress axis functioning, thereby providing one explanation of the apparent increased sensitivity of the stress system in females in some circumstances. Future research will likely pursue this further, as the concept of HPA axis dysregulation and disorders of homeostasis as central to psychiatric disorders, developed over the last decade, is further delineated. The attraction of this approach is that, in conjunction with differences in biology, it embraces the type and duration of stressor, the genetic makeup of an individual, social and environmental influences, as modulators of the psychopathology manifested and the related stress system dysregulation. In short, a seemingly reductionist approach to an understanding of women's mental health can comfortably embody the importance of social, psychological and personality factors.

REFERENCES

Abou-Samra, A., Pugeat, M. and Dechaud, H. *et al.* (1984) 'Increased plasma concentrations of N-terminal beta-lipotropin and unbound cortisol during pregnancy', *Clinical Endocrinology (Oxford)* 20: 221–8.

Akil, H., Haskett, R. and Young, E. *et al.* (1993) 'Multiple HPA profiles in endogenous depression: effect of age and sex on cortisol and beta-endorphin', *Biological Psychiatry* 33: 73–85.

Ashby, C.R., Carr, L.A., Cook, C.L., Steptoe, M. and Franks, D. (1988) 'Alteration of platelet serotonergic mechanisms and monoamine oxidase activity on premenstrual activity', *Biological Psychiatry* 24: 225–33.

Backstrom, T. (1995) 'Symptoms related to the menopause and sex steroid treatments', in: G.R. Bock and J.A. Goode (eds) *Non-reproductive Actions of Sex Steroids, Ciba Foundation Symposium 191*, Chichester: John Wiley & Sons, 171–80.

Baker, A., Simpson, S. and Dawson, D. (1997) 'Sleep disruption and mood changes associated with menopause', *Journal of Psychosomatic Research* 43: 359–69.

Biver, F., Lotsa, F., Monclus, M. and Wikler, D. *et al.* (1996) 'Sex differences in 5HT2 receptors in the living human brain', *Neuroscience Letters* 204: 25–8.

Bloch, M., Schmidt, P. and Rubinow, D. (1997) 'Premenstrual syndrome: evidence for symptom stability across cycles', *American Journal of Psychiatry* 154: 1741–6.

Bloch, M., Schmidt, P., Tung-Ping, S., Tobin, M. and Rubinow, D. (1998) 'Pituitary-adrenal hormones and testosterone across the menstrual cycle in women with premenstrual syndrome and controls', *Biological Psychiatry* 43: 897–903.

Blum, M., McEwen, B. and Roberts, J. (1987) 'Transcriptional analysis of tyrosine hydroxylase gene expression in the tuberoinfundibular neurons of the arcuate nucleus after estrogen treatment', *Journal of Biological Chemistry* 262: 817–21.

Born, J., Ditschuneit, I., Schreiber, M., Dodt, C. and Fehm, H. (1995) 'Effects of age and gender on pituitary-adrenocortical responsiveness in humans', *European Journal of Endocrinology* 132: 705–11.

Boyce, P., Parker, G., Barnett, B., Cooney, M. and Smith, F. (1991) 'Personality as a vulnerability factor to depression', *British Journal of Psychiatry* 159: 106–14.

Brace, M. and McCauley, E. (1997) 'Oestrogens and psychological well-being', *Annals of Medicine* 29: 283–90.

Brezezinski, A., Wurtman, R., Wurtman, R., Gleason, R., Greenfield, J. and Nader, T. (1990) 'D-fenfluramine suppresses the increased calorie and carbohydrate intakes and improves the mood of women with premenstrual depression', *Obstetrics and Gynaecology* 76: 29996–301.

Buchanan, C., Becker, J. and Eccles, J. (1992) 'Are adolescents the victims of raging hormones? Evidence for activational effects of hormones on moods and behavior at adolescence', *Psychological Bulletin* 111: 62–107.

Butler, P., Weiss, J., Stout, J. and Nemeroff, C. (1990) 'Corticotropin-releasing factor produces fear-enhancing and behavioral activating effects following injection into the locus coeruleus', *Journal of Neuroscience* 10: 176–83.

Casper, R.F., Yen, S. and Wilkes, M. (1979) 'Menopausal hot flushes: a neuroendocrine link with pulsatile luteinizing hormone secretion', *Science* 205: 823–5.

Chrousos, G.P. and Gold, P.W. (1992) 'The concepts of stress and stress system disorders', *Journal of the American Medical Association* 267: 1244–52.

Condon, J. (1993) 'The premenstrual syndrome: a twin study', *British Journal of Psychiatry* 162: 481–6.

De Bellis, M., Chrousos, G.P. and Dorn, L. *et al.* (1994) 'Hypothalamic-pituitary-adrenal axis dysregulation in sexually abused girls', *Journal of Clinical Endocrinology and Metabolism* 78: 249–55.

Dinan, T.G. (1996) 'Serotonin and HPA function', *Life Sciences* 58: 1683–94.

Dorn, L., Burgess, E. and Susman, E. *et al.* (1996) 'Response to oCRH in depressed and non-depressed adolescents: does gender make a difference?', *American Journal of Academic Child and Adolescent Psychiatry* 35: 764–73.

Earls, F. (1987) 'Sex differences in psychiatric disorders: origins and developmental influences', *Psychtriatric Developments* 1: 1–23.

Eriksson, E., Alling, C., Andersch, B., Andersson, K. and Berggen, U. (1994) 'Cerebrospinal fluid levels of monoamine metabolites. A preliminary study of their relationship to menstrual cycle phase, sex steroids and pituitary hormones in healthy women and in women with premenstrual syndrome', *Neuropsychopharmacology* 11: 201–13.

Faratian, B., Gaspar, A., O'Brien, P., Johnson, I., Filshie, G. and Prescott, P. (1984) 'Premenstrual syndrome: weight, abdominal swelling, and perceived body image', *American Journal of Obstetrics and Gynaecology* 150: 200–4.

Finegan, J., Bartleman, B. and Wong, P. (1988) 'A window for the study of prenatal sex hormone influences on postnatal development', *Journal of Genetics and Psychology* 150: 101–12.

Fitzgerald, M., Malone, K., Li, S. and Harrison, W.M. *et al.* (1997) 'Blunted serotonin response to fenfluramine challenge in premenstrual dysphoric disorder', *American Journal of Psychiatry* 154: 556–8.

Frank, R.T. (1931) 'The hormonal basis of premenstrual tension', *Archives of Neurology and Psychiatry* 26: 1053–7.

Freeman, E., Sondheimer, S. and Rickels, K. (1997) 'Gonadotropin-releasing hormone agonist in the treatment of premenstrual symptoms with and without ongoing dysphoria: a controlled study', *Psychopharmacological Bulletin* 33: 303–9.

Funk, J., Mortel, K. and Meyer, J. (1991) 'Effects of oestrogen replacement therapy on cerebral perfusion and cognition amongst postmenopausal women', *Dementia* 2: 268–72.

Gallucci, W., Baum, A. and Laue, L. *et al.* (1993) 'Sex differences in the sensitivity of the hypothalamic-pituitary-adrenal axis', *Health Psychology* 12: 40–5.

Goland, R., Jozak, S. and Conwell, I. (1994) 'Placental corticotropin-releasing hormone and the hypercortisolism of pregnancy', *American Journal of Obstetrics and Gynaecology* 171: 1287–91.

Goland, R.S., Wardlaw, S., Stark, R., Brown, L. and Frantz, A. (1986) 'High levels of corticotropin-releasing factor immunoreactivity in maternal and fetal plasma during pregnancy', *Journal of Clinical Endocrinology and Metabolism* 63: 1199–203.

Gorwood, P., Leboyer, M., Jay, M., Payan, C. and Feingold, J. (1995) 'Gender and age of onset of schizophrenia: impact of family history', *American Journal of Psychiatry* 152: 208–12.

Graber, A., Ney, R., Nicholson, W., Island, D. and Liddle, G. (1965) 'Natural history of pituitary-adrenal recovery following long-term suppression with corticosteroids', *Journal of Clinical Endocrinology and Metabolism* 25: 11–16.

Grossman, A.B. (1983) 'Brain opiates and neuroendocrine function', *Journal of Clinical Endocrinology and Metabolism* 12: 725–46.

Hafner, H. and Van der Heiden, W. (1997) 'Epidemiology of schizophrenia', *Canadian Journal of Psychiatry* 42: 139–51.

Halbreich, U. and Smoller, J. (1997) 'Intermittent luteal phase sertraline treatment of dysphoric premenstrual syndrome', *Journal of Clinical Psychiatry* 58: 399–402.

Harris, A. (1997) 'Menstrually related symptom changes in women with schizophrenia', *Schizophrenic Research* 27: 93–9.

Harris, T., Surtees, P. and Bancroft, J. (1991) 'Is sex necessarily a risk factor for depression', *British Journal of Psychiatry* 83: 327–31.

Henderson, V., Paganini-Hill, A., Emanuel, C., Dunn, M. and Buckwalter, J. (1994) 'Estrogen replacement therapy in older women', *Archives of Neurology* 51: 896–900.

Hultman, C., Ohman, A., Cnattingius, S., Wieselgren, I. and Lindstrom,

L. (1997) 'Prenatal and neonatal risk factors for schizophrenia', *British Journal of Psychiatry* 170: 128–33.

Janowsky, D., Davis, J., El-Yousef, M. and Sekerke, H. (1972) 'A cholinergic-adrenergic hypothesis of mania and depression', *Lancet* ii: 632–5.

Kendler, K., Silberg, J., Neale, M., Kessler, R., Heath, A. and Eaves, L. (1992) 'Genetic and environmental factors in the aetiology of menstrual, premenstrual and neurotic symptoms: a population-based twin study', *Psychological Medicine* 22: 85–100.

Kessler, R.C., McGonagle, K., Schwartz, M., Blazer, D. and Nelson, C. (1993) 'Sex and depression in the National Co-morbidity Survey, I: lifetime prevalence, chronicity and recurrence', *Journal of Affective Disorder* 29: 85–96.

Lesch, K., Rupprecht, R. and Poten, B. *et al.* (1989) 'Endocrine responses to 5HT1a receptor activation in humans', *Biological Psychiatry* 28: 203–5.

Lesch, K., Mayer, S. and Dieselkamp-Tietze, J. *et al.* (1990) '5HT1a receptor responsivity in unipolar major depression: evaluation of ipsapirone induced ACTH and cortisol secretion in patients and controls', *Biological Psychiatry* 28: 620–8.

Luger, A., Deuster, P. and Kyle, S. *et al.* (1987) 'Acute hypothalamic-pituitary-adrenal responses to the stress of treadmill exercise: physiological adaptations to physical training', *New England Journal of Medicine* 316: 1309–15.

Maggi, A. and Perez, J. (1986) 'Estrogen-induced upregulation of gamma-amino butyric receptors in the CNS of rodents', *Journal of Neurochemistry* 47: 1793–7.

Magiakou, M.-A., Mastorakos, G., Rabin, D., Dubbert, B., Gold, P. and Chrousos, G. (1996) 'Hypothalamic corticotropin-releasing hormone suppression during the post-partum period: implications for the increase in psychiatric manifestations at this time', *Journal of Clinical Endocrinology and Metabolism* 81: 1912–17.

Magos, A., Brincat, M. and Studd, J.W. (1986) 'Treatment of the premenstrual syndrome by subcutaneous oestradiol implants and cyclical oral norethisterone: placebo controlled study', *British Medical Journal* I: 1629–33.

Monteleone, P., Catapano, F., Tortorello, A. and Maj, M. (1997) 'Cortisolresponses to d-fenfluramine in patients with obsessive-compulsive disorder and in healthy subjects: evidence for a gender-related effect', *Neuropsychobiology* 36: 8–12.

Montgomery, J., Appleby, L. and Brincat, M. *et al.* (1987) 'Effects of oestrogen and progesterone implants on psychological disorders of the climacteric', *Lancet* i: 297–9.

Morrison, J. (1989) 'Childhood sexual history of women with somatization disorder', *American Journal of Psychiatry* 146: 239–41.

Mullen, P.E., Romans-Clarkson, S., Walton, V. and Herbison, G. (1988) 'Impact of sexual and physical abuse on women's mental health', *Lancet* 2: 841–5.

Narbone, M., Ruello, C. and Oliva, A. *et al.* (1990) 'Hormonal dysregulation and catamenial epilepsy', *Functional Neurology* 5: 49–53.

Nelen-Hoeksema, S. (1990) *Sex differences in depression*, Stanford, CA, Stanford University Press.

Nemeroff, C. (1996) 'The corticotropin-releasing factor (CRF) hypothesis of depression: new findings and new directions', *Molecular Psychiatry* 1: 336–42.

O'Hara, M., Schlechte, J., Lewis, D. and Wright, E. (1991) 'Prospective study of post-partum blues: biological and psychosocial factors', *Archives of General Psychiatry* 48: 801–6.

O'Keane, V. and Dinan, T.G. (1992) 'Sex steroid priming effects on growth hormone responses to pyridostigmine throughout the menstrual cycle', *Journal of Clinical Endocrinology and Metabolism* 75: 11–14.

O'Keane, V. and Dinan, T.G. (1991) 'Prolactin and cortisol responses to d-fenfluramine in major depression: Evidence for diminished responsivity of central serotonergic function', *American Journal of Psychiatry* 148: 1009–15.

O'Keane, V., O'Hanlon, M., Webb, M. and Dinan, T.G. (1991) 'D-fenfluramine/prolactin responses throughout the menstrual cycle: evidence for oestrogen-induced alteration', *Clinical Endocrinology* 34: 289–92.

Palego, L., Marazziti, D. and Rossi, A. *et al.* (1997) 'Apparent absence of aging and gender effects on serotonin 1A receptors in human neocortex and hippocampus', *Brain Research* 758: 26–32.

Paulmyer-Lacroix, O., Hery, M., Pugeat, M. and Grino, M. (1996) 'The modulatory role of oestrogens on corticotropin-releasing factor gene expression in the hypothalamic paraventricular nucleus of ovariectomized rats: role of adrenal gland', *Journal of Neuroendocrinology* 8: 515–19.

Paykel, E.S. (1991) 'Depression in women', *British Journal of Psychiatry* 158 (suppl. 10): 22–9.

Pearce, M. and Hawton, K. (1996) 'Psychological and sexual aspects of the menopause and HRT', *Baillieres Clinical Obstetrics and Gynaecology* 10: 385–99.

Pearlstein, T., Rosen, K. and Stone, A. (1997) 'Mood disorders and the menopause', *Endocrine Clinics of North America* 26: 279–94.

Pedersen, C., Stern, R., Pate, J., Senger, M. and Bowes, W. (1993) 'Thyroid and adrenal measures during late pregnancy and the puerperium in women who have been majorly depressed or who have become dysphoric post-partum', *Journal of Affective Disorder* 29: 201–11.

Reid, R.L. (1985) 'Premenstrual syndrome', in: Leventhal, J.M. (ed.) *Current problems in obstetrics, gynaecology and fertility*, vol VIII, Chicago: Year Book Medical Publishers, 1–57.

Rubinow, D., Roy-Byrne, P., Hoban, C., Gold, P. and Post, R. (1984) 'Prospective assessment of menstrually related mood disorders', *American Journal of Psychiatry* 141: 684–6.

Schmidt, P., Nieman, L., Danaceau, M., Adams, L. and Rubinow, D. (1998) 'Differential behavioral effects of gonadal steroids in women with and in those without premenstrual syndrome', *New England Journal of Medicine* 338: 209–16.

Scott, E., McGarrigle, H. and Lachelin, G. (1990) 'The increase in plasma and salivary cortisol levels in pregnancy is not due to an increase in corticosteroid binding globulin levels', *Journal of Clinical Endocrinology and Metabolism* 71: 639–44.

Seeman, M.V. (1997) 'Psychopathology in women and men: focus on female hormones', *American Journal of Psychiatry* 154: 1641–7.

Selye, H. (1974) *Stress without distress*, Philadelphia, PA: Lippincott, Raven.

Shaw, J., Kennedy, S. and Joffe, R. (1995) 'Gender differences in mood disorders: a clinical focus', in: Seeman, M. (ed.) *Gender and Psychopathology*, Washington DC: American Psychiatric Press, pp. 89–111.

Smith, R., Owens, P., Brinsmead, W., Singh, B. and Hall, C. (1987) 'The non-suppressability of plasma cortisol persists after pregnancy', *Hormone and Metabolic Research* 19: 41–2.

Stein, M., Yehuda, R., Koverola, C. and Hanna, C. (1997) 'Enhanced dexamethasone suppression of plasma cortisol in adult women traumatized by childhood sexual abuse', *American Journal of Psychiatry* 42: 680–6.

Streck, W. and Lockwood, D. (1979) 'Pituitary-adrenal recovery following short-term suppression with corticosteroids', *American Journal of Medicine* 66: 910–14.

Su, T., Schmidt, P. and Danaceau, M. (1997) 'Fluoxetine in the treatment of premenstrual dysphoria', *Neuropsychopharmacology* 16: 346–56.

Su, T.P., Schmidt, P., Danaceau, M., Murphy, D. and Rubinow, D. (1997) 'Effect of menstrual cycle phase on neuroendocrine and behavioral responses to the serotonin agonist m-chlorophenylpiperazine in women with pre-menstrual syndrome and controls', *Journal of Clinical Endocrinology and Metabolism* 82: 1220–8.

Sunblad, C., Wikander, I., Andersch, B. and Eriksson, E. (1997) 'A naturalistic study of paroxetine in pre-menstrual syndrome: efficacy and side effects during ten cycles of treatment', *European Neuropsychopharmacology* 7: 201–6.

Sundstrom, I., Ashbrook, D. and Backstrom, T. (1997) 'Reduced benzo-diazepine sensitivity in women with premenstrual syndrome: a pilot study', *Psychoneuroendocrinology* 22: 25–38.

Toran-Allerand, C.D. (1996) 'The estrogen/neurotrophin connection during neural development: is co-localization of estrogen receptors with the neurotrophins and their receptors biologically relevant?', *Developmental Neuroscience* 18: 36–41.

Wurtmann, J.J., Brezezinski, A., Wurtman, R. and Laferrere, B. (1989) 'Effect of nutrient intake on pre-menstrual depression', *American Journal of Obstetrics and Gynaecology* 161: 1228–34.

Yehuda, R., Southwick, S., Krystal, J., Bremner, D. and Mason, J. (1993) 'Enhanced suppression of cortisol following dexamethasone adminis-tration in post-traumatic stress disorder', *American Journal of Psychiatry* 150: 83–6.

Yonkers, K. and Ellison, J. (1996) 'Anxiety disorders in women and their pharmacological treatment', in: Jensvold, M., Halbreich, U. and Hamilton, J. (eds) *Psychopharmacology and Women*, Washington DC: American Psychiatric Press, pp. 261–85.

Yonkers, K., Halbreich, U. and Freeman, E. *et al.* (1997) 'Symptomatic improvement of premenstrual dysphoric disorder with sertraline treat-ment. A randomized controlled trial', Sertraline Premenstrual Dysphoric Collaborative Study Group, *Journal of the American Medical Association* 278: 983–8.

Chapter 3

Gender and culture: a sociological perspective to mental health problems in women

Janet Holmshaw and Sheila Hillier

The social role of women has varied considerably in different cultures and at different times, but nowhere in the world is there a society where women hold the primary positions of power and authority, and there is little evidence that such a human society has ever existed. Certain aspects of male and female roles seem more or less universal. For men this means taking the major role in politics, religion and the military. For women it involves childrearing and caring for the health, development, and wellbeing of the family. These clearly distinguished roles are accompanied by clearly differentiated status, with women's social roles usually being accorded the lower status.

How did this all come about? By what mechanisms have social roles evolved? And what is the contribution of women's social role to mental health and illness? This chapter sets out to explore the social and cultural concomitants to women's mental health, and to explain the greater prevalence of mental illness apparent in women in contemporary Western industrial society.

BACKGROUND

There is historical speculation rather than evidence about the reasons for the general social subordination of women. Drawing upon myth and archaeological findings, writers have posited a Neolithic European matriarchy that was displaced over 10,000 years ago. Much of the 'history' remains hazy; and artefactual evidence of religious veneration of the female does not necessarily imply a socially superior status. Feminist writers have deemed the generally androcentric character of Western society as 'patriarchy', but there is dispute about how valid the term is to describe women's general lesser access to power and resources. Some have argued that the description of 'women' as a group places too much stress upon an essential biological commonality that ignores differences in class, race and ethnicity. In so far as these differences do exist, however, they seem only to differentiate forms of oppression. A more powerful argument, which especially concerns the social conditions of women and their contribution to women's mental illness, is the argument that to treat women as universal and essential victims ignores well documented examples of the exercise of female power through dominance and resistance. The label of 'mental illness' (see below) has been applied to some of these female behaviours.

Although it is generally assumed by historians and sociologists that cultural, social and ideological factors will influence definitions and perceptions of disease, relatively little is known about the gender aspects of mental illness in the past.

In classical times the female sex was identified with the unknown, mysterious and fearful. The Furies who brought madness to others were female, as were the Maenads, expressors of ecstasy. These characterizations linked women with the irrational in the rational/ irrational dichotomy that characterizes Western thought. There is no suggestion amongst classical writers that women were more susceptible than men to mental malady, but some of the causes were believed to be different, and marriage was recommended as a cure for hysteria.

The division in mediaeval Christianity between the fallen figures of Eve and Lilith and the impossible perfection of the Virgin Mary was an expression of the same polarity. A new amatory and romantic discourse of southern Europe in the twelfth century for the first time expressed in troubadours' song and poetry a statement about the female as a human being with qualities. This regulation of emotional expression within a language, which combined respect and desire, produced, at least for rich women, a powerful and positive identity, elements of which are still strongly present today. More prevalent, however, was the representation of women as vain, timorous, lazy and fragile, despite clear historical evidence to the contrary. These latter views seemed to coincide with those periods of social change that had resulted in increased prosperity; men generally controlled this process and benefited from it more than women and amongst the richer classes a woman became the fragile, delicate and indulged object of her husband's prosperity.

Towards the end of the eighteenth century there was a significant shift in the way that madness was viewed. Lunatics were no longer perceived as ferocious animals to be locked up, but sick human beings, objects of pity to be cared for. However, it was not until the Victorian era that madness itself became firmly conceptualized as mental illness under the jurisdiction of the rising medical establishment (of men) and the close association between femininity and pathology became firmly established within scientific and popular thinking.

Before the middle of the century records showed that men were far more likely than women to be confined as insane; in 1845 it was estimated that male patients outnumbered female patients by about 30 per cent. By 1872 women made up 31,822 of the 58,640 certified lunatics in England and Wales (Showalter, 1987) though men still made up the majority of middle- and upper-class patients in private asylums. However, by the 1890s the predominance of women had spread to include all classes of patients in all kinds of institutions except for asylums for the criminally insane, a dominance that has continued ever since.

The reasons for this increase were fiercely debated among asylum reformers and asylum superintendents. It was argued that poor people were more likely to be committed than the well-off and that women were more likely than men to be poor, and that illnesses associated with poverty, e.g. malnutrition and anaemia, could also lead to madness. Further, not all women committed were insane; asylum populations also included many women with physical illnesses or who were physically and mentally handicapped. Finally, doctors' expectations may have determined patient supply in designing asylums with more dormitory spaces for women.

However, despite their awareness of poverty and illness, the dominant view amongst Victorian psychiatrists was that women were more vulnerable to insanity than men because the instability of their reproductive systems interfered with their sexual, emotional and rational control.

Very little exploration of gender issues in the history of psychiatry can be found in medical journals, textbooks, records etc. Such information occurs in the books, biographies, diaries and letters of women writers like Charlotte Bronte, Virginia Woolf and Florence Nightingale. These personal accounts suggest that madness is the price that women artists have had to pay in trying to express their creativity in a male dominated society. Such works present female insanity both in its social context, and as a reaction to the limitations of the feminine role itself. Unmarried middle-class women were widely considered a social problem by the Victorians, and as being particularly subject to mental disorders. Whilst doctors blamed menstrual problems or sexual abnormality, women writers suggested that it was the lack of meaningful work, hope, or companionship that led to depression. In her book, *The Female Malady*: Showalter (1987) explores these texts and suggests that the rise of the 'Victorian madwoman' was one of history's self-fulfilling prophecies.

> In a society that not only perceived women as childlike, irra-
> tional and sexually unstable but also rendered them legally
> powerless and economically marginal, it is not surprising that
> they should have formed the greater part of . . . the asylum
> populations (Showalter, 1987: 73)

In the nineteenth century a number of circumstances led to a concentration on the mental susceptibility of women. Scandals about the use of private mad houses for the incarceration of awkward women of property revealed the ease with which people could be convinced of the greater vulnerability of women to mental disorder, and their relative powerlessness. Moreover the medical belief that women were more vulnerable to madness than men had extensive social consequences. It became a reason to keep women out of the professions, to deny them political rights and education, and to keep them under male control in the family and by the state.

The contemporary picture continues to display higher rates of mental disorder for women, especially depression and anxiety. Weissman and Klerman's 1977 review of clinical research reports showed that depression was twice as common in women. More recent evidence supports this. The prevalence of treatment for anxiety and depression in the UK shows rates for women just over double the rates for men (ONS, 1997). GP statistics show even greater gender differences with four times as many women than men being diagnosed with psychological problems (Ussher, 1994). Rates for attempted suicide and deliberate self harm are also greater for women, though rates for completed suicide are higher for men (Moscicki, 1994).

Epidemiological data from national surveys and community studies confirm these findings. The Household Survey for Great Britain showed that psychiatric disorder was more common in women with the peak prevalence of disorders between 25 and 54 years. From 55 years there was a rapid decline both in prevalence generally and also in the sex ratio (Jenkins, 1997). Since the 1980s the use of consistent diagnostic assessments and better quality epidemiological methods has confirmed these higher rates, especially for depression. The 1990 Cross National Collaborative Group (USA, Canada, New Zealand and Germany) found lifetime rates of major depression were higher in women (Weissman *et al.*, 1993). Most community studies show that young married women with small children are particularly at risk.

ARTEFACT EXPLANATIONS

It has been argued that gender differences in mental health are artefactual, that they do not reflect real differences in the prevalence of mental illness but are the result of bias in the way that prevalence is measured. Bias may arise because of differences between women and men in reporting psychological problems, or in the way that mental illness is identified and diagnosed by GPs and other health professionals. The apparent overrepresentation of women in mental health statistics may also occur because of methodological bias in the conduct of surveys and compilation of statistics.

One of these explanations relates to the area of illness behaviour. From this perspective women's apparent higher rates of mental illness are seen to reflect gender differences in help-seeking behaviour because women have a greater willingness to admit to psychological distress and to seek treatment. This argument receives considerable support from studies that have shown that women are more likely to recognize a psychiatric problem in themselves (Horowitz, 1977) and more likely to consult their GP with psychological and emotional problems (Briscoe, 1982; Corney, 1990).

Following on from this it is argued that women's less structured working day and flexible hours allow them to visit their doctors more easily when not feeling well. Women also have more contact with their GPs over children's health matters and so have a greater opportunity to report their own symptoms. This view has received little support from research. Gove (1984) points to the many studies showing that women work longer hours than men (whether or not employed outside the home) and are under much greater time restraints. Brown and Harris' (1978) community study of depression in women found that one reason for depression being left unreported and untreated in women with young children at home was the lack of time the women had to visit the doctors for their own problems.

Another argument in favour of the 'illness behaviour' hypothesis is that increased rates of depression and anxiety in women are due to differences in the way that men and women react to psychological upset. Therefore, women differentially report more stress and distress and seek medical help more often, whereas men get into trouble with the courts because of alcohol, drug misuse, arguments or violence. Yet in their community study of couples who had recently experienced at least one 'shared' life event, severe enough potentially to provoke an episode of depression, Nazroo and associates did not find any evidence of men developing substance misuse as an alternative to depression, or of men's depression being 'masked' by substance misuse. This led them to conclude: 'Whilst in a national sample women's greater rates of depression may be compensated by other disorders in men this is not the result of a differential response to the same situation' (Nazroo, Edwards and Brown, 1998: 315).

The use of community surveys, rather than rates of treatment and hospitalization, is said to avoid the bias of help-seeking patterns of behaviour. Thus higher rates of depressed women found in community samples is regarded as a truer reflection of prevalence. However, it is possible that the same factors involved in help seeking may also bias the findings of community samples. Women may more readily identify psychological problems in themselves and be more willing to talk about these to an interviewer (often a female interviewer) as part of a community survey.

It has also been argued that women's higher rates of psychological symptoms in community samples are the result of women being more likely to remember and to amplify the severity of past episodes of depression and anxiety, or that men will tend to underplay these. However in their community sample of couples Nazroo et al. (1998) found no evidence that women were more likely than men to recall past episodes of depression.

Most community studies focus on certain types of mental illness (depression, anxiety, phobias). When a larger range of conditions is included a different pattern emerges. Cleary (1987) found women and men had similar overall rates of psychiatric disorder when antisocial personality and substance misuse were taken into account. Many community studies have focused only on women. Large-scale health surveys include wives' reports of their husbands' health as well as their own, rather than including each family member separately. Overrepresentation of women recorded in mental illness surveys has in part been blamed on the methodology used in some community surveys that average scores across the study population. This results in women scoring an average that is higher than men because of the greater reporting of mild symptoms. Newmann (1984) showed that women were more likely to report mild symptoms of depression but not severe symptoms. Using a categorical or threshold approach to identify depression avoids this average score bias. However Nazroo et al. (1998) found that using a threshold approach showed an increase rather than a decrease in gender differences in depression.

Higher rates of mental illness in women may also be due to differences in the detection and diagnosis of mental illness in men and women. Women's apparent higher rates of mental illness could be because GPs and other health professionals diagnose mental illness more readily in women. Marks et al. (1979) found that GPs were more likely to detect psychological problems in women than in men. This may, in part, be the result of stereotypical expectations about the expression of psychological distress (see above) held by health professionals, and by society as a whole. Depression and anxiety where women's rates are higher are usually seen as illness, whereas alcoholism, drug misuse and personality disorder where men predominate are still ambiguously seen as illness and/or wrongdoing. Moreover, similar symptoms and behaviour are often treated differently in men and women. The increased rates of hospital admission for women diagnosed as suffering from personality disorder is probably because men with similar conditions are more likely to be dealt with through the police and courts.

Differential detection and diagnosis may also be the result of decision-making processes amongst health professionals. In identifying something as a problem, or in making diagnoses, GPs and others rely upon their judgements about coping, the extent to which someone's ability to carry out their normal social role is affected by their mental state. As women's social roles are often more complex and demanding they may be more likely to be seen as being affected or disrupted, or potentially disrupted, by women's psychological distress. Contextual factors will also be very influential in the process of making a diagnosis. Proportionately more women than men are diagnosed as having dementia. However older women are more likely to be living alone and so there is greater concern about their ability to look after themselves. Older men are much less likely to be living alone. Many more will have an often younger spouse at home with them. Men are also more likely to receive help from the family when they do live on their own and so deterioration in their abilities is less likely to cause concern, or even be noticed.

Notwithstanding the evidence presented above it is now more generally accepted that the higher level of psychological distress in women is real and not simply a result of illness behaviour or other artefactual effects.

THE SOCIAL CONSTRUCTION OF MENTAL ILLNESS

Two main sociological approaches have been taken to explain the aetiology of mental illness. The first sees mental illness as a social construct: the result of how certain behaviour is viewed, defined and acted upon by others. The second emphasizes the role of social factors in producing mental illness.

The first of these approaches was very influential in the 1960s in the USA and to a lesser extent in Europe and the UK. It was associated with the anti-psychiatry movement, which developed as a reaction to the perceived coercive nature of psychiatry, the dominance of the biomedical model, and the increasing recognition of the importance of social factors in mental health. Critical sociologists such as Thomas Szasz (1962) argued that the concept of madness/mental illness was a social construction, a means of defining behaviour that society finds unacceptable. Mental illness is seen primarily as an ascribed status, determined chiefly by external circumstances, and the label of mental illness is a convenient way of describing what are, basically, problems of living.

The labelling approach drew attention to the construction of mental illness as a social state. It also described the process whereby people come to be formally labelled (or diagnosed) and also come to accept this deviant identity themselves. In his book *Being Mentally Ill* (1966) another American sociologist, Thomas Scheff, claimed that labelling was the most important cause of mental illness and put forward the following explanation as to how this process occurred. Cultural stereotypes of mental illness exist that provide a variety of images, labels and definitions to describe how someone with a mental illness might behave. They are available both to those observing someone's strange behaviour, and to people experiencing disturbing feelings and thoughts that they cannot otherwise explain. These stereotypes provide a template for conceptualizing behaviour as mental illness and also a repertoire of behaviours for someone who is deeply distressed or disturbed. Society contains what Scheff described as 'residual rules' – rules of contact which are expected to be followed in social situations that are not covered by specific religious, legal or moral constraints. Initially certain odd or unusual behaviours, which can include many psychiatric symptoms, can be categorized as 'residual rule breaking'. Scheff considered residual rule breaking to be quite common, but that most of the time, and for most people, such behaviour is accommodated and explained away.

However, a person may be labelled and responded to as if mentally ill should the residual rule breaking become public knowledge and the person is referred to the police or psychiatrists. That situation depends on several factors, which are outside the control of the affected individual, such as the level of tolerance in the community and the social distance between the rule breaker and the agencies referred to (police, psychiatrist). Those of lower social status, and especially people on the margins of society, are most likely to be dealt with by the official system.

Referral to an official agency is thus seen as a crucial step in determining whether such residual rule breaking leads to long-term changes in someone's life situation and their own self-image. Once someone has been referred there is a strong chance that they will be channelled through the system and officially labelled as mentally ill. This is because psychiatrists are more sensitive to signs of mental illness than are members of the public and less likely to ignore or dismiss unusual behaviour. There is also a tendency among professionals to assume illness in situations even where the diagnosis is uncertain, in the belief that it is safer to treat someone who may not be ill than to release someone who may be ill.

There is some room for negotiation in when or how such labels are applied, but they have an extremely powerful effect. By helping to make sense of problems in a seemingly objective way they provide a way of expressing unexplainable feelings and, more importantly, they provide a basis for diagnosis and treatment. Scheff would argue that to a large extent psychiatry is about persuading people to accept one of a limited number of mentally ill roles. Diagnostic labels are rarely neutral, however, and the use of some diagnoses can have serious consequences for people, especially when the conditions diagnosed are stigmatizing. Stigmatizing conditions can be defined as conditions that mark people as being inferior or socially unacceptable, and set them apart from 'normal' people. People's stigma can come to dominate the way that they are seen by others and how they are treated in society. For instance, after discharge from a mental hospital someone carries the label of 'ex-mental patient', a stigma that can overshadow whatever else someone is, or has done in their lives, in a way that would not happen with most other diagnoses.

From the social construction perspective therefore, mental illness is seen as a social role. Illness is not seen as being within the individual but within the system. Feminist theory takes forward these ideas in explaining gender differences in mental health. From this perspective women are seen as being more often labelled as mentally ill than men. Women's feelings and behaviours are more likely to be diagnosed as psychological symptoms than are men's. It is argued that women are more vulnerable to such labelling due to both the general sexism in society as a whole, and also the sexism of professional attitudes. Medicine, including psychiatry, is regarded as being male dominated and underpinned by stereotypes of female inferiority. This is demonstrated in GPs' greater readiness to identify psychological problems in women and also in the differential treatment for men and women once such problems are diagnosed. Studies have shown GPs to be more sympathetic towards psychological problems in men. Viewing them as more unusual, and therefore more serious. Women are more likely to be prescribed psychotropic drugs (Ashton, 1991), to be given electroconvulsive therapy (ECT) (Frank, 1990), and are less likely to be referred to a specialist mental health worker following psychological diagnosis from their GP (Brown et al., 1988). Even in schizophrenia where most studies show that the incidence is about equal in women and men, treatments have strong symbolic associations with the female role. From the 1930s to the 1950s in the UK the main treatments for schizophrenia were insulin shock, electroshock and lobotomy. These were used far more for women than men patients with the justification that the resulting damage to memory and cognitive ability would have less important consequences for women's lives (Showalter, 1987).

In her book *Women and Madness* (1972) Phyllis Chesler argues that what is considered to be madness or mental illness is tied to the performance of sex roles. Under pressure men and women exaggerate their normal responses, so that women, who in normal circumstances show more anxiety, fear and sadness, are likely, under pressure, to become overanxious or depressed and be given the label of mental illness. In contrast men may become too angry and violent, and be referred to the police or the courts. In society the female role is less valued than the male. 'Madness' in women and men is the label given to behaviour acting out the devalued female role. However women are also labelled 'mad' if they reject the female sex role. This results in the so-called Catch 22 of female mental health – women can be labelled as mentally ill for both conforming to, and not conforming to, sex roles, whereas for men it is only when they do not conform to their sex role that they will be given such a label.

The social constructionist approach has been criticized for ignoring the reality of distress that people experience. Feminist theory has also been taken to task for providing only long-term solutions about changing the structure and inequalities in society, whilst failing to offer any immediate help for women facing these problems. Szasz has been criticized by psychiatrists for exaggerating the role of social factors, and by other sociologists for not taking his analysis far enough – where Szasz draws a distinction between functional and organic illness other sociologists would also argue for the role of labelling in the social construction of physical as well as mental illness. In the UK where the experience of commitment for mental illness has been far less than in the USA, the labelling approach has been criticized for offering too general and all-encompassing an explanation for the development of mental health problems.

This examination of the power and process of labelling has offered important insights into how behaviour can be interpreted, and the extent to which this interpretation can continue to exert considerable impact on someone's behaviour and their life circumstances. It has also raised important questions as to the neutrality of psychiatry and the negative effects of diagnosis, treatment and hospitalization.

Further evidence of how mental health/illness may be socially constructed occurs when we consider the social context of mental symptoms and disorders. The content of delusions and hallucinations often mirrors the concerns of society as a whole, and changes accordingly. For example, delusions concerning electricity were prevalent at the beginning of this century, and of being controlled by television and radio waves in the 1950s and 1960s. The Cold War was reflected in a plethora of people experiencing delusions/ hallucinations concerning spies or the KGB that is rarely seen today. Instead there exists a growing number of people whose delusions are concerned with AIDS and contact with extra terrestrials.

Psychological symptoms and disorders themselves have also changed. An example of this is the presentation of Conversion Hysteria commonly seen by Freud and his contemporaries. The young women with unexplainable paralysis or complete loss of voice with their spirits seemingly unaffected by such symptoms (the reported *belle indifference*) are no longer seen in clinical practice. What has happened to such conditions? Have they disappeared, or emerged as a new set of symptoms?

Less subtle is the way that certain behaviours and symptoms are reclassified by psychiatry and society. At the beginning of this century homosexuality was considered a mental disorder and alcoholism seen as a moral issue. Attitudes within psychiatry, and in society as a whole, have now changed considerably but people who were diagnosed as homosexual felt the power of this label not just in the various unpleasant treatments that were prescribed, but also in coming to see themselves as mentally disordered.

The influence of social constructs on definitions of mental health can also be seen in the appearance of new mental health problems, e.g. anorexia nervosa and bulimia, and in the reclassification of other deviant behaviours as mental health problems. This is described as the 'medicalization' hypothesis – the tendency for an increasing number of behaviours to be subject to medical definition and control. Attention Deficit Disorder in children is an example of this, as is the current debate about the inclusion of extremely violent behaviour, like mass killings, and behaviours such as paedophilia as mental disorder. In the absence of recognizable symptoms of mental illness such behaviours would have been labelled as evil acts several decades ago. Yet now society, including psychiatry, seems more willing to describe such actions as 'sick', and therefore in need of medical/psychiatric treatment. This has sparked the current debate about the best way of dealing with people diagnosed with personality disorders, and the forthcoming legislation about their confinement.

In examining the social construction of mental illness we could also consider how women themselves construct ideas and explanations for their mental health problems. In their study of stress, anxiety and depression in a community sample of Canadian women, Walters (1993) collected qualitative information on women's own understanding of their mental health problems. Overall women's explanations for mental health problems highlighted the social basis of mental health and the links between physical and mental health. There was a distinct move away from the traditional medical model. Very little importance was placed on individual psychological development for mental health. Women's explanations for poor mental health centred on three main themes: the heavy workload of women, issues of identity and social legacy. The heavy workload included the multiple demands faced by women: 'Trying to be everything everyone wants you to be . . . Not only the "double day of work" but other complications too'; for example caring for sick relatives/spouses, economic pressures etc.; also feeling overloaded: 'caring for others and receiving little in return . . . no time for oneself and lack of support' (Walters, 1993: 397).

Issues of identity included the cultural pressures of images of femininity and what it is to be woman – the process of ageing, increasing weight, symptoms of menopause, feeling less valued and less attractive. Mental health problems were usually referred to in terms of the particular situations that women were trying to cope with and also of longer-term struggles. For example, the social legacy of being a lone parent, or of being an immigrant, or the long-term effects of childhood sexual abuse and violence.

THE SOCIAL PRODUCTION OF MENTAL ILLNESS

The second major sociological approach to explaining mental illness is to view mental illness as a social product. This has become more influential since the 1970s. The social production perspective considers social factors to be the major cause of mental illness, and stresses the importance of socio-economic status, ethnicity, family structure and participation in paid employment for mental health and illness. Numerous studies have shown the most common risk factors for depression to be low socio-economic status (incorporating lower education levels, low household income and unemployment) disrupted marital status, and poor physical health (itself strongly related to social factors).

Whereas the social construction hypothesis focused on the role of sexism in psychiatry in explaining gender differences in mental health, in the social production approach the focus is on sexism in society as a whole and the way that it generates mental suffering and disturbance. From this perspective it is argued that whilst social disadvantage affects mental health generally, some things affect women more often than men. For instance the link between poverty and ill health is well established (Bruce, 1991) and women are far more likely to be living in poverty. The World Health Organization's much quoted statistic that whilst women do 90 per cent of the work in the world they own 1 per cent of the wealth demonstrates that this is a world-wide phenomenon. In 1995 the United Nations reported that over 70 per cent of the 1.3 billion people living in poverty in the world are women. Even when not actually living below poverty level women are more likely to be living in relative poverty, or on a much lower income, compared to men. This is especially so for women with young children at home. Studies in the UK have shown that women are more likely than men to be in low income households at all age groups (Popay, Bartley and Owen, 1993). The proportion of women living in poverty has risen steadily over the last 30 years despite the overall reduction in poverty in the 1980s.

Popay et al.'s study found that men and women in low income households had higher rates of affective disorder, but that a greater proportion of women (22 per cent of younger women and 24 per cent of older women) were in these groups compared to men (16 per cent of younger and 18 per cent of older men). Brown and Harris' earlier community study of the social origins of depression found that working-class women were four times more likely than their middle-class counterparts to have symptoms of clinical depression.

Another general social effect shown to increase the risk for mental illness, especially depression, is the occurrence of upsetting life events. Brown and Harris suggest that women may be subject to more upsetting life events than men, though other studies have not found this. However it is also possible that women have a special susceptibility to life events and that particular events may have greater impact on women, for instance those that affect close emotional ties. This is the 'cost of caring' hypothesis, which states that women care more for others and so are more affected by events affecting others. Turner and Avison (1989) found that men and women were equally vulnerable to events affecting themselves, but that women were more disturbed by events affecting others.

The occurrence of positive life events has been found to be strongly related to recovery from depression. Consequently the lack of positive events is related to an increased chance of chronicity for episodes of depression (61 per cent compared to 15 per cent among those experiencing a positive event during the episode [Brown, Adler and Bifulco 1988]). The likelihood of experiencing a positive life event, rather than just more negative events, during an episode of depression is much less amongst socially disadvantaged women.

Sexual discrimination

Women are more exposed both to general social risk factors for mental illness, and those like sexual discrimination that have specific impact on women. In most societies males are valued more highly than females. Because of the strong preference for male children, in many parts of the world women receive inferior nutrition and health care from birth. This is compounded subsequently by inferior education, employment opportunities and rights. Rights to land ownership, inheritance, marriage and divorce discriminate against women in many countries. Traditional cultural practices, like female genital mutilation, dowry and bride price, and the marriage of physically immature young girls may cause physical and mental harm to women (Craft, 1997), as may the general attitudes and values of cultures that view girls and women as having varying degrees of inferiority, inequality and uncleanliness, even contamination and unholiness.

Discrimination and negative attitudes towards women can have an indirect as well as a direct impact on health, for example inequalities in employment opportunities. It is well accepted that employment generally has a beneficial effect on psychological health. It brings interest and fulfilment, structure and a sense of control, as well as income, social status and social contacts. Women are much less likely to be employed than men or are to be in poorly paid routine jobs. Even within the same occupational category women have on average much lower salaries than men. Women clerical workers are paid on average 60 per cent of their male counterparts' earnings and women sales workers are paid 57 per cent of male wages. In studies where groups of men and women are carefully matched along social and economic categories, the increased rate of women with affective disorder disappears, and in some instances there is an increased rate for men (Jenkins, 1985).

The beneficial effects of employment for women are attenuated by marital status and childcare responsibilities. Least benefit accrues to married women with young children who are in full-time employment. Studies have shown that depression in women may be related to both the extra stresses of employment and unemployment (Bebbington, 1998). Occupations vary in the rewards they provide and the demands and hazards they produce. These interact with other demands to influence women's mental health in a complicated way. Even the least satisfying type of work is seen to have a protective effect against depression and even the most satisfying and rewarding work can increase the stress and anxiety experienced by women (Walters, 1993). Bebbington (1998) indicates that being unemployed made more impact on women's mental health than men's, a finding supported by Popay (1993). But the latter study also showed that next to unemployment the second highest rate of affective disorder was in housewives. It is also important to note that in this study a third of women occupied the housewife role compared with fewer than 10 per cent of women and 4 per cent of men who were unemployed.

Violence and abuse towards women

There are also experiences that are specific to women, or that occur far more often for women, that are a reflection of general sexism in society and the way that this is translated into personal relationships. The World Development Report (1993) estimates that 5–16 per cent of the healthy years of life lost to women of reproductive age can be linked to victimization based on gender, rape and domestic violence.

It is clear that violence can result in long-term mental, physical and sexual health problems. In the UK domestic violence is estimated to occur in 1 in 4 households, mostly inflicted on women by their male partners (Mental Health Act Commission, 1997). This is probably an underestimate as there is much underreporting, but it accounts for nearly a quarter of all reported violence. Studies conducted by the Women's Aid Federation have found that such violence is often long-standing (73 per cent of the women in their sample suffered violence for at least 3 years [Binney, Harkell and Nixon, 1981]).

The exact figures for rape are also difficult to assess, as there is gross underreporting in this area, especially rape occurring within relationships. Rape within marriage is often not included, and is still not illegal in many countries. Hall's (1989) study in London found that 1 in 6 women had been raped and 1 in 5 of the remainder had fought off an attempted rape. There is a sense that all women are victims of rape; in their fears and anxieties, in the restrictions placed on girls by fearful parents, and the ways that women restrict their own lives out of fear. This is seen in the official advice given to female students and employees by safety officers, and the police.

Sexual harassment is also very common and difficult to assess. On the basis of self-report studies MacKinnon (1979) found that 7 out of 10 women in the UK were affected by sexual harassment in a prolonged way during the course of their working lives.

The experience of sexual abuse is far more common amongst females. There are clearly direct effects on the child of physical and sexual abuse during childhood. There are also strong links with adult depression and other mental illnesses. As many as 50 per cent of women receiving psychiatric services are found to have experienced sexual or physical abuse as children and adults (Williams, 1993). Such events are related strongly to severe mental illness and high service use. For instance 80 per cent of women patients in high security hospitals have been sexually abused in childhood or adolescence. Strong links are now being seen between a history of abuse and self-harm or suicide attempts (Koss, 1990). Such factors may explain the gender differences in rates of suicide and attempted suicide noted earlier. Attempted suicide and deliberate self-harm are much more common in women and are related to poverty, deprivation, psychological distress, and a history of physical and sexual abuse. Rates of completed suicide are higher for men and are related to alcoholism, drug abuse and occupations with access to more certain means of death (doctors, farmers).

Society is not only stratified by gender; women in different social groups face multiple discrimination and disadvantage and particular mental health consequences (black and ethnic minority groups, older women and lesbians). At the same time there is reduced likelihood that the needs of these women will be met by mental health services.

Engendered roles

Men and women differ in terms of the range and status of the roles they carry out and in the satisfaction that they get from them. Most human behaviour can be defined as role-related and roles have a central significance for people's self-definition and self-evaluation and thus with mental health and illness. The lack of autonomy and the limited nature of many women's social roles produces frustration, tension and is the source of psychological distress for many women.

Broad measures of social role, however, fail to reveal the full explanation for higher rates of mental illness in women. For example Weich and associates (1998) have looked at the prevalence of common mental symptoms with regards to 'role strain' (the number of social roles experienced by individuals). Whilst they found that women clearly occupied more social roles than men during early and middle adult life, the 'role strain' hypothesis that women have higher prevalence of mental disorders because of their tendency to be over- or under-occupied compared to men was not demonstrated. Clearly a more qualitative exploration of social roles is required to provide further illumination, for even within vulnerable social positions that are occupied by both men and women (e.g. low income groups) there are higher rates of affective disorder in women. This suggests that the experience of a particular social position may be qualitatively different for women and men.

The ways in which social roles of men and women may affect their health have been explored by several writers. Gove and his associates hypothesized the 'nurturant role' that women in most societies are expected to occupy (Gove and Hughes, 1979). This involves having responsibility for performance of essential household tasks and major responsibility for the care of children, spouse and elderly relatives. The result is that women confront more demands from others, experience less privacy and time to themselves, and have a tendency to become physically run down. As a consequence women are more vulnerable to mental health problems. In their study for all living situations except where someone lived alone, women were more likely to occupy a nurturant role than men, especially when children were also living there. For subjects living alone, when controlled for socio-economic factors there were no gender differences in physical and mental health. The experience of social demands and lack of privacy was seen as being strongly related to poor mental health (Gove, 1984).

There is a substantial literature on the gendering of domestic tasks measuring the amount of time spent on different tasks by men and women. These show differential assignment of domestic duties with women spending more time on such tasks, but also being more likely to perform the majority of these on their own. Men's involvement in domestic chores usually involves accompanying or helping their wives, for example going shopping. Even when men are assigned the same domestic tasks as women, such as the care of elderly relatives, the expectations placed upon them are very different.

Alongside such quantitative measurement it is important to take account of the social context of the performance of domestic tasks. This means considering who takes the responsibility for, and manages, tasks and what time pressures are experienced. Sullivan (1997) found that women have less time for rest or leisure activities than men, and were more likely to be interrupted during these activities. They also considered the intensity of the domestic tasks and found that women, especially those with small children, carry out more activities at the same time.

Not only do women living with others experience more social demands and intrusions into their privacy, but they may also be more reactive than men to these social demands. In their community study of couples who had recently experienced a 'shared' life event that was severe enough to have the potential to provoke depression, Nazroo (1998) and associates found gender differences in the onset of depression following these shared events. Women were at 80 per cent greater risk of depression than men. However when they explored the effects of different types of event they found that the increased risk for women was five times greater following a crisis involving children, housing and reproduction, but that there was no gender difference in risk of depression for other types of 'shared' crisis (finances, work, marital relationships). They investigated this further by assessing the role differences in terms of responsibility, involvement and commitment, and showed that women were more involved and felt greater responsibility (but not necessarily greater commitment) than men for roles involving childcare and housekeeping. Differences in social roles therefore resulted in women being more likely to hold themselves responsible for events and crises in these areas, and at the same time enabled men to distance themselves from them. The salience of the crisis or life event to role identity was the chief explanation of gender differences. Women had no greater risk of depression following a crisis that lacked role salience for them, but had a ten-fold increased risk for crises that did. These findings related to the salience of current roles for individual women. They do not demonstrate a general increase in sensitivity of women to particular types of event (which would be the case with a general socializing effect), or that women possess increased sensitivity to crises generally (as would be explained by premenstrual mood changes). It also showed that women with children were no more likely to develop depression for non-salient crisis than women without children – it is just that children are a significant source of salient life event or crises.

This evidence has strong implications for the quality of women's lives, in particular about stress induced by 'the pressure of time', and relates well with the accounts given by women to describe the causes of mental ill health in the study by Walters (1993). In their responses women tended to try and 'normalize' mental health problems such as anxiety and depression as something to put up with, part of everyday life. With other problems, they found the opposite. For instance more women were worried about being overweight than actually were, or said they were, overweight. This reflects the stronger social support for women's worries about weight and attractiveness and in presenting such worries as 'healthy' worries, but not for stress, anxiety, depression etc. There was also the sense that doctors and husbands tend to minimalize the importance of women's stress, fatigue and low mood.

> Women receive more reinforcement to slim and attend to their appearance than they do to leave the dishes or the cooking or the shopping or the parental or child care to their male partners. And women who are single parents have no such options available as well as limited public support. (Walters, 1993: 401).

CULTURAL/TRANSCULTURAL ASPECTS

As the prevalence of depression and other mental illnesses varies by gender, marital status, involvement in childcare and employment it is therefore linked to the things that people do. Social roles vary and so does the value placed upon these roles. For example married women are much more at risk for depression in many North European industrial societies. Research in the UK has demonstrated that carers in general have higher levels of anxiety and depression, and most carers are women. There is a link between caring for children or dependent relatives and isolation, low social value and lack of resources (Brown and Harris, 1978). In most modern industrial societies women are taught to conform and to please others in a culture that places most value on self-serving individualism. In cultures that value the home-making role, e.g. Mediterranean countries or British Orthodox Jews, married women are at a much lower risk of depression.

The position of ethnic minority women is of particular interest. Women in this group include migrants who have come to be married, to work, to escape poverty, or to seek refuge from war in their homeland. They also include women who have been born in this country. They may be women of colour (like Sikh women) or they may share the skin colour, but not the ethnicity, of the dominant white majority (like Irish women). The numbers of women in white, Indian and black groups who work full time are about the same (nearly 40 per cent) with Pakistani/Bangladeshi women forming a smaller group. Indian and black women are more likely to be working when they have children, including children under 5 years. While the public services, like health, housing and administration form the chief source of employment for black and white women, South Asian women work predominantly in manufacturing, shops, hotels and restaurants. Without exception, women in all ethnic groups earn, on average, less than men, although black women tend to have the highest earnings (ONS, 1996).

Marriage patterns among women of different ethnicities vary; black women are most likely to be lone mothers, and tend to marry after the age of 30 to men of their own age or younger. South Asian women marry earlier, to older men, are unlikely to be lone parents, and have more children on average than other groups. One in ten South Asian households consists of more than one family. This pattern is rare in other groups. Marriage, parenthood and employment may function as positive supports, or sources of stress, especially since ethnic minority families including almost half the Bangladeshis live in overcrowded housing. What is without doubt is the negative influence of racially motivated crime, which affects the quality of women's lives. For all forms of crime, the 1996 British Crime Survey found fear was greater in minority ethnic groups, and this was reflected in the greater likelihood of their being victims of crime than white people.

Therefore a number of social risk factors mentioned earlier, poverty, low-paid employment, overcrowded housing, as well as racial discrimination and fear of racial attack, should impact on ethnic minority women's mental health.

Because data is usually presented without reference to research that would show direct influences of gender, the impact of social factors on the mental health of minority ethnic group women is scanty. A national survey of psychiatric morbidity showed that for non-white women the rates were considerably lower, around half of the white group, but were always higher than for men, with the exception of Pakistani men. Psychotic illness showed some interesting patterns: rates for black Caribbean women were higher than for all other women and considerably higher than for black Caribbean men. Whether this is an artefact or the consequence of greater likelihood of seeking treatment or being 'labelled' is currently unknown. For the other groups, rates for psychosis prevalence were the same, or lower among women than men (Nazroo, 1997).

The picture is therefore not a simple one; membership of a minority ethnic group appears to be protective in some cases but not in others. Although gender confers vulnerability for neurosis, it does not do so for psychosis. The latest data did not support the view that minority ethnic group women have poorer mental health, although black Caribbean psychosis rates are relatively high. The possibility must remain, for South Asian women in particular, that there has been a failure in studies and clinical practice, which have used inappropriate diagnostic categories to identify mental illness across different cultures. Different pathways to treatment with ineffective response leading to a low rate of utilization could also contribute to the observed differences in rates. There is little research that shows us how psychological distress may be differently expressed. Krause's work (1989), which describes how Punjabi women speak of a 'sinking heart', is one of the few pieces of research which shows us how psychological distress may be differently expressed in different ethnic groups.

VULNERABILITY – STRESS MODEL

The vulnerability–stress model has become increasingly influential in explaining the aetiology of mental illness and combines biological and psychosocial perspectives. Mental illness is seen as the result of the interaction between two sets of factors. First there is the amount that someone is predisposed towards certain illness(es), and second the occurrence of extra pressures which 'tip the balance' of health status into illness. Thus a greater degree of vulnerability requires less stressful experiences to trigger the onset or relapse of mental illness. This model can be used to explain not just how stress may be a determining factor in explaining the onset of a particular mental health problem, e.g. schizophrenia, but also in explaining the incidence of mental health problems in general. It is the stressors that precipitate onset or relapse of any kind of mental health problem and that particular vulnerabilities then determine the type of mental health problem that is experienced. Thus the socio-economic and environmental pressures facing people in lower social classes leads to an increase in incidence of mental health problems of almost every kind. However, the type of illness experienced is determined by the specific vulnerability factors (biological, social, genetic, psychological) of different people within this group. Mental health and illness therefore is largely the product of social influences. Where biological and psychological factors are also involved these cannot be separated from their social settings. Social factors, including social roles, influence the problems and difficulties that people face in their everyday lives and also their ability to manage them.

Using this model the greater incidence of mental health problems in women can be explained as either being due to the greater vulnerability of women or because of their greater stress. Women's engendered role can be seen as adding to both greater vulnerability and greater stress. Women's social role makes them more vulnerable to developing mental illness, especially depression and anxiety. Putting others first, taking primary care and responsibility for children, home, spouse and dependent relatives, especially in societies which do not award much value to these roles, has a negative impact on women's self-esteem and self-image. This becomes compounded when women themselves internalize society's negative attitudes towards their sex (again with some cultural variation). The long-term effects of childhood neglect and abuse continue into adult lives, possibly by affecting women's self-esteem or ability to form good supportive adult relationships. Women's lives are also mainly lived within areas of experience where opportunity, autonomy creativity, stimulation and acknowledged success are limited leading to frustration and tension. At the same time women's social roles also lead to women experiencing more stress (greater burden of work and pressure of time, lack of uninterrupted time for rest and leisure activities, poverty, violence and abuse).

In many parts of the world women's social roles have changed considerably over the last 100 years. In the UK women now have greater opportunities for education, employment, and greater roles and rights within society. They now have fewer children, which has had a positive effect on health and mortality. Men's roles have also changed, although to a much lesser extent than women's, especially men's involvement in childcare. Whilst we are a long way from the 'blurring' of gender roles that has been popularly heralded, if social roles do become more equal then gender differences in mental health will also be reduced, and reflect only the remaining psychological and biological differences between the sexes.

REFERENCES

Ashton, H. (1991) 'Psychotropic drug prescribing for women', *British Journal of Psychiatry* 158: 30–5.

Bebbington, P.E., Dunn, G., Jenkins, R., Lewis, G., Brugha, T., Farrell, M. and Meltzer, H. (1998) 'The influence of age and sex on the prevalence of depressive conditions: report from the National Survey of Psychiatric Morbidity', *Psychological Medicine* 28(1): 9–20.

Binney, V., Harkell, G. and Nixon, J. (1981) *Leaving Violent Men: A Study of Refuges and Housing for Battered Women*, London: Women's Aid Federation England.

Briscoe, M. (1982) 'Sex differences in psychological well-being', *Psychological Medicine Monograph Supplements*, 1.

Brown, G.W., Adler, A. and Bifulco, A. (1988) 'Life events, difficulties and recovery from chronic depression', *British Journal of Psychiatry* 152: 487–98.

Brown, G.W. and Harris, T.O. (1978) *Social Origins of Depression: A Study of Psychiatric Disorder in Women*, London: Tavistock.

Bruce, M.L., Takenchi, D.T. and Leaf, P.J. (1991) 'Poverty and psychiatric status: longitudinal evidence from the New Haven Epidemiologic Catchment Area Study', *Archives of General Psychiatry* 48(5): 470–4.

Chesler, P. (1972) *Women and Madness*, New York: Doubleday.

Cleary, P.D. (1987) 'Gender differences in stress-related disorders', in R.C. Barnett, L. Biener and G.K. Baruch (eds) *Gender and Stress*, New York: Free Press.

Corney, R. (1990) 'A survey of professional help sought by patients for psychosocial problems', *British Journal of General Practice* 40: 365–8.

Craft, N. (1997) 'Women's health is a global issue', *British Medical Journal* 315: 1154–7.

Frank, L.R. (1990) 'Electroshock: death, brain damage, memory loss and brainwashing', *Journal of Mind and Behaviour* 11: 489–512.

Gove, W.R. (1984) 'Gender differences in mental and physical illness: the effects of fixed roles and nurturant roles', *Social Science and Medicine* 19(2): 77–91.

Gove, W. and Hughes, M. (1979) 'Possible causes of the apparent sex differences in physical health: an empirical investigation', *American Sociological Review* 44: 126–46.

Horowitz, A. (1977) 'The pathways into psychiatric treatment: some differences between men and women', *Journal of Health and Social Behaviour* 18: 169–78.

Jenkins, R. (1985) 'Sex differences in minor psychiatric morbidity', *Psychological Medicine Monograph Supplements* 7.

Jenkins, R., Lewis, G., Bebbington, P., Brugha, T., Farrell, M., Gill, B. and Meltzer, H. (1997) 'The National Psychiatric Morbidity Surveys of Great Britain: initial findings from the household survey', *Psychological Medicine* 27: 775–89.

Koss, M. (1990) 'The women's mental health research agenda: violence against women', *American Psychologist* 45(3): 374–80.

Krause, I-B. (1989) 'Sinking heart – a Punjabi communication of distress', *Social Science and Medicine* 563–73.

MacKinnon, C.A. (1979) *Sexual Harassment of Working Women*, New Haven and London: Yale University Press.

Marks, J., Goldberg, D.P. and Hillier, V.F. (1979) 'Determinants of the ability of general practitioners to detect psychiatric illness', *Psychological Medicine* 11: 535–50.

The Mental Health Act Commission (1997) *Seventh Biennial Report 1995–1997*, London: HMSO.

Moscicki, E.K. (1994) 'Gender differences in completed and attempted suicide', *Annals of Epidemiology* 4(92): 152–8.

Nazroo, J. (1997) *Ethnicity and Mental Health*, London, Policy Studies Institute.

Nazroo, J.Y., Edwards, A.C. and Brown, G.W. (1998) 'Gender differences in the prevalence of depression: artefact, alternative disorders, biology or roles?', *Sociology of Health and Illness* 20(3): 312–30.

Newmann, J.P. (1984) 'Sex differences in symptoms of depression: clinical disorder or normal distress?', *Journal of Health and Social Behaviour* 25: 136–59.

ONS (1996) *Social Trends*, 26. London: The Stationery Office.

ONS (1997) *Social Trends*, 27. London: The Stationery Office.

Popay, J., Bartley, M. and Owen, C. (1993) 'Gender inequalities in health: social position, affective disorders and minor physical morbidity', *Social Science and Medicine* 36(1): 21–32.

Scheff, T. (1966) *Being Mentally Ill*, Chicago, IL: Aldine.

Showalter, E. (1987) *The Female Malady: Women, Madness and English Culture 1830–1980*, London: Virago.

Sullivan, O. (1997) 'Time waits for no (wo)man: an investigation of the gendered experience of domestic time', *Sociology* 31(2): 221–39.

Szasz, T.S. (1962) *The Myth of Mental Illness*, St Albans: Paladin.

Turner, R.J. and Avison, W.R. (1989) 'Gender and depression: assessing exposure and vulnerability to life events in a chronically strained population', *Journal of Nervous and Mental Diseases* 177: 443–55.

Ussher, J.M. (1994) 'Women's conundrum: feminism or therapy?', *Clinical Psychology Forum*, February, 2–5.

Walters, V. (1993) 'Stress, anxiety and depression: women's accounts of their health problems', *Social Science and Medicine* 36(4): 393–402.

Weich, S., Sloggett, A. and Lewis, G. (1998) 'Social roles and gender difference in the prevalence of common mental disorders', *British Journal of Psychiatry* 173: 489–93.

Weissman, M.M., Bland, R., Joyce, P.R., Newman, S., Wells, J.E. and Wittchen, H-U. (1993) 'Sex differences in rates of depression: cross-national perspectives', *Journal of Affective Disorders* 29: 77–84.

Weissman, M.M. and Klerman, G.L. (1977) 'Sex differences and the epidemiology of depression', *Archives of General Psychiatry* 34: 98–111.

Williams, J. and Watson, G. (1994) 'Mental health services that empower women: the challenge to clinical psychology', *Clinical Psychology Forum* February, 6–12.

Williams, J.A., Watson, G., Smith, H., Copperman, J. and Wood, D. (1993) *Purchasing Effective Mental Health Services for Women: A framework for action*, Canterbury: University of Kent/Mind Publications.

Chapter 4

Psychological perspectives on women's vulnerability to mental illness

Catherine Haw

INTRODUCTION

Gender differences in mental illness

There is a general agreement in the literature that women report more psychiatric disorder than men and vastly outnumber them in certain disorders such as depression, anorexia and bulimia nervosa, somatic disorders and some anxiety disorders (Seeman, 1995). However, there is considerable disagreement as to how to explain this. One position holds that gender differences in overall rates of mental disorder are more apparent than real and can be attributed to gender bias of different kinds operating at all levels of the problem recognition–help seeking–diagnostic–treatment process. Feminists have also argued that the attribution of madness to women represents a process of labelling or social construction, and that mental illness in women can only be fully understood within a particular historical and social context. These arguments, which form a powerful critique and alternative view of gender differences in mental disorder, can be contrasted with vulnerability models of mental disorder which suggest (a) women have specific vulnerabilities to some disorders, and (b) are more generally vulnerable to mental illness than are men. These contrasting views do not entirely map onto the *constructionist* and *essentialist* distinction discussed in the literature on gender (e.g. Bohan, 1997) as vulnerability models include social models (Brown and Harris, 1978) which explicitly locate the vulnerability in the social context and not in the woman herself. However, generally speaking, both biological and psychological models suggest that women are, or become, vulnerable to mental illness by virtue of some 'essential' aspect of their person, whether this is because of their biology, personality, perception or thinking. This particular debate can be greatly exaggerated. It also illustrates the dangers of selecting one paradigm in the search for clarity and the 'correct' view at a time when the study of gender and its relation to mental illness is characterized by multiple views which have their roots in very different epistemologies (see Martin, 1998). In this chapter I briefly review some of the evidence for the 'no difference' school referring to the feminist and social constructionist critiques before presenting three examples of psychological approaches to gender and psychopathology: psychodynamic theory; attachment theory; and cognitive theory.

Mental illness in the eye of the beholder?

The question of bias

Feminists have been most assiduous in their observation and discussion of the issue of bias in social research on gender differences and women, pointing to the various threats to the validity of research findings (see Jacklin, 1981). Biases occur both when differences are exaggerated or when they are minimized because assumptions of gender neutrality are made. Specific biases have been highlighted in studies of gender and mental disorder which question the validity of observed differences in rates of mental illnesses.

Sampling bias[1]

This occurs when community studies exclude prisons and other institutions in which men at risk for psychiatric disorder predominate or where there is a systematic bias for men to decline to take part in surveys and treatment.

Self report bias

Women in the US and UK are more likely to recognize, admit to and seek help for psychologically defined difficulties and may also forget, neglect or deny symptoms in a different way to men (e.g.

---

[1] This classification of the most important forms of sex bias is adapted from Becker (1997).

Briscoe, 1982). These phenomena are likely to yield higher rates of disorder among women on self report scales, frequently used in community epidemiological research, as well as influencing attendance at GP surgeries and other treatment centres (Busfield, 1996). However, when men and women report similar symptom levels it seems that they are equally likely to consult their GP with the exception of men in social classes V and VI, who are particularly *unwilling* to admit to symptoms (Williams *et al.*, 1987; Amenson and Lewinsohn, 1981). Moreover, women may differ among themselves in their recognition and labelling of symptoms depending on their employment status (Haw, 1995) marital status (Williams *et al.* 1987) and other social variables. This suggests that gender is not the only social variable affecting self report and help seeking, and that the influence of gender may, in some cases, be exaggerated. Furthermore, it is unlikely that biases of these kinds can explain the extent of the differences observed in some disorders.

Diagnostic sex-bias

There has been considerable debate as to whether and how much clinicians' own sex-role views influence their judgement about what is pathological in men and women and the role of the process of social negotiation that occurs in consultation in the potential over-diagnosis of some disorders in women, such as depression (Potts *et al.*, 1991; Lopez, 1989), depression in schizophrenia (Loring and Powell, 1988), borderline personality disorder (Becker and Lamb, 1994) and histrionic personality disorder (Loring and Powell, 1988). The evidence for clinician bias is mixed with both positive and negative results reported in mainly analogue studies. Garb (1997), reviewing the literature, concluded that although 'gender bias will undoubtedly be found in the future' (p. 113) when greater attention is paid to, for example, the sex and other characteristics of the clinician and the sex of the client, the only *consistent* demonstration of gender bias found was in the diagnosis of histrionic (female) and antisocial (male) personality disorder.

Construct or criterion bias

Construct bias or *criterion bias* occurs when the criteria for a particular disorder are themselves 'male' or 'female'. Measures such as the General Health Questionnaire (GHQ) when used as an index of psychiatric disorder in the community can lead to the overrepresentation of women as 'cases' as they include symptoms of distress which are common in women and exclude symptoms such as heavy drinking which are common in men (Newman, 1984). Bias of this kind also occurs when traits and behaviours which are stereotypically feminine, and are emphasized in the socialization of girls but not boys, form the basis of the diagnosis. For example, one criterion for histrionic personality disorder is uncontrollable sobbing on minor sentimental occasions (Golombok and Fivush, 1994).

Busfield (1996) argues that definitions of mental disorder are subject to gender bias because the delineation of the construct is based on ideas about intentionality, reason and rationality which are themselves associated with gender. Redrawing these boundaries are likely to result in changes in the sex ratios. Indeed, the Epidemiological Catchment Area (ECA) Study which was based on standardized clinical interviews and included alcohol related disorders, using the DSM III classification, suggested six month prevalence figures of 16.6 per cent for women and 14 per cent for men which is considerably lower than the commonly presented ratio of 2:1 (Regier et al., 1988). As this model would predict, diagnostic sex bias is extreme at the boundaries, in the prediction of violence- or sex-linked personality disorders (deviancy/psychiatric disorder), and in the differential diagnosis of depression and organic disorder (psychiatric disorder/organic disorder) (Garb, 1997).

Can gender be considered on its own?

The presentation of overall gender differences in rates of mental disorder can obscure the effects of other demographic factors known to influence rates of disorder both independently and in interaction with gender. When socio-economic class is controlled for gender, differences are reduced (Kaplan et al., 1984; Larson et al. ,1990). Gender differences in mental disorder also vary with age. Although women predominate in the adult psychiatric population, before adolescence, boys show an excess in emotional and behavioural problems, gender identity disorders, learning disorders, anxiety disorders, psychotic and affective disorders and adjustment disorders (Nolen-Hoekshema, 1990; Eme, 1979). The precise age at which this switch is reported to occur varies between 12 and 15. Women's vulnerability to a particular disorder may also vary with the changing demands of the family life cycle (Bebbington *et al.*, 1998; Haw, 1995). Cultural differences are also important as some diagnoses common in women in the West are seen less frequently in women elsewhere in the world. For example of those who receive a diagnosis of irritable bowel syndrome, 70-90 per cent in the West versus only 20–30 per cent in the East are women (Thompson and Heaton, 1989). This suggests that if responses to difficulties are patterned by gender, they are also patterned by race, social class, age and social role.

FEMINIST AND SOCIAL CONSTRUCTIONIST CRITIQUES

Feminists, presenting their case from a rather different perspective, also argue that the higher incidence of psychiatric disorders in women cannot be accepted at face value. They suggest 'mental illness' should be seen as a label, or a social construct, which serves to maintain an oppressive, misogynous system reinforcing sexual inequality and disempowering women by defining them as mentally ill (e.g. Chesler, 1972; Fulani, 1987; Ussher, 1991). Behaviour which is unacceptable, either because it is stereotypically feminine and, hence, devalued (Broverman *et al.*, 1970), or because it challenges the traditional female role (Showalter, 1987) is held to be deviant and hence 'mad'. Rejecting any heuristic necessity for intrapsychic explanation, social constructionists present a related, but more sophisticated, argument stressing the connection between meaning and power, with language as a sign system used by the powerful to label and define to the disadvantage of women and others with less access to power (Foucault, 1973). Theorists adopting this position point out that gender does not reside in the person, but is a social construct that is constituted in social interaction (e.g. Hare-Mustin and Macerek, 1990). It is something you 'do', not what you 'are' (West and Zimmerman, 1998). From this perspective, mental disorders, such as 'depression' are created as discursive objects which serve to decontextualize women's experience and subsequently reconstitute it as a symptom. Thus, social constructionists have examined anxiety disorders (Fodor, 1992), depression and affective disorders (Hamilton and Jensvold, 1992) and trauma (Root, 1992), in order to elaborate how these problems are manifested in women's lives, to *re-link* them to experiences of oppression, discrimination and relative powerlessness and to uncouple them from psychiatric discourse which locates the difficulty within the person.

VULNERABILITY MODELS OF MENTAL ILLNESS IN WOMEN

The contrasting view of gender differences in both overall rates of mental disorder and the patterning of women's disorders assumes that these differences are not spurious or due to bias and that diagnostic categories validly reflect women's vulnerability to mental illness in general and specific disorders in particular. There are three major explanations of this kind which address different questions, make use of different methodologies and highlight different processes: *biological* explanations which involve explanations about women's bodies, *social* explanations which look to the social circumstances in women's lives and *psychological* explanations which have traditionally concerned themselves with the mind and behaviour.

Psychological theories of women's vulnerability differ, not only in their specific proposals but also in the epistemological framework within which their ideas are framed and presented. They also take very different approaches to the question of gender. Attachment theory and cognitive theories of psychiatric disorder have tended to assume gender neutrality and have not included a consideration of women's development as a central aspect of theory even though the social and developmental literature would allow them to do so. Psychoanalytic theory has always assumed that gender is central to development and mental health, however these theories are highly speculative and have been criticized for their negative impact on women. Nevertheless, all three say something about women's vulnerability and all posit internal, relatively stable mental constructs. As Unger (1998) points out, in contrast to constructivist and social constructionist positions, these explanations share a common commitment to a fixed past as a major determinant of current behaviour and share the assumption that reality constructs the person, that is, they are investigated within a positivist/realist epistemological framework. It is these characteristics that allow social, biological and psychological factors to be combined in stress-diathesis or psychosocial models of disorder that are prominent in psychology today (e.g. Gotlib and Hammen, 1992).

PSYCHOANALYTIC THEORIES

Psychoanalytic views of gender development and their relation to psychopathology

Psychoanalytic views of gender and their relation to mental illness have changed considerably over the course of this century and can be divided into three periods. The first period, dominated by Freud and his critics, such as Karen Horney,[2] presented male psychosocial development as the norm with the Father as the key parental figure and the struggle to come to terms with his authority as the key psychological issue. The second period dominated by the object relations school emphasized the role of the Mother in psychic development and posited differentiation and separation from this powerful figure as the key issues. Lacan, who reworked Freud's theory in terms of the symbolic role of the Phallus and the Law of the Father, was a major critic of an exclusive preoccupation with the mother–infant relationship which neglected the role of the symbolic father and obscured the psychological accommodations women have had to make to the cultural system of patriachy. The third, contemporary, period is perhaps more difficult to define in this way, but attempts to give both mothers and fathers a role in development, emphasizes the importance of accepting their relation with each other and acknowledges the loss involved in heterosexual object choice and the resolution of the Oedipus Complex.

Freud

In classical psychoanalytic theory feminine development could only be understood in terms of a *lack* of something. In the first instance, this was the lack of a penis, but, as a result of the consequent

---

[2] Horney was a key critic of Freud's position on women. However, Freud had many critics of this aspect of his theory (see Raphael-Leff and Perelberg, 1997).

difficulties in coming to terms with this in the Oedipus Complex,[3] initial disappointment was followed by a lack in other areas, such as super-ego development, capacity for sublimation and moral judgement. Freud argued there were no developmental differences between the sexes until children recognized anatomical differences and observed that girls, and their mothers, did not have a penis.[4] Both sexes come to view girls as being castrated and inferior. This discovery was seen as a major blow to girls' primary narcissism resulting in a wave of repression and a temporary renunciation of sexuality (Freud, 1925).

In the Oedipus Complex, girls are said to achieve 'normal' sexuality if they relinquish active impulses in favour of a passive femininity through their acceptance of the absence of a penis and a desire to make up for their deficiency by finding a natural substitute – a penis-baby. However, Freud felt that the polarity of gender was only fully established at puberty when maleness comes to be 'subject, activity and possession of the penis' and femaleness becomes 'object and passivity' (Freud, 1923). Failure to overcome penis envy leads to two alternative and less desirable developmental trajectories. The first is the *masculinity complex* in which the girl rebels against 'the anatomical reality of her castration' and the passivity associated with it, refuses to give up the clitoris, and seeks to appropriate 'masculine' libido and associated qualities. The second path, involves the rejection of sexuality altogether, the devaluation of women and womanhood in general, resulting in frigidity, inhibition and neurosis.

Freud felt that feminine development predisposed women to hysteria and depression. Since women are seeking a penis or penis substitute in their relationships with men, and, moreover, have already suffered a narcissistic blow to their ego in discovering their castration, they are more likely to form over-dependent and narcissistic love relations and more likely to suffer melancholia on the experience of their loss. Freud also characterized hysteria as a

---

[3] Said to occur around ages 2 or 3.

[4] Naturalistic studies note that boys tend to discover their penis between 6 and 8 months shortly before girls discover their genitals. Following a period of curiosity about sexual difference, both appear to have a shock-like reaction leading to increased ambivalence in girls towards their mothers (Galenson, 1986). This reaction is much more extreme when the initial relationship with the mother has been less adequate.

'feminine' neurosis and related it to the difficulties women had in negotiating the Oedipus Complex and transferring their love from their mothers to their fathers. Freud (1926) argued that loss of love played much the same role in the genesis of anxiety in hysteria as the threat of castration played in phobias and obsessional neurosis. The implication is that the loss of love plays a greater role in female anxiety and the genesis of 'feminine' disorders such as hysteria, while castration anxiety plays a greater role in the 'masculine' obsessional disorders.

Horney's early papers reflect her distaste for Freud's anti-feminist stance and her social theorizing. She argued that women respond to the actual social limitations of their role rather than being driven by penis envy. She also pointed out that both men and women have something unique to be identified with and that both envy each other. Nevertheless, her own theories drew largely from those of Freud. She acknowledged the existence of primary penis envy but distinguished between the observable reaction of little girls to the discovery of the penis[5] or *primary envy* and *secondary envy* of men that derives from 'all that has miscarried in the development of womanhood' to clarify how 'a biological handicap' was compounded by a social reality of actual disadvantage (Horney, 1973: 14).

Melanie Klein, object relations and the mother–daughter relationship

The second period of interest in women's development, in the 1960s and 1970s, coincided with the rebirth of the feminist movement and was dominated by analysts who placed the mother in a more central position as the most powerful, enviable and influential parent. Melanie Klein reworked the Oedipus Complex in a completely new way, placing the mother centre stage in the earliest period and shifting her attention away from a sole interest in erotic desire to a new interest in emotional and intellectual development. She felt that the more persecuting and primitively cruel the early maternal identification, the less adequately the child, girl or boy, is able to negotiate the demands and losses of the Oedipus Complex (Mitchell, 1986).

---

[5] Said to have onanistic and scotophillic advantages.

Object relations theorists, such as Winnicott, Fairburn, Guntrip and Kohut rejected Freud's and Klein's emphasis on instinctual drives. They presented a more purely psychological formulation of development based on the idea of a central ego seeking to relate itself with objects through which it could find satisfaction and support. In this view, development is seen as a process of separation and growing away from infantile dependency; from a primary identification with the object to a mature state of relatedness based on the differentiation of the self from the object, the internalizations of object attachments and development of the self structure.[6]

Feminist psychoanalysts have developed more extensive views of women's development within the framework of object relations theory. These positions suggest that the issues of identification with and separation from the mother are key to understanding both men's and women's development. Chodorow (1978) has argued that as a result of 'asymmetrical parenting' both girls and boys come to define themselves in relation to the mother. However, the need to differentiate into two different genders means that the process is quite different for the two sexes. Girls' psychic structure develops within a context of identification on the basis of *similarity* with the mother, whereas boys construct their identity on the basis of *difference*. This negation is held to create difficulties for masculine identity which is seen as being threatened by experiences that re-evoke early maternal identifications, whereas girls are seen as being more secure in their positive identification with their mothers. However, girls are not exempt from difficulty in this analysis. Since women come to define themselves in terms of their relationships, they are consequently more dependent on them; more vulnerable to their loss and less likely to express dissatisfaction and anger towards their love objects. A non-autonomous self concept of this kind will lead to helplessness, self denigration and depression. Further difficulties arise for girls as a result of the need to identify with a figure who is devalued by societies that place a higher value on the male. Eichenbaum and Orbach (1982) see this as the root cause of women's sense of inferiority and low self-esteem. In their article on love and violence, Goldner *et al.* suggest that this identification with a less valued figure creates problems for women's sense of power and agency rather than their gender identity as girls

---

[6] See Summers (1994) for a review of these theories.

must 'struggle to claim for herself what her mother was denied: a voice of her own, a mind of her own, a life of her own' (Goldner *et al.*, 1990: 555).

Lacan and attempts to revive the father

Lacan sought to revitalize Freud's emphasis on sexuality and the unconscious through an examination of the way in which the unconscious is structured by language rather than instinct. He construed the pre-verbal child as living in fantasized dyadic union with the mother. The role of the father as representative of the patriarchic Law of the Father was to disrupt the illusion of unity and initiate the child's entry into culture, the use of language and the Symbolic Order. The Phallus[7] as the central signifier in development is the mark which positions individuals in terms of their sex, their power and the position from which they are able to speak. The manner in which girls and boys come to take up their positions in relation to it forms the basis of gender identity. Identity is seen as illusory as both sexes are destined to seek the appearance of either 'having' or 'being' the Phallus in what Lacan describes as a comedy of appearance and reality. What appears to be an identity, as a man or as a woman, is an illusion created through identifications with the desires and expectations of the other as determined by the Law defining patriarchal society.

The girl becomes feminine by identifying with that part of her mother that the boy *disidentifies* with (Benjamin, 1998: 8). As a result she may have difficulties in articulating her feminine identity and distinguishing it from the pre-oedipal relation with the mother, characterized as an unrepresentable presymbolic condition, and may be caught between the temptations of the latter associated with psychotic illusion and the impossibility of defining herself in relation to the Phallus. This also leaves women prone to the speechlessness of hysteria. 'Anorexia, bulimia and 'complaint' (lack of direction) are seen as modern manifestations of hysteria and treated as such in Lacanian clinics' (McGuire, 1995: 186).

---

[7] That is the symbolic representation of the penis as opposed to the concrete, 'real' penis.

Some themes in contemporary views

Psychoanalysts continue to argue that passivity, narcissism and masochism on the one hand, and dependency and the inability to find a voice of one's own on the other, pose particular problems for women. They also argue that these personality styles are associated with the 'feminine' (internalizing) disorders such as depression, somatic disorders, eating disorders and aggression against the self. However, contemporary analysts attempt to free the association between these vulnerabilities from gender, through the development of a psychology of women which allows for a more active female subject. For example, Jessica Benjamin (1998) attempts to overturn the 'Oedipal' construction of gender as the opposition of passivity and activity by proposing a representation of a co-operative 'penis-as-link' (Birkstead-Breen, 1996). This allows for an appreciation of an active view of the vagina (signifying female sexuality) as representing the containment and holding of desire and excitement which she links with the early (active) mother who combines structure, regulation and recognition before the oedipal split into phallic and receptive (see also Stern, 1985; Beebe and Lachman, 1988). The search for a more active female subject is also seen in the presentation of pregnancy and maternity as important stages of development (Breen, 1974; Pines, 1997; Raphael-Leff, 1991); the attempt to find a symbolic bodily representation of women's experience (Irigaray, 1977) and the elaboration of the more active component of the maternal relationship which includes the possibility of perverse aims (Welldon, 1988; Parker, 1995).

Contemporary Kleinians also stress the importance of considering both parents in understanding gender, albeit from a different point of view. They argue that incestuous sexual wishes and their prohibition are less important than the child's need to tolerate a sexual relationship between the parents that excludes him, in the resolution of the Oedipus Complex (Britton, 1989). Recognition of one's own separateness in this triangular set of relationships, and coming to terms with one's position in the generational hierarchy and as male or female, is thought to provide a basis for symbolic thought (Temperley, 1997). However, unlike Lacanians, symbolic thought is not equated with the Law of the Father which consigns women to be objects in a male world, even though these theorists share the view that it is the entry of the father which leads to a greater capacity to symbolize. Temperley argues 'there is no intrinsic reason why parental intercourse need confer the man with qualities of subject and the woman with those of object unless the child is still, in her or his unseparateness, projectively identified with the phallus and seeking thereby to control the mother' (ibid: 265). These integrative formulations, which imply a separation from concrete representations of gender, allow for the construction of a creative gender identity that can incorporate identifications with *both* parents and do not necessitate an 'adhesive identification' with the surface qualities and superficial aspects of societally defined gender codes (Waddell, 1989).

ATTACHMENT THEORY

Attachment theory posits that the failure to form a secure attachment to a central parental figure, usually the mother, in infancy impairs the individual's later capacity to make affectional bonds, leaving them vulnerable to the development of particular emotional disorders. Drawing from his studies of separation and loss, Bowlby (1969; 1973; 1979; 1980) suggested that individuals respond in characteristic ways to parental insensitivity and lack of responsiveness. All individuals with insecure attachments were said to be vulnerable to stressful life events even though the expression of distress and the particular form a disorder takes might vary. Thus, those with *anxious* attachments might respond to the loss of a loved one through incessant mourning and depression, the *compulsively self reliant* might not mourn for years, yet fall prey to intermittent depression and irritability (Parkes, 1972). Ainsworth *et al.* (1978) developed a way of measuring the proposed underlying attachment in infancy and further clarified these different attachment styles. She observed children in the *Strange Situation Task*, an artificially produced separation experience, and classified children's' responses into *secure, insecure/resistant or ambivalent*, and *insecure/avoidant*. Further investigation revealed a fourth disorganized attachment strategy (Main and Solomon, 1986).[8]

---

[8] Roughly 65 per cent of 'normal' children are judged secure, 21 per cent insecure/avoidant and 15 per cent insecure/ambivalent (Van IJzendoorn and Kroonenburg, 1988). Studies of at-risk children show higher proportions of insecurely attached and disorganized attachments (Crittenden, 1985).

Bowlby hypothesized that children form internal representations of their early interactions with their attachment figure that form the basis of their view of themselves and others. These *internal working models* provide the intrapsychic mechanism by which the effects of early experience are carried forward into later life. Main *et al.* (1985) have explored adults' internal working models of attachment using the Adult Attachment Interview (AAI).[9] Adults who presented a single and coherent model of their attachment history and were better able to access early memories and to perform other cognitive functions, were found to have children who were securely attached to them (Main, 1991). In contrast, insecure adults, especially those with unresolved experiences of loss or those with multiple models of their experience, were more likely to have children judged insecure in the Strange Situation. Individuals with poor reflective functioning and limited metacognitive capacities appear to be prey to the unpredictability of their own minds and the discontinuity of their affective worlds leaving them vulnerable to stressful events, chronic interpersonal difficulties and episodic disorders (see also, Fonagy, 1997). This formulation suggests that the same processes underlie cognitive integration, the ability to recognize the mental state of another, the ability to parent and vulnerability to mental illness.

Attachment theory and gender

Despite a relative neglect of the issue of gender, a number of gender hypotheses have been put forward in attachment-related theory and research. Relational theorists such as Gilligan (1982), Miller (1976) and Kaplan (1986), among others, have argued that, in contrast to men, attachment and affiliation play a dominant and continuing role in women's lives as their sense of self and identity develops within a context of relationships, or 'being-in-relation', and judge themselves against a standard of care and responsibility.

---

[9] The AAI categorizes individuals into four groups. Dismissive individuals tend to deny the importance of relationships and minimize the importance of feelings. Secure individuals have access to their feelings and are free to talk about them. Preoccupied individuals seem to be caught up in their relationships often experiencing contradictory and incoherent feelings about them. Individuals classified as unresolved give disorganized or inconsistent accounts and appear to have suffered trauma or loss.

This, it is proposed, leaves them more vulnerable to the impact of loss and the disruption of interpersonal ties.

A second issue concerns the role of gender in the intergenerational transmission of secure/insecure attachment and psychopathology. Research contrasting mother and father attachments suggests that mother attachment is primary in predicting children's security (Van IJzendoorn, 1995) and takes precedence in the internal hierarchy of working models (Main *et al.*, 1985). However, the work of Doane and her colleague Diamond suggests that gender identification may influence the adoption of styles of emotional expression that underpin the transmission of attachment security (Diamond and Doane, 1994; Doane *et al.*, 1991). Finally, the extension of the attachment model past early infancy requires us to address the question of what happens to attachment relationships *following* gender differentiation and the issue of the relationship between attachment, gender identity and sexuality. I confine myself here to a consideration of gender differences in attachment security and their relation to psychopathology at different stages of the life cycle.

Some gender differences in attachment research and their relation to psychopathology

Infants and young children

Male and female infants and young children do not seem to differ in their propensity to become attached, or their attachment style (Ainsworth, 1991; Lamb *et al.*, 1985). However, the same set of attachment behaviours may have different antecedents and consequences for boys and girls. One well-established link appears to be an association between insecure, avoidant attachment and later behavioural problems in boys but not girls (Cohn, 1990; Renken *et al.*, 1989; Erickson *et al.*, 1985; Lewis *et al.*, 1984). Research examining the link between maternal depression and children's cognitive, emotional and social development also suggests that boys are more vulnerable to disrupted early interaction (Hay, 1997; Murray *et al.*, 1993; 1996). Although some studies have noted an association between insecure attachment and internalizing behaviours in girls (e.g. Turner, 1991; Fagot and Kavanagh, 1993) most studies have failed to demonstrate any association. Moreover, in a recent study, the majority of secure children with significant disorders were girls (Goldberg, 1997). Greenberg et al. (1997) suggest that the absence of an association between insecure (resistant) attachment and internalizing disorders may be due to the relative rarity of resistant attachments, and the invisibility of internalizing disorders in children as well as their covariance with externalizing disorders. Others have suggested that cultural pressures on girls in the direction of internalizing behaviour may obscure associations between attachment security and either passive withdrawal or aggression in girls (e.g. Renken et al., 1989).

Research with infants and older children demonstrates that parents, teachers and peer groups all respond differently to the insecure behaviours of boys and girls (Weinberg et al., 1999; Fagot and Hagan, 1991; Fagot and Kavanagh 1993;Turner 1991). While the reciprocal response of adults to insecurity in boys and girls may systematically encourage the development of externalizing behaviours in boys and internalizing and dependent behaviours in girls, in line with sex-role norms, the relative lack of support insecure boys receive in these interactions is likely to contribute to the stronger relationship between insecurity (avoidant) and psychopathology (externalizing syndromes) observed in boys.

Adolescence and adulthood

It is in adolescence that girls and women begin to report internalizing symptoms (somatic problems, depressed mood, eating disorders and aggression against the self) in excess of boys, whereas adolescent boys and men continue to exhibit higher levels of externalizing symptoms (e.g. aggression, delinquent and antisocial acts, behaviour problems, stealing, bullying) (Leadbeater, 1995). Moreover, although girls may not develop stronger attachments than boys, patterns of attachment may vary with gender in a way that is less true of younger children. Thus, some studies suggest that, in adolescence, girls tend to be more preoccupied and boys more avoidant, and these strategies are differentially associated with internalizing and externalizing disorders (Kenny et al., 1993; Kobac and Sceery, 1988; Rosenstein and Horowitz, 1996).

The adult research literature confirms that clinical groups show a high proportion of individuals with insecure attachments (Van IJzendoorn and Bakermans-Kranenburg, 1996; Fonagy et al., 1997; Rubin and Lollis, 1988). Research using measures such as the

Parental Bonding Instrument (PBI) (Parker *et al.*, 1979) have also fairly consistently reported an association between adult depression and the recall of an early lack of care and/or overprotection (e.g. Gotlib *et al.*, 1988; see also review by Blatt and Homann, 1992). Gerlsma *et al.*, (1990) reported similar findings in a meta-analysis of recalled parenting practices in depressed and anxious patients. Although one might expect the retrospective recall of depressed patients to be highly biased by their negative cognitive set, the research literature suggests that this may not be the case (Parker, 1981; 1986).

The relationship between attachment style and a particular type of disorder – externalizing or internalizing – is less clear. Although some studies have shown a link between externalizing behaviours and a dismissive style of adult attachment and between a preoccupied style and internalizing disorders such as depression, particularly in adolescent groups (e.g. Rosenstein and Horowitz, 1996). Van IJzendoorn and Bakermans-Kranenburg (1996) they were unable to show any systematic relation between type of adult insecurity and type of clinical disorder. Clinical subjects had higher levels of unresolved or contradictory attachment strategies although the preoccupied and dismissive styles, particularly the former, were not unrepresented. These authors found no gender differences in attachment style in their non-clinical samples but did not examine gender in relation to their clinical groups.

Despite this, some studies have suggested a stronger association between attachment security and psychological wellbeing among male adult subjects in a manner which parallels the findings in the infant and childhood literature. For example, attachment security was more important as a buffer against stress for males in some adolescent samples (Papini *et al.*, 1991; Kobak *et al.*, 1991; Gjerde, Block and Block, 1988; Kenny *et al.*, 1993). Dozier and her colleagues who looked at attachment security in adult clinical populations, also suggested that security may not provide as powerful a protective factor for women as it does for men (Dozier, 1990; 1991). Harris and Bifulco (1991) found that there was an association between lack of care, vulnerable attachment style and depression with the exception of a 'detached' group of women who were not vulnerable to depression even though they had experienced a loss. These studies of adult attachment suggest a possible link between insecure attachment and inflexible gender roles. Both the Harris and Bifulco (1991) and the Kenny *et al.* (1993) studies suggest that insecure women may benefit from masculine strategies. Similarly, the greater sensitivity of males to secure attachments may, paradoxically, reflect the importance of connectedness in the lives of men who dismiss their needs for attachment. Moreover, we may need to look beyond attachment security if we are to predict psychological disturbance in women.

Attachment theory, gender and interpersonal vulnerability

Bowlby (1973) proposed that children form working models of attachment figures in their early years and these tend to shape the way in which individuals construct later relationships. Thus, attachment theory proposes an interpersonal vulnerability – a tendency to form insecure relationships – which is associated with an internal and relatively stable representational map of relationships at the level of language and thought. Work on the AAI has provided evidence for individual differences in the way in which adults organize specific memories into an overall view of their early relationships (Main et al., 1985). However, the tendency to form relationships which are not supportive can be considered a risk factor in its own right, and provides one mechanism by which distress is perpetuated across the life cycle and across generations. Attachment insecurity is associated with early pregnancy in girls (Harris and Bifulco, 1991). The lack of a supportive partner is a well-documented risk factor for women (Brown and Harris, 1978; Brown et al., 1986). Several studies have reported non-random pairing with respect to attachment in couples (Senchak and Leonard, 1992; Crittenden et al., 1991; Kirkpatrick and Davis, 1994). However, although secure partners tend to form relationships with each other, gender appears to affect the pairings of insecure individuals with a higher frequency of anxious women marrying avoidant men (Kirkpatrick and Davis, 1994). Although these relationships were rated as poor they also appeared to be stable. This result would suggest that insecure women find themselves in relationships in which they are less likely to receive support. Given the association between insecure avoidant styles and externalizing behaviours in males, women may be at further risk for depression and psychiatric disorder due to the added risk created by the stressful behaviours of their mates such as domestic violence, alcoholism, etc. (Wheaton et al., 1997).

COGNITIVE THEORY

Cognitive models of psychiatric disorder propose that dysfunctional assumptions and their resulting biases in other systems lead to, and maintain, disorder. Symptomatic behaviour, mood disturbance and lack of motivation are all seen as secondary to maladaptive assumptions, negative schema, cognitive distortions and attentional biases (Hawton et al., 1989). Despite an extensive literature on gender development (see Golombok and Fivush, 1994), cognitive theorists of mental disorder have not paid very much attention to the issue of gender until recently. Moreover, the clinical and developmental literature is not as well integrated as is the case for attachment theory. For example, Beck's (1967) work on adults makes several developmental assumptions about the origins of maladaptive schemas which have not been the focus of research in the adult field and which ignore altogether the issue of gender socialization. Some cognitive theorists have attempted to rectify this, arguing that gender is a culture that profoundly influences beliefs, behaviours and emotional reactions (Beall and Sternberg, 1993; Davis and Padesky, 1989). Gender role socialization has also been put forward as a partial explanation for gender-linked cognitive vulnerabilities proposed by different theorists. This work has demonstrated gender differences at all levels of the appraisal process. That is, it has been proposed that women are more vulnerable to depression,[10] as a result of primary (event-focused) and secondary (coping-focused) appraisal processes (Folkman and Lazarus, 1986) as well as self-appraisals. Although some social theorists have argued that a concept of a *self-system* is needed to interpret gender differences in personality, development and behaviour (e.g. Cross and Madson, 1997), cognitive theory has, to date, not provided us with a theoretical integration of this kind. Nevertheless, several sex-linked vulnerabilities, reflecting primary, secondary and self-appraisal processes, have been put forward to explain the 2 : 1 ratio of women to men experiencing depression. The four receiving most attention in the recent literature are presented here.

---

[10] I confine myself to a discussion of unipolar depression in this section, for reasons of space, and because gender-linked vulnerabilities have primarily been discussed in relation to depression.

Gender, attributional style and learned helplessness

Sex-role socialization is seen by some authors as promoting learned helplessness in women (Heshusius, 1980). In his study of women and attempted suicide, Jack (1992) argued that sex-role socialization promotes learned helplessness in two main ways. First, females experience more non-contingency between response and outcome in diverse areas in their lives and, second, women are actively trained to identify with a female stereotype that emphasizes passivity and helplessness. Women, it is argued, have a more negative cognitive style and are more likely to make stable, global and internal causal attributions for negative events predisposing them to helplessness and hopelessness in the face of unpleasant life events (Abramson *et al.*, 1978; Abramson *et al.*, 1989). There is considerable agreement that the tendency to make global, stable and internal attributions for negative events is associated with motivational and behavioural deficits. Although some studies have been able to predict depressive affect following the prior assessment of attributional style, there is more agreement that dysfunctional attributions influence the course of clinical depression rather than cause it (Coyne and Gotlib, 1983; Dent and Teasdale, 1988).

Abramson *et al.* (1978) suggested that their theory might be able to explain sex differences in depression. There are, however, some differences of opinion about whether men and women have different attributional styles. Many studies of children do indeed suggest that girls have more dysfunctional attributional styles, either because they attribute failure to internal stable and global causes or they attribute success to external, unstable causes (see Jack, 1992). However, not all studies have shown this, and as Nolen-Hoekshema (1990) points out, girls' negative attributional style seems to be confined to a narrow band of cognitive task – the tasks most frequently used in these studies – and when children are asked to account for bad events in a number of other domains, it appears that boys are sometimes more likely to give maladaptive explanations.

Studies of adults also provide mixed evidence. There is fairly consistent evidence to suggest that women make more external attributions than men, attributing outcomes to luck or task difficulty, although this difference is small (Frieze *et al.*, 1982; Sohn, 1982) and some studies have shown no differences (McHugh *et al.*,

1982). Several studies using Bem's Sex Role Inventory (BSRI) (Bem, 1974) suggest that sex-role orientation or sex-role stereotypy is more important than sex *per se* in predicting performance deficits following failure (Gannon *et al.*, 1985, Erkut, 1983; Welch *et al.*, 1986).[11] In particular, subjects, whether they are male or female, who score low on the masculinity scale were more likely to demonstrate the expected effects. The predominance of masculine-typed tasks in these experiments has also lead some authors to suggest that women might not give maladaptive attributions for their performances if feminine-typed tasks were also included (McHugh *et al.*, 1982). These reservations suggest that gender may influence causal attributions and these may have an effect on both depressive mood and coping behaviours likely to influence the persistence of low mood and depressive disorders. However, research needs to investigate the attributions made by ordinary men and women in a variety of domains if any definite conclusions are to be drawn.

Dependency and 'sociotropy'

Speculation that dependency plays a role in the development of a psychiatric disorder, and more particularly, may predispose women to psychological difficulties, has a long history. More recently, a substantial literature has accumulated that brings together psychoanalytic and cognitive theorists in proposing two contrasting personality styles which are held to create specific psychological vulnerabilities to depression. Beck *et al.* (1983) described individuals who organized their sense of mastery and worth around interpersonal relatedness as sociotropic, and contrasted them with *autonomous* individuals concerned with freedom and independence and relatively impervious to external feedback. Blatt's (1974) dependent ('anaclitic') and self-critical ('introjective') and Arieti and Bemporad's (1980) other-oriented or goal-oriented personality types describe a similar contrast. Both personality orientations are hypothesized to predispose one to depression: whereas the dependent individual is at risk when sources of interpersonal support are

---

[11] A number of studies have also suggested that the endorsement of masculine traits on Bem's inventory is a good predictor of depression in adolescents and can substantially account for sex differences in depression (e.g. Allgood-Merton *et al.*, 1990; Peterson *et al.*, 1991).

threatened, the autonomous person is sensitive to setbacks in achievement and situations reflecting self-definition.

Recent reviews have tended to confirm the value of dependency-sociotropy as a vulnerability factor for depression (e.g. Nietzel and Harris, 1990). In particular, there is evidence of elevated sociotropy/ dependency and, less reliably, self-criticism, among clinically depressed individuals as compared with remitted patients and controls (e.g. Franche and Dobson, 1992; Fairbrother and Moretti, 1998). Some prospective studies of college students have provided evidence for the event-vulnerability *congruency hypothesis*, that is the proposal that highly sociotropic individuals will be susceptible to negative interpersonal events whereas events involving failure, goal frustration or threats to self definition will be particularly challenging for autonomous individuals (Hammen *et al.*, 1985).

Finally, although longitudinal studies have failed to predict depression directly from sociotropy/dependency or autonomy/self-criticism, longitudinal studies using clinical samples have found an association between sociotropy/dependency, congruent life events and subsequent depression (Segal *et al.*, 1989; 1992). However, despite the seeming consistency of these results they have been criticized for their failure to distinguish the effects of sociotropy/ dependency and/or autonomy/self criticism from the effects of stable features of the social context, poor assessment of acute life events and an inability to resolve the issue of whether these 'personality features' are simply markers of an episode (Coyne and Whiffen, 1995).

Given the long psychodynamic history of dependency as a key vulnerability factor for depression and psychiatric disorder in women, and the close association between sociotropy and gender (Luthar and Blatt, 1993) it is somewhat surprising that more attention has not been paid to this issue. Moreover, it would seem particularly important to distinguish between pathological dependency and an interdependent orientation in order to avoid the tendency to devalue and define feminine characteristics as deficiencies (Kaplan, 1986). Rude and Burnham (1995) were able to distinguish between 'connectedness' and 'neediness' in a factor analytic study of Beck's sociotropy and Blatt's dependency scale measures. They also demonstrated that gender was related to connectedness but not to depression, whereas neediness was related to depression but not gender. However, if this is the case, then 'sociotropy' may be associated with depression as a result of some other factor whether this is a personality characteristic such as neuroticism, as suggested by some, or a marker of the depression itself as suggested by others.

A related but alternative hypothesis rejects any notion of a stable intrapsychic vulnerability and suggests that identities based on roles are important in determining a sense of self and that events that disrupt these roles are likely to be depressogenic (Thoits, 1991; Oatley and Bolton, 1985). Consistent with this hypothesis, Brown *et al.* (1987) found that women were more likely to become depressed if a precipitating event matched a valued role domain. Nazroo *et al.* (1997) found that the greater risk for women was associated with events involving children, housing or reproductive problems, and that differences in risk in married couples was restricted to couples with gender-segregated roles. Kessler and McLeod (1984) noted that women were vulnerable to events that happen to others in their social network whereas men were typically only affected by events that directly affected themselves and referred to this as the 'cost of caring'. This argument suggests that 'connectedness' may increase vulnerability through an exposure to a larger group of 'identity related stressors' (Thoits, 1991).

Self discrepancy theory

Self discrepancy theory suggests that when individuals experience their capacities, characteristics and behaviours as not meeting their goals or *self guides* (the *ideal* self and the *ought* self), they experience emotional distress (Higgins, 1987). Higgins and his colleagues argue that discrepancies between the actual self and the ideal self increase vulnerability to depression, and are associated with the absence of positive outcomes, while actual–ought discrepancies increase vulnerability to anxiety symptoms and are associated with the presence of negative outcomes. These predictions have been demonstrated among college students (Higgins *et al.*, 1985) and clinically depressed and phobic subjects (Strauman, 1989; Scott and O'Hara, 1993).

Hankin *et al.* (1998) suggest that as adolescents enter the stage of formal operations they develop the capacity to think abstractly and reflect from multiple viewpoints which may open up the possibility of discrepancies in the way they view themselves. Since this process occurs at a time when they are maturing physically, a process that begins later in boys, girls may be particularly vulnerable to developing excessive self standards and self-ideal discrepancies, particularly in the area of body image (Allgood *et al.*, 1990; Dornbusch *et al.*, 1984; Strauman *et al.*, 1991). Pressures on women to attend to social judgements about their appearance increases the likelihood that adolescent girls will experience discrepancies in their self judgements both from their own standpoint and from the viewpoint of others. Research on interactions in same-sex and mixed-sex groups shows that girls and women are less assertive, take less than their share of scarce resources and are ignored more frequently by both sexes than males in mixed-sex groups but are equally active in same-sex groups (Maccoby, 1990). This suggests a further reason why girls should develop self discrepancies, particularly in adolescence when interest in forming sexual relationships becomes salient and mixed-sex contacts increase. Actual–ideal discrepancies of this kind have been found to partially mediate gender differences in depressive symptomology (Hankins *et al.*, 1998) and are related to the development of eating disorders (Strauman *et al.*, 1991).

Self-focus and maladaptive response styles

A further theory put forward to explain gender differences in depression suggests that women have a more *self-focused attentional style*, which may lead to less effective coping with minor dysphoric reactions (e.g. Nolen-Hoekshema, 1987; Pyszczynski and Greenberg, 1987). Nolen-Hoekshema (1987; 1991) has proposed that individuals who respond to dysphoric moods with a ruminative response style will be vulnerable to persistent dysphoria. She has reported several studies of non-clinical populations which demonstrate that ruminative response styles are able to predict higher levels of dysphoria over time (Nolen-Hoekshema and Morrow, 1991; Nolen-Hoekshema *et al.* 1993, 1994). Roberts *et al.* (1998) presented further evidence in support of the hypothesis in a college sample of students who met DSM-IV criteria for major depression. They proposed that rumination may reflect a cognitive manifestation of neuroticism that increases vulnerability to episodes of persistent dysphoria.

Nolen-Hoekshema and her colleagues have also shown that men and women differ in their response styles to depressed mood (Nolen-Hoekshema, 1987; Nolen-Hockshema *et al.*, 1993). Men tended to make use of more active strategies to distract themselves from their concerns whereas women made use of a ruminative style which focused attention onto depressive concerns and led to the amplification and continuation of negative mood. In a further study, this author found that rumination explained gender differences in changes in dysphoric mood over a 6-month period (Nolen-Hoekshema *et al.*, 1994). Although women's tendency to ruminate may lead them to suffer higher rates of depression, men's distracting style can also lead to pathology, albeit of a different kind, such as aggression, or alcoholism (e.g. Gjerde *et al.*, 1988). Nolen-Hoekshema's work suggests, therefore, that male and female socialization will lead to very different styles of coping with emotional distress, a conclusion that attachment and developmental research increasingly demonstrates.

CONCLUSION

Psychoanalytic positions on gender tend to assume difference. In contrast, attachment and cognitive theories make assumptions of similarity between the sexes. These differing stances are reflected in the extensive theorizing of psychoanalysts and in the failure of cognitive and attachment theorists to provide any substantial discussion of gender and how it might influence psychological vulnerability and the expression of mental illness. Nevertheless, gender differences have emerged within both traditions and we can legitimately ask to what extent do these findings provide support for the vulnerability model of gender differences in mental disorder.

Women outnumber men in a number of mental disorders, suggesting they may possess a general vulnerability to a range of disorders. However, the predominance of women in disorders such as depression, anorexia and bulimia nervosa and other 'feminine' disorders may result from traits or cognitive characteristics or other vulnerabilities specific to those disorders. Although attachment theory has proposed a rather general vulnerability in the hypothesized relation between anxious attachments and internalizing disorders in women, the evidence for this association is weak, and those studies which do demonstrate an association confine themselves to measures of depression alone. Similarly, the research on gender-related cognitive vulnerabilities is largely restricted to the study of depression. There is, therefore, little evidence to date to support any general psychological vulnerability to psychiatric disorder, and most research reviewed here concerns a specific vulnerability to depression.

Gender linked personality styles

Passivity, excessive dependency and aggression turned inwards have been theorized and highlighted as feminine personality traits with psychopathological consequences by successive analytic schools of thought. More recently, psychoanalysts have rejected any necessity for concluding that these characteristics are the necessary outcome of feminine development, but continue to argue they have negative consequences for mental health. Both psychoanalytic and cognitive researchers have now presented evidence to suggest that individuals, predominantly women, with a sociotropic or dependent orientation are prone to depression, particularly in the presence of congruent stressful life events. However, not only can this research be criticized for various methodological failings (Coyne and Whiffen, 1995), the evidence does not provide an entirely satisfactory explanation of gender differences in depression and there has been little extension to other 'internalizing' disorders. Although there is an association between gender and sociotropy-dependency, there has been little discussion of how gender might affect the expression of sociotropy-dependency and autonomy-self criticism and their relationship to depression. Many other questionnaire measures do not reveal sex differences in passivity-dependence (e.g. Levit, 1991; Steinberger and Silverberg, 1986). Moreover, because the importance of relationships to women has been so misunderstood, their propensity to engage with others has been portrayed as dependency but needs to be distinguished from 'neediness' or pathological dependency which may be associated with depression but unrelated to gender (Stiver, 1994; Rude and Burnham, 1995).

Cognitive psychologists in the clinical field have documented many female specific findings (see Barnett and Gotlib, 1990). However, the lack of a theoretical framework within which to view gender leads to difficulties in the assessment of their significance and their relation to each other. The lack of an integrating principle also suggests a mental chaos which could make of the individual an unstable 'Skinnerian' creature buffeted by external forces. It also profoundly underestimates the role of culture, a position from which psychoanalytic thinkers have increasingly freed themselves. Self discrepancy theory provides one attempt to present a theoretical formulation of gender as well as demonstrating that self discrepancies can partially explain sex differences in depression. This theory has the advantage of referring to the organizing principle of a central self which avoids a fragmentation of the individual into an assortment of attitudes, beliefs and traits, and provides some explanation of how both external (social) and internal (biological, psychological) developments can lead to negative evaluations of the self and consequent distress.

Attachment styles

Bowlby was careful to distinguish between dependency and attachment which he saw as a general human need unrelated to gender. Although it has been suggested that the expression of insecurity and the attachment styles of males and females may differ as a result of sex-role socialization, few gender differences have emerged in either strength and security of attachment or male and female attachment styles. Despite this, an association between avoidant and externalizing disorders in boys has frequently been reported and a parallel association between anxious attachment and internalizing disorders has now been reported among adolescent girls at a time when rates for these disorders increase dramatically in the female population. However, no such pattern has been reported in the adult literature even though attachment security is itself associated with psychiatric disorder for both sexes.

These associations are not well understood at the moment. Although attachment research suggests that attachment insecurity represents a gender-free vulnerability to psychiatric disorder, gender appears to influence its antecedents and consequences including the form the disorder takes. While this may be closely tied to the socialization of males and females to express emotion in different ways and differences in the reciprocal roles of their social partners, it is also likely that other factors are influencing the determination of a given disorder which may themselves relate to gender. Two further alternative hypotheses also need to be evaluated. First, it may be that the association between attachment style is more strongly associated with a particular disorder when gender norms dictate an intolerance of insecurity, as in the case of young boys and possibly adolescent girls, leading to a lack of support and structure. Second, there may be a tendency for poorly supported and insecure individuals to find their way into unhelpful relationships which expose them to further stresses and difficulties.

Negative cognitions and coping styles

Research on the causal attributions children and adults make for success and failure and their subsequent tendencies towards help-lessness and hopelessness has not provided consistent evidence to support the view that women make more negative attributions thereby increasing their risk for depression. This extensive litera-ture shows rather clearly how the choice of task, sex-role beliefs and bias arising from the perceived need to report behaviours that are consistent with gender norms influence the likelihood that women will report negative cognitions to a greater extent than men. Moreover, research using Bem's sex-role inventory suggests it is not the presence of 'feminine' traits such as sociability that leads to depression but the absence of 'masculine' traits, indexing instrumental and assertive behaviours, that increases the likelihood of hopelessness and depression in face of uncontrollable events.

Another promising area of research suggests that women have a more ruminative coping style than men, leading them to dwell on negative thoughts for longer periods of time and facilitating the persistence of low mood and depression. This less active coping style may have its roots in female socialization. However, as Nolen-Hoekshema and Girgus (1994) point out, these sex differences in coping style are present in pre-adolescent children whereas gender differences in depression in particular, and the female excess in psychiatric disorder in general, do not emerge until adolescence, making it unlikely that the former can fully explain the latter. If psychological vulnerabilities such as less assertiveness and rumina-tive response style contribute to women's tendency to depression, then they must do so in interaction with other forces in early adolescence. These authors suggest that the challenges faced by girls but not boys include hormonal dysregulation and the need to confront restrictions in their sex role as well as the challenge of sexuality including the threat and reality of an increase in sexual abuse.

The search for psychological vulnerability thus comes back to the need to refer to ongoing interactions in the social world. In their review, Coyne and Whiffen (1995) suggest that the emphasis on sociotropy-dependency as a trait should be replaced by one on the quality of attachment in order to reflect not only 'what is sought from relationships but . . . what is provided and received' (p. 386). However, while it is true that men and women may differ in what they provide each other in attachment terms, the effects of contemporary relationships on functioning include many aspects of relationships besides attachment qualities. Moreover, the concept of internal working models relates less to contemporary relationships than to the internal representation of earlier ones. Given that disadvantaged women may find their way into further situations of disadvantage, and women's propensity to engage with others may lead to inequalities in the amount of caring and support offered and received, particularly in a society which is stratified by gender, researchers with an interest in psychological vulnerability may need to turn their attention to the nature of exchange in contemporary relationships and their relation to the internal representation of earlier ones.

REFERENCES

Abramson, L.Y., Seligman, M.E.P. and Teasdale, J.D. (1978) 'Learned helplessness in humans: critique and reformulation', *Journal of Abnormal Psychology* 81: 49–74.

Abramson, L.Y., Metalsky, G.I. and Alloy, L.B. (1989) 'Hopelessness depression: a theory-based subtype of depression', *Psychological Review* 96: 358–72.

Abramson, L.Y., Alloy, L.B. and Hogan, M.E. (1997) 'Cognitive personality subtypes of depression: theories in search of disorders', *Cognitive Therapy and Research* 21: 247–65.

Ainsworth, M.D.S., Blehar, M.C., Waters, E. and Wall, S. (1978) *Patterns of attachment: a Psychological Study of the Strange Situation*, Hillsdale, NJ: Erlbaum.

Ainsworth, M.D. (1991) 'Attachments and other affectional bonds across the life cycle', in C.M. Parkes, J. Stevenson-Hinde and P. Marris (eds) *Attachment Across the Life Cycle*, London: Routledge.

Allgood-Merton, B., Lewinsohn, P.M. and Hops, H. (1990) 'Sex differences and adolescent depression', *Journal of Adolescent Psychology* 99: 55–63.

Amenson, C.S. and Lewinsohn, L.Y. (1981) 'An investigation of the observed sex difference in unipolar depression', *Journal of Abnormal Psychology* 90: 1–13.

Arieti, S. and Bemporad, J.R. (1980) 'The psychological organization of depression', *American Journal of Psychiatry* 137: 1360–5.

Barnett, P.A. and Gotlib, I.H. (1988) 'Psychosocial functioning and depression: distinguishing among antecedents, concomitants and consequences', *Psychological Bulletin* 104: 97–126.

Barnett, P.A. and Gotlib, I.H. (1990) 'Cognitive vulnerability to depressive symptoms among men and women', *Cognitive Therapy and Research* 14: 47–61.

Beall, A.E. and Sternberg, R.J. (1993) *The Psychology of Gender*, New York: The Guilford Press.

Bebbington, P.E., Dunn, G., Lewis, G., Brugha, T., Farrell, M. and Meltzer, H. (1998) 'The influence of age and sex on the prevalence of depressive conditions: report from the National Survey of Psychiatric Morbidity', *Psychological Medicine* 28: 9–19.

Beck, A.T. (1967) *Depression: Clinical, Experimental, and Theoretical Aspects*, New York: Hoeber (republished as *Depression: Causes and Treatment*, Philadelphia: University of Pennsylvania Press, 1972).

Beck, A.T., Epstein, N. and Harrison, R.P. (1983) 'Cognitions, attitudes and personality dimensions in depression', *British Journal of Cognitive Psychotherapy* 1: 1–16.

Becker, D. (1997) *Through the looking glass: Women and Borderline Personality Disorder*, Boulder, CO: Westview Press.

Becker, D. and Lamb, S. (1994) 'Sex bias in the diagnosis of borderline personality disorder and post-traumatic stress disorder', *Professional Psychology: Research and Practice* 25: 55–61.

Beebe, B. and Lachman, F. (1988) 'The contribution of mother–infant mutual influence to the origins of self and object representations', *Psychoanalytic Psychology* 5: 305–37.

Bem, S.L. (1974) 'The measurement of psychological androgyny', *Journal of Consulting and Clinical Psychology* 42: 155–62.

Benjamin, J. (1998) *Shadow of the Other: Intersubjectivity and Gender in Psychoanalysis*, London: Routledge.

Birkstead-Breen, D. (1996) 'Phallus, penis and mental space', *International Journal of Psychoanalyis* 77: 649–57.

Blatt, S.J. (1974) 'Levels of object representation in anaclitic and introjective depression', *The Psychoanalytic Study of the Child* 24: 107–57.

Blatt, S.J. and Homann, E. (1992) 'Parent–child interaction in the etiology of dependent and self-critical depression', *Clinical Psychology Review* 12: 47–91.

Bohan, J.S. (1997) 'Regarding gender: Essentialism, constructivism and feminist psychology', in M.M. Gergan and S.N. Davis (eds) *Toward a New Psychology of Gender*, London: Routledge.

Bowlby, J. (1969) *Attachment and Loss: Vol. 1, Attachment*, London: Hogarth Press.

Bowlby, J. (1973) *Attachment and Loss: Vol. 2, Separation, Anxiety and Anger*, London: Hogarth press.

Bowlby, J. (1980) *Attachment and Loss: Vol. 3, Loss Sadness and Depression*, London: Hogarth Press.

Bowlby, J. (1979) *The Making and Breaking of Affectional Bonds*, London: Tavistock Publications.

Briscoe, M. (1982) 'Sex differences in psychological well-being', *Psychological Medicine Monograph Supplement 1*.

Breen, D. (1974) *The Birth of a First Child*, London: Tavistock Publications.

Britton, R. (1989) 'The missing link: parental sexuality in the Oedipus complex', in: R. Britton, M. Feldman and E. O'Shaughnessy (eds) *The Oedipus Complex Today*, London: Karnac Books.

Broverman, K., Broverman, D., Clarkson, F., Rosencrantz, P. and Vogel, S. (1970) 'Sex-role stereotyping and clinical judgement of mental health', *Journal of Consulting and Clinical Psychology* 34: 1–7.

Brown, G.W. and Harris, T. (1978) *The Social Origins of Depression: A Study of Psychiatric Disorder in Women*, Cambridge: Cambridge University Press.

Brown, G.W., Andrews, B., Harris, T., Adler, Z. and Bridge, L. (1986) 'Social support, self esteem and depression', *Psychological Medicine* 16: 813–31.

Brown, G.W., Bifulco, A. and Harris, T. (1987) 'Life events, vulnerability and depression: some refinements', *British Journal of Psychiatry* 150: 30–42.

Busfield, J. (1996) *Men, Women and Madness*. Basingstoke: The Macmillan Press.

Chesler, P. (1972) *Women and Madness*, New York: Doubleday.

Chodorow, N. (1978) *The Reproduction of Mothering: Psychoanalysis and the Sociology of Gender*, Berkeley: University of California Press.

Cohn, D.A. (1990) 'Child–mother attachment of six year olds and social competence at school', *Child Development* 61: 152–62.

Coyne, J.C. and Gotlib, I.H. (1983) 'The role of cognition in depression: a critical appraisal', *Psychological Bulletin* 94: 472–505.

Coyne, J.C. and Whiffen, V.E. (1995) 'Issues in personality as diathesis for depression: the case of sociotropy-dependency and autonomy-self-criticism', *Psychological Bulletin* 118: 358–78.

Crittenden, P.M. (1985) 'Maltreated infants: vulnerability and resilience', *Journal of Family Issues* 13: 432–49.

Crittenden, P.M., Partridge, M.F. and Claussen, A.H. (1991) 'Family patterns of relationships in normative and dysfunctional families', *Development and Psychopathology* 3: 491–512.

Cross, S.E. and Madson, L. (1997) 'Models of the self: self-construals and gender', *Psychological Bulletin* 122: 5–37.

Davis, D. and Padesky, C. (1989) 'Enhancing cognitive therapy with women', in A. Freeman, K.M. Simon, Beutler and H. Arkowitz (eds) *Comprehensive Handbook of Cognitive Therapy*, New York: Plenum Press, pp. 535–57.

Dent, J. and Teasdale, J.D. (1988) 'Negative cognition and the persistence of depression', *Journal of Abnormal Psychology* 97: 29–34.

Diamond, D. and Doane, J. (1994) 'Disturbed attachment and negative affective style: an intergenerational spiral', *British Journal of Psychiatry* 164: 770–81.

Doane, J.A., Hill, A.W. and Diamond, D. (1991) 'A developmental view of therapeutic bonding in the family', *Family Process* 30: 155–75.

Dornbusch, S.M., Carlsmith, J.M., Duncan, P.D., Gross, R.T., Martin, J.A., Ritter, P.L. and Siegel-Gorelick, B. (1984) 'Sexual maturation, social class, and the desire to be thin among adolescent females', *Developmental and Behavioural Paediatrics* 5: 308–14.

Dozier, M. (1990) 'Attachment organisation and treatment use for adults with serious psychopathological disorders', *Development and Psychopathology* 2: 47–60.

Dozier, M., Stevenson, A.L., Lee, S.W. and Velligan, D.J. (1991) 'Attachment organisation and familial overinvolvement for adults with serious psychopathological disorders', *Development and Psychopathology* 3: 475–89.

Eichenbaum, L. and Orbach, S. (1982) *Understanding Women: A Feminist Psychoanalytic Approach*, New York: Basic Books.

Eme, R.F. (1979) 'Sex differences in childhood psychopathology: a review', *Psychological Bulletin* 865: 574–95.

Erickson, M., Sroufe, L.A. and Egeland, B. (1985) 'The relationship between quality of attachment and behaviour problems in pre-school in a high risk sample', in I. Bretherton and E. Waters (eds) *Growing points of attachment theory and research*, *Monographs of the Society for Research in Child Development*, no. 209, 50 (1–2).

Erkut, S. (1983) 'Exploring sex differences in expectancy, attributions and academic achievement', *Sex Roles* 9: 217–31.

Fagot, B.I. and Hagan, R. (1991) 'Observations of parent reactions to sex-stereotyped behaviours', *Child Development* 62: 617–28.

Fagot, B.I. and Kavanagh, K. (1993) 'Parenting during the second year: effects of children's age, sex and attachment', *Child Development* 64: 258–71.

Fairbrother, N. and Moretti, M. (1998) 'Sociotropy, autonomy and self-discrepancy: status in depressed, remitted depressed and control participants', *Cognitive Therapy and Research* 22: 279–96.

Fodor, I.G. (1992) 'The agoraphobic syndrome: from anxiety neurosis to panic disorders', in L.S. Brown. and M. Ballou (eds) *Personality and*

Psychopathology: Feminist Reappraisals, New York: The Guilford Press, pp. 177–205.

Folkman, S. and Lazarus, R.S. (1986) 'Stress processes and depressive symptomatology', *Journal of Abnormal Psychology* 95: 105–13.

Fonagy, P., Target, M., Steele, M., Steele, H., Leigh, T., Levinson, A. and Kennedy, R. (1997) 'Morality, disruptive behaviour, borderline personality disorder, crime and their relationship to security of attachment', in L. Atkinson and K.J. Zucker (eds) *Attachment and Psychopathology*, New York: The Guilford Press, pp. 223–76.

Foucault, M. (1973) *The Birth of the Clinic: An Archaeology of Medical Perception*, London: Tavistock.

Franche, R. and Dobson, K. (1992) 'Self criticism and interpersonal dependency as vulnerability factors to depression', *Cognitive Therapy and Research* 16: 419–35.

Freud, S. (1923) 'The infantile genital organisation: an interpolation into the theory of sexuality', in A. Richards and A. Dickson (1991) *On Sexuality*, Harmondsworth: The Penguin Freud Library, vol. 7, pp. 303–12.

Freud, S. (1925) 'Some psychical consequences of the anatomical distinction between the sexes', in A. Richards and A. Dickson (1991) *On Sexuality*, Harmondsworth: The Penguin Freud Library, vol. 7, pp. 323–44.

Freud, S. (1926) 'Inhibitions, symptoms and anxiety', in A. Richards and A. Dickson (1993) *On Psychopathology*, Harmondsworth: The Penguin Freud Library, vol. 10, pp. 229–329.

Frieze, I.H., Whitley, B., Hanusa B. and McHugh, M. (1982) 'Assessing the theoretical models for sex differences in causal attributions for success and failure', *Sex Roles* 3: 333–43.

Fulani, L. (1987) *The Psychopathology of Everyday Racism and Sexism*, New York: Harrington Press.

Galenson, E. (1986) 'Early pathways to female sexuality in advantaged and disadvantaged girls', in T. Bernay and D.W. Cantor (eds) *The Psychology of Today's Women*, Cambridge, MA: Harvard University Press.

Gannon, L., Heiser, P. and Knight, S. (1985) 'Learned helplessness versus reactance: the effects of sex-role stereotypy', *Sex Roles* 12: 791–806.

Garb, H.N. (1997) 'Race bias, social class bias and gender bias in clinical judgement', *Clinical Psychology: Science and Practice* 4: 99–120.

Gerlsma, C., Emmelkamp, P.M.G. and Arrindell, W.E. (1990) 'Anxiety, depression and perception of early parenting: a meta-analysis', *Clinical Psychology Review* 10: 251–77.

Gilligan, C. (1982) *In a Different Voice: Psychological Theory and Women's Development*, Cambridge, MA: Harvard University Press.

Gjerde, P.F., Block, J. and Block, J.H. (1988) 'Depressive symptoms and personality during late adolescence: Gender differences in the externalisation-internalisation of symptom expression', *Journal of Abnormal Psychology* 97: 475–86.

Goldberg, S. (1997) 'Attachment and childhood behaviour problems in normal, at-risk, and, clinical samples', in L. Atkinson and K.J. Zucker (eds) *Attachment and Psychopathology*, New York: The Guilford Press, pp. 171–95.

Goldner, V., Penn, P., Sheinberg, M. and Walker, G. (1990) 'Love and violence: gender paradoxes in volatile attachments', *Family Process* 29: 343–64.

Golombok, S. and Fivush, R. (1994) *Gender Development*, Cambridge: Cambridge University Press.

Gotlib, I.H., Mount, J.H., Cordy, N.I. and Whiffen, V.E. (1988) 'Depression and perceptions of early parenting: a longitudinal investigation', *British Journal of Psychiatry* 152: 24–7.

Gotlib, L.H. and Hammen, C. (1992) *Psychological aspects of depression: towards a cognitive-interpersonal integration*, Chichester: John Wiley and Sons.

Greenberg, M.T., DeKlyen, M., Speltz, M.L. and Endriga, M.C. (1997) 'The role of attachment processes in externalising psychopathology in young children', in L. Atkinson and K.J. Zucker (eds) *Attachment and Psychopathology*, New York: The Guilford Press, pp. 196–222.

Hamilton, J.A. and Jensvold, M. (1992) 'Personality, psychopathology, and depression in women', in L.S. Brown and M. Ballou (eds) *Personality and Psychopathology: Feminist Reappraisals*, New York: Guilford, pp. 116–43.

Hammen, C., Marks, T., Mayol, A. and DeMayo, R. (1985) 'Depressive self-schemas, life stress and vulnerability to depression', *Journal of Abnormal Psychology* 94: 308–19.

Hankin, B.L., Roberts, J. and Gotlib, I.H. (1997) 'Elevated self standards and emotional distress during adolescence: emotional specificity and gender differences', *Cognitive Therapy and Research* 21: 663–79.

Hare-Mustin, R.T. and Marecek, J. (eds) (1990) *Making a difference: Psychology and the Construction of Gender*, New Haven: Yale University Press.

Harris, T. and Bifulco, A. (1991) 'Loss of parent in childhood, attachment style, and depression in adulthood', in C.M. Parkes, J. Stevenson-Hinde and P. Marris (eds) *Attachment Across the Life Cycle*, London: Routledge, pp. 127–59.

Haw, C.E. (1995) 'The family life cycle: a forgotten variable in the study of women's employment and well-being', *Psychological Medicine* 25: 727–38.

Hawton, K., Salkovskis, J.K. and Clark, D.M. (1989) *Cognitive Behaviour Therapy for Psychiatric Problems*, Oxford: Oxford University Press.

Hay, D.F. (1997) 'Postpartum depression and cognitive development', in L. Murray and P.J. Cooper (eds) *Postpartum Depression and Child Development*, New York: The Guilford Press, pp. 85–110.

Heshusius, L. (1980) 'Female self-injury and suicide attempts: culturally reinforced techniques in human relations', *Sex Roles* 6: 843–55.

Higgins, E.T., Klein, R. and Strauman, T. (1985) 'Self concept discrepancy theory: a psychological model for distinguishing among different aspects of depression and anxiety', *Social Cognition* 3: 51–76.

Higgins, E.T. (1987) 'Self-discrepancy: a theory relating self and affect', *Psychological Review* 94: 319–40.

Horney, K. (1973) 'The flight from womanhood: the masculinity complex in women as viewed by men and by women', in J.B. Miller (ed.) *Psychoanalysis and Women*, London: Penguin, pp. 5–20.

Irigaray, L. (1977) 'The sex which is not one', in C. Zanardi (ed.) *Essential Papers in the Psychology of Women*, New York: New York University Press.

Jack, R. (1992) *Women and Attempted Suicide*, Hillsdale, NJ: Erlbaum.

Jacklin, C.N. (1981) 'Methodological issues in the study of sex-related differences', *Developmental Review* 1: 266–73.

Kaplan, A. (1986) 'The "self-in-relation": implications for depression in women', *Psychotherapy* 23: 234–42.

Kaplan, S.L., Hong, G.K. and Weinhold, C. (1984) 'Epidemiology of depressive symptomology in adolescents', *Journal of the American Academy of Child Psychiatry* 23: 91–8.

Kenny, M.E., Moilanen, D.L., Lomax, R. and Brabeck, M.M. (1993) 'Contributions of parental attachments to view of self and depressive symptoms among early adolescents', *Journal of Early Adolescence* 13: 408–30.

Kessler, R.C. and McLeod, J.D. (1984) 'Sex differences in vulnerability to undesirable life events', *American Sociological Review* 49: 629–31.

Kirkpatrick, L.A. and Davis, K.E. (1994) 'Attachment style, gender, and relationship stability: a longitudinal study', *Journal of Personality and Social Psychology* 66(3): 502–12.

Kobac, R.R. and Sceery, A. (1988) 'Attachment in late adolescence: working models, affect regulation, and representations of self and others', *Child Development* 59: 135–46.

Kobak, R.R., Sudler, N. and Gamble, W. (1991) 'Attachment and depressive symptoms during adolescence: a developmental pathway analysis', *Development and Psychopathology* 3: 461–74.

Lamb, M.E., Thompson, R.A., Gardner, W. and Charnov, E.L. (1985) *Infant–Mother Attachment: The Origins and Developmental Significance of Individual Differences in Strange Situation Behaviour*, Hillsdale, NJ: Erlbaum.

Larson, R.W., Raffaelli, M., Richard, M.H., Ham, M. and Jewell, L.

(1990) 'Ecology of depression in late childhood and early adolescence: a profile of daily states and activities', *Journal of Abnormal Psychology* 99: 92–102.

Leadbeater, B.J., Blatt, S.J. and Quinlan, D.M. (1995) 'Gender-linked vulnerabilities to depressive symptoms, stress and problem behaviours in adolescents', *Journal of Research on Adolescence* 5: 1–29.

Levit, D.B. (1990) 'Gender differences in ego defences in adolescence: sex roles as one way to understand the differences', *Journal of Personality and Social Psychology* 61: 992–99.

Lewis, M., Feiring, C., McGuffog, C. and Jaskir, J. (1984) 'Predicting psychopathology in six year olds from early social relations', *Child Development* 55: 123–36.

Lopez, S.R. (1989) 'Patient variable biases in clinical judgement: conceptual overview and methodological considerations', *Psychological Bulletin* 106: 104–203.

Loring, M. and Powell, B. (1988) 'Gender, race and DSM-III: a study of the objectivity of psychiatric diagnostic behaviour', *Journal of Health and Social Behaviour* 29: 1–22.

Luthar, S.S. and Blatt, S.J. (1993) 'Dependent and self-critical depressive experiences among inner-city adolescents', *Journal of Personality* 61: 365–86.

Maccoby, E.E. (1990) 'Gender and relationships: a developmental account', *American Psychologist* 45: 513–20.

Maguire, M. (1995) *Men, Women, Passion and Power: Gender Issues in Psychotherapy*, London: Routledge.

Main, M., Kaplan, N. and Cassidy, J. (1985) 'Security in infancy, childhood and adulthood: a move to the level of representation', in I. Bretherton and E. Waters (eds) Growing points of attachment theory and research. *Monographs of the Society for Research in Child Development*, no. 209, 50 (1–2).

Main, M. and Solomon, J. (1986) 'Discovery of a new, insecure-disorganised/disoriented attachment pattern', in M. Yogman and T. B. Brazelton (eds) *Affective Development in Infancy*, Norwood, NJ: Ablex, pp. 95–124.

Main, M. (1991) 'Metacognitive knowledge, metacognitive monitoring, and singular (coherent) vs. multiple (incoherent) model of attachment: findings and directions for future research', in C.M. Parkes, J. Stevenson-Hinde and P. Marris (eds) *Attachment Across the Life Cycle*, London: Routledge, pp. 127–59.

Martin, J.R. (1988) 'Methodological essentialism, false differences, and other dangerous traps', in B.M. Clinchy and J.K. Noram (eds) *The Gender and Psychology Reader*, New York University Press, pp. 10–33.

McHugh, M.C., Frieze, I.H. and Hanusa, B.H. (1982) 'Attributions and sex differences in achievement', *Sex Roles* 8: 467–79.

Miller, J.B. (1976) *Toward a New Psychology of Women*, Boston: Beacon Press.

Mitchell, J. (1986) *The Selected Melanie Klein*, London: Penguin.

Murray, L., Kempton, C., Woolgar, M. and Hooper, R. (1993) 'Depressed mothers' speech to their infants and its relation to infant gender and cognitive development', *Journal of Child Psychology and Psychiatry* 34: 1083–101.

Murray, L., Fiori-Cowley, A., Hooper, R. and Cooper, P.J. (1996) 'The impact of post-natal depression and associated adversity on early mother–infant interactions and later infant outcomes', *Child Development* 67: 2512–26.

Nazroo, J.Y., Edwards, A.C. and Brown, G.W. (1997) 'Gender differences in the onset of depression following a shared life event: a study of couples', *Psychological Medicine* 27: 9–19.

Newman, J.P. (1984) 'Sex differences in symptoms of depression: clinical disorder or normal distress', *Journal of Health and Social Behaviour* 25: 136–59.

Nietzel, M.T. and Harris, M.J. (1990) 'Relationship of dependency and achievement/autonomy to depression', *Clinical Psychology Review* 20: 279–97.

Nolan, S.A., Roberts, J. and Gotlib, I.H. (1998) 'Neuroticism and ruminative response style as predictors of change in depressive symptomology', *Cognitive Therapy and Research* 22(5): 455–555.

Nolen-Hoekshema, S. (1987) 'Sex differences in unipolar depression: evidence and theory', *Psychological Bulletin* 101: 259–82.

Nolen-Hoekshema, S. (1990) *Sex Differences in Depression*, Stanford, CA: Stanford University Press.

Nolen-Hoekshema, S. (1991) 'Responses to depression and their effects on the duration of depressive episodes', *Journal of Abnormal Psychology* 100: 569–82.

Nolen-Hoekshema, S., Morrow, J. and Fredrickson, B.L. (1993) 'Response styles and the duration of episodes of depressed mood', *Journal of Abnormal Psychology* 102: 20–8.

Nolen-Hoekshema, S. and Morrow, J. (1991) 'A prospective study of depression and post-traumatic stress symptoms after a natural disaster: the 1989 Loma Prieta earthquake', *Journal of Personality and Social Psychology* 61: 115–21.

Nolen-Hoekshema, S. and Girgus, J.S. (1994) 'The emergence of sex differences in depression in adolescence', *Psychological Bulletin* 115: 424–43.

Nolen-Hoekshema, S., Parker, L.E. and Larson, J. (1994) 'Ruminative coping with depressed mood following loss', *Journal of Personality and Social Psychology* 67: 92–104.

Oatley, K. and Bolton, W. (1985) 'A social-cognitive theory of depression in reaction to life events', *Psychological Review* 92: 372–88.

Papini, D.R., Roggman, L.A. and Anderson, J. (1991) 'Early adolescent perceptions of attachment to mother and father: a test of the emotional-distancing and buffering hypotheses', *Journal of Early Adolescence* 11(2): 258–75.

Parkes, C.M. (1972) *Bereavement: Studies of Grief in Adult Life*, London: Tavistock Publications.

Parker, G., Tupling, H. and Brown, L.B. (1979) 'A parental bonding instrument', *British Journal of Medical Psychology* 52: 1–10.

Parker, G. (1981) 'Parental reports of depressives: an investigation of several explanations', *Journal of Affective Disorders* 3: 131–40.

Parker, G. (1986) 'Validating an experiential measure of parental style. The use of a twin sample', *Acta Psychiatrica Scandinavica* 73: 22–7.

Parker, R. (1995) *Torn in Two: The Experience of Maternal Ambivalence*, London: Virago.

Peterson, A.C., Sarigiani, P.A. and Kennedy, R.E. (1991) 'Adolescent depression: why more girls?', *Journal of Youth and Adolescence* 20: 247–72.

Pines, D. (1997) 'The relevance of early psychic development to pregnancy and abortion', in Raphael-Leff, J. and Perelberg, R.J. (1997) *Female Experience: Three Generations of British Women Psychoanalysts on Work with Women*, London: Routledge, pp. 131–43.

Potts, M.K., Burnham, M.A. and Wells, K.B. (1991) 'Gender differences in depression detection: a comparison of clinical diagnosis and standardised assessment', *Psychological Assessment* 3: 609–15.

Pyszczynski, T. and Greenberg, J. (1987) 'Self-regulatory perseveration and the depressive self-focusing style: a self-awareness theory of reactive depression', *Psychological Bulletin* 102: 122–38.

Raphael-Leff, J. (1991) *Psychological Processes of Childbearing*, London: Chapman & Hall.

Raphael-Leff, J. and Perelberg, R.J. (1997) *Female Experience: Three Generations of British Women Psychoanalysts on Work with Women*, London: Routledge.

Regier, D.A., Boyd, J.M., Burke, J.D., Rae, D.S., Myers, J.K., Kramer, M., Robins, L.N., George, L.K., Karno, M. and Locke, B.Z. (1988) 'One month prevalence of mental disorders in the United States', *Archives of General Psychiatry* 45: 977–86.

Renken, B., Egeland, B., Marvinney, D., Mangelsdorf, S. and Sroufe, L.A. (1989) 'Early childhood antecedents of aggression and passive-withdrawal in early elementary school', *Journal of Personality* 57: 257–80.

Roberts, J.E., Gilboa, E. and Gotlib, I.H. (1998) 'Ruminative response style and vulnerability to episodes of dysphoria: gender, neuroticism, and episode duration', *Cognitive Therapy and Research* 22(4), 401–23.

Root, M.P.P. (1992) 'Reconstructing the impact of trauma on personality', in L.S. Brown and M. Ballou (eds) *Personality and Psychopathology: Feminist Reappraisals*, New York: The Guilford Press, pp. 229–65.

Rosenstein, D.S. and Horowitz, H.A. (1996) 'Adolescent attachment and psychopathology', *Journal of Consulting and Clinical Psychology* 64: 244–53.

Rubin, K.H. and Lollis, S.P. (1988) 'Origins and consequences of social withdrawal', in J. Belsky and T. Nezworski (eds) *Clinical Implications of Attachment*, Hillsdale, NJ: Erlbaum, pp. 219–52.

Rude, S.S. and Burnham, B.L. (1995) 'Connnectedness and neediness: factors of the DEQ and SAS dependency scales', *Cognitive Therapy and Research* 19(3): 323–40.

Scott, L. and O'Hara, M.W. (1993) 'Self discrepancies in clinically anxious and depressed university students', *Journal of Abnormal Psychology* 102: 282–7.

Seeman, M.V. (1995) *Gender and Psychopathology*, Washington DC: American Psychiatric Press.

Segal, Z.V., Shaw, B.F. and Vella, D.D. (1989) 'Life stress and depression: a test of the congruency hypothesis for life events and depressive subtype', *Canadian Journal of Behavioural Science* 21: 389–400.

Segal, Z.V., Shaw, B.F., Vella, D.D. and Katz, R. (1992) 'Cognitive and life stress predictors of relapse in remitted unipolar depressed patients', *Journal of Abnormal Psychology* 101: 26–36.

Senchak, M. and Leonard, K.E. (1992) 'Attachment styles and marital adjustment among newlywed couples', *Journal of Social and Personal Relationships* 9: 51–64.

Showalter, E. (1987) *The Female Malady: Women, Madness and English Culture, 1830–1980*, London: Virago.

Sohn, D. (1982) 'Sex differences in achievement self-attributions: an effect–size analysis', *Sex Roles* 8: 345–57.

Steinberg, L. and Silverberg, S.B. (1986) 'The vicissitudes of autonomy in early adolescence', *Child Development* 57: 841–51.

Stern, D. (1985) *The Interpersonal World of the Infant: a View from Psychoanalysis and Developmental Psychology*, New York: Basic Books.

Stiver, I.P. (1994) 'The role of gender in dependency: an invited commentary', *American Journal of Orthopsychiatry* 64: 636–9.

Strauman, T.J. (1989) 'Self-discrepancies in clinical depression and social phobia: cognitive structures that underlie emotional disorders', *Journal of Abnormal Psychology* 98: 14–22.

Strauman, T.J., Vookles, J., Berenstein, V., Chaiken, S. and Higgins, E.T. (1991) 'Self-discrepancies and vulnerability to body dissatisfaction and disorder eating', *Journal of Personality and Social Psychology* 61: 946–56.

Summers, F. (1994) *Object Relations Theory and Psychopathology: A Comprehensive Text*, Hillside, NJ: The Analytic Press.

Temperley, J. (1997) 'Is the Oedipus Complex bad news for women?', in J. Raphael-Leff and R.J. Perelberg (eds) *Female Experience: Three Generations of British Women Psychoanalysts on Work with Women*, London: Routledge, pp. 258–65.

Thoits, P.A. (1991) 'On merging identity theory and stress research', *Social Psychology Quarterly* 54: 101–12.

Thompson, W.G. and Heaton, K.W. (1989) 'Functional bowel disorders in apparently healthy people', *Gastroenterology* 79: 283–8.

Turner, P.J. (1991) 'Relations between attachment, gender, and behaviour with peers in pre-school', *Child Development* 62: 1475–88.

Unger, R.K. (1998) 'Sex, gender and epistemology', in B.M. Clinchy and J.K. Noram (1998) *The Gender and Psychology Reader*, New York University Press, pp. 481–97.

Ussher, J. (1991) *Women's Madness: Misogyny or Mental Illness?*, London: Harvester Wheatsheaf.

Van IJzendoorn, M.H. (1995) 'Adult attachment representations, parental responsiveness, and infant attachment: a meta-analysis on the predictive validity of the adult attachment interview', *Psychological Bulletin* 117(3): 387–403.

Van IJzendoorn, M.H. and Bakermans-Kranenburg, M.J. (1996) 'Attachment representations in mothers, fathers, adolescents and clinical groups: a meta-analytic search for normative data', *Journal of Consulting and Clinical Psychology* 64: 8–21.

Van IJzendoorn, M.H. and Kroonenburg, P.M. (1988) 'Cross-cultural patterns of attachment. A meta-analysis of the Strange Situation', *Child Development* 59: 147–56.

Waddell, M. (1989) 'Gender identity – fifty years on from Freud', *British Journal of Psychotherapy* 5: 381–90.

Weinberg, M.K. and Tronick, E.Z. (1992) 'Sex differences in emotional expression and affective regulation in 6-month-old infants', *Society for Paediatric Research* 31(4): 15A.

Weinberg, M.K., Tronick, E.Z., Cohn, J.F. and Olson, K.L. (1999) 'Gender differences in emotional expressivity and self regulation during early infancy', *Developmental Psychology* 35: 175–88.

Welch, R., Gerrard, M. and Huston, A. (1986) 'Gender related personality attributes and reaction to success/failure: an examination of mediating variables', *Psychology of Women Quarterly* 10: 221–133.

Welldon, E.V. (1988) *Mother, Madonna, Whore: The Idealisation and Denigration of Motherhood*, London: Free Association Books.

West, C. and Zimmerman, D.H. 'Doing gender', in B.M. Clinchy and J.K. Noram (1998) *The Gender and Psychology Reader*, New York University Press, pp. 104–24.

Wheaton, B., Roszell, P. and Hall, K. (1997) 'The impact of twenty childhood and adult traumatic stressors on the risk of psychiatric illness', in I.H. Gotlib and B. Wheaton (1997) *Stress and Adversity over the Life Course*, Cambridge: Cambridge University Press, pp. 50–72.

Williams, P., Tarnopolsky, A., Hand, D. and Shepherd, M. (1987) 'Minor psychiatric morbidity and general practice consultations: the West London survey', *Psychological Medicine Monographs Suppl. 9*, 1–37.

Chapter 5

Depression in women

Eleni Palazidou

INTRODUCTION

Depression is one of the most common psychiatric conditions, yet it remains frequently unrecognized and undertreated and its impact on the sufferers, their families and society is underestimated. Although an 'eminently treatable' disorder a substantial number of cases either do not seek help, go unrecognized, are not treated or are undertreated.

The Royal College of Psychiatrists and the Royal College of General Practitioners in the UK, launched a 5-year 'Defeat Depression' campaign (1991–96). All forms of media activities were employed with the aim to increase awareness of the wide presence of this condition, its illness status and its treatability, and to reduce the stigma attached to it. The results were reported as showing significant positive changes regarding attitudes to depression, reported experience of depression and attitudes to antidepressant drugs. Although statistically significant these changes were only in the magnitude of 5–10 per cent.

Why not seek help?

The stigma attached to depressive illness remains unchanged despite the 'Defeat Depression' campaign. About 10 per cent of people surveyed by Market and Opinion Research International (MORI) in 1991 considered depressed people to be often 'mad/unstable'. This persisted in the 1997 MORI survey at the end of the campaign, despite the increase in awareness that depression is a medical condition. About two-thirds of the subjects surveyed considered psychosocial problems to be responsible for depression and only about 45 per cent thought of it as an illness and 33 per cent as due to biological changes in the brain. The strong association the public makes between depression and psychosocial adversity encourages a sense of fatalism and helplessness. The assumption is made by the depressed woman, particularly if she has experienced recent or past adverse life events or is surrounded by other stresses (personal, family problems, difficulties with living conditions or work), that her mood state is 'understandable' and inevitable. The sense of hopelessness usually associated with depressed mood plus the fear of being dismissed by professionals and possibly family or friends discourage any considerations of seeking healthcare attention. Even in cases where the depressed mood state may not be 'understandable' in the absence of adversity, seeking help may be perceived by the depressive as admission to weakness of character. The fear of being dismissed as a 'neurotic woman' and the possible label of mental illness discourage further any considerations of contact with healthcare professionals.

Nevertheless, it should be noted that women are more likely to seek treatment than men! According to the Zurich study (Ernst and Angst, 1992) two-thirds of females with major depressive disorder sought healthcare compared to only one-third of males.

Depression unrecognized

It is well known that most depression seen in primary care in the UK goes unrecognized. Only about 50 per cent of patients presenting to primary care with depressive symptoms are diagnosed. Depressive symptomatology is commonly masked by physical symptom presentation. According to Kroenke and Spitzer (1998) most physical symptoms, including somatoform, are at least 50 per cent more often reported by women than by men and this is not accounted for by the higher prevalence of mental illness in women. However, this does not appear to affect detection of depression by general practitioners in women compared to men; a recent international WHO study failed to find differences in detection of depressive disorders between males and females in primary care (Gater et al., 1998).

Depression untreated/undertreated

The European DEPRESS (Depression Research in European Society) study which investigated a total of 78,463 subjects from the normal population in 5 countries (Belgium, France, Germany, the Netherlands and the UK), found that only 69 per cent of the 6.9 per cent of subjects with major depressive disorder (6-month prevalence) consulted healthcare professionals (Lepine, 1997). Of those seen by healthcare professionals only 41 per cent were prescribed medication and only 18 per cent were given antidepressants. Similar results were shown by the Zurich study (Ernst and Angst, 1992) which found that even fewer (55 per cent) of the major depressives sought treatment and only 40 per cent of them received medication, half of these given antidepressants and the rest given benzodiazepines. Females were more likely to seek help (two thirds of the females and only one third of the males sought professional help) but again only half of either females or males received antidepressant drug treatment. These are disheartening findings considering the high response of this condition to antidepressant drug treatment. The importance of treating depression should not be underestimated. When treated and untreated patients with major depressive episodes (including bipolar cases) were compared, although the treated subjects were more severely ill, they had a significantly better outcome (Angst, 1998).

EPIDEMIOLOGY

Depression may present in the form of Major Depressive Disorder in the context of a bipolar or unipolar illness, Minor Depressive Disorder, Brief Recurrent Depression or Dysthymia and in women also as depressive mood state related to reproductive cycle/events – Premenstrual Dysphoric Disorder and Postpartum Depression.

Major depressive illness has the highest prevalence rates amongst the major mental disorders. Prevalence rates as well as incidence rates, however, show a fair amount of variance between studies and sites. Angst (1998) lists 22 studies published between 1978 and 1995, carried out in different parts of the world including Europe (Paris, Basle, Sardinia, Mainz, Munich and Iceland), the United States (including the Epidemiological Catchment Area (ECA) study – five sites), Canada (Edmonton), Puerto Rico, New Zealand

(Christchurch) and the Far East (Taiwan, Hong Kong and Korea). These showed lifetime prevalence rates, ranging from as low as 0.9 per cent (women: 1.0; men: 0.7) (Taiwan) to as high as 18.0 per cent (women: 25.8 per cent; men: 12.3 per cent) (USA). This marked variability is to a great extent accounted for by methodological differences. The most commonly used instrument for assessment of depression in these studies was the DIS (Diagnostic Interview Schedule) although some studies used the CIDI (Composite International Diagnostic Interview) or the SADS-RDC (Schedule for Affective Disorders and Schizophrenia – Research Diagnostic Criteria). Differences in the sensitivity of these instruments may account for some of the discrepancy (the DIS tends to yield lower rates than the others) although other factors, such as differences in interview methodology, may also be responsible.

Lifetime prevalence rates have been criticized as less accurate because they rely on long-term recall. A meta analysis of the ECA study (Simon and von Korf, 1995) revealed a systematic loss of information due to poor recall. For this reason point prevalence rates are considered more reliable than period prevalence rates and current prevalence rates (usually meaning symptoms present in the past four weeks) are most commonly used. The ECA study (Weissman et al., 1990) yielded current prevalence rates for major depressive disorder of 2.4 per cent, the National Comorbidity Study also in the US (Blazer et al., 1994) 4.9 per cent and in the UK using the Present State Examination (PSE) (Bebbington et al., 1989) 7 per cent. The incidence data from the ECA study collected during one year follow-up from four sites (Eaton et al., 1989) found a rate of 1.56 per cent (women: 1.98 per cent; men: 1.1 per cent).

Gender differences

Despite the variability in the overall prevalence rates of depression a very consistent and well-replicated finding emerging from all quoted studies is the striking female preponderance, with a female to male ratio from 1.5 to 3.0. Weissman and Klerman (1977) were the first to note the significant gender differences in the prevalence of depression after a review of the available reports from the 1970s. These included data from community surveys in the US which concentrated mainly on symptoms related to depression (as the DSM diagnostic criteria were not available until 1980) in addition to data from studies carried out elsewhere which used the ICD classification. More recent studies which had the benefit of defined diagnostic criteria and standardized assessments confirmed the higher prevalence rates for women compared to men.

The gender differences in the prevalence of depression appear to emerge in the mid-teens. In a 10-year longitudinal, prospective study, Hankin *et al.* (1998) found small differences with female preponderance emerging at age 13–15 and becoming greatest at age 15–18. In contrast, anxiety symptoms are twice as common in girls as in boys by the age of 6 (Lewinsohn *et al.*, 1998). A reversal of sex differences in the prevalence of depression is observed after the age of 55 (Bebbington *et al.*, 1998).

It should be noted that gender differences exist in the prevalence of unipolar depression but not in bipolar disorder where males and females are equally at risk. Prevalence rates of the milder or more chronic forms of depression (minor depressive disorder and dysthymia) are considered higher in women, although it should be noted that such studies are fraught with difficulties because of differences in definition and reliability of diagnosis and in the case of dysthymia the reliance on memory.

AETIOLOGY

Depressive illness is probably the best example of a psychobiological disorder where nature and nurture interact in its genesis. Although many aetiological factors including genetic, biochemical, physical, psychological, social, cultural and other have been implicated, no single factor has been identified that by itself and in the absence of any others can bring about depressive illness. Even in bipolar disorder where strong genetic vulnerability has been demonstrated (in twin, family and adoption studies) the concordance rates in monozygotic twins varies between studies with an average of about 65 per cent, suggesting that factors other than genetic are also, perhaps to a lesser extent, important in the manifestation of the disorder. In unipolar depression the genetic vulnerability is smaller with concordance rates in monozygotic twins below 50 per cent.

It has been suggested that major depressive disorder is aetiologically a heterogeneous disorder consisting of genetic and non-genetic forms. Andrew *et al.* (1998) investigated this possibility based on the hypothesis that if such heterogeneity exists, the first-degree relatives of discordant twins should have lower rates of major depressive disorder, consisting largely of the non-genetic form of the condition, than the first-degree relatives of concordant twins. Their findings showed no differences in the lifetime prevalence and age-corrected risk of depression between relatives of concordant and discordant twin pairs, providing evidence against the presence of two distinct forms (genetic and non-genetic). These results support the notion that depressive illness in general results from a combination of genetic vulnerability and associated chemical brain abnormalities and environmental adversity.

Central neurotransmitter system abnormalities consisting mainly of impaired activity within the noradrenergic and serotonergic systems have been shown but it is not clear whether these are genetically determined or acquired. The role of stress and stress hormones is also considered of importance. The neurobiological and psychosocial causes of depression are discussed elsewhere in this book.

What determines the gender differences?

Methodological factors

The gender differences in the prevalence of depressive illness are by no means universally accepted. Studies supporting the 2 : 1 female to male ratio have been criticized and the sex differences in prevalence have been attributed by some to an artefact, the product of methodological error. Indeed the international data show some inconsistency; some of the studies in the third world – for example in two African villages (Orley and Wing, 1979) and in Uttar, Pradesh, in India (Dube, 1970) as well as studies in certain western populations where women and men enjoy equal social status, for example in college samples (Wilhelm and Parker, 1989), fail to demonstrate a difference in the prevalence of depression between the genders.

The possibility that these gender differences may be explained by a bias in diagnosis, i.e. the clinicians being more likely to diagnose depression in women than in men, is not supported by evidence. The WHO Collaborative Study on Psychological Problems in General Health Care, aiming to improve understanding of the relevance of biological and social factors to sex differences in the prevalence of depression and anxiety symptoms, examined the detection rates in fifteen primary care centres from four continents. No gender differences were found in detection of current depression, agoraphobia or panic disorder (Gater *et al.*, 1998). The results of this study are also consistent with the conclusion that biological and psychological factors, operating alone or interacting, have similar effects across cultures irrespective of local psychosocial factors, which may differ from country to country, in contributing to sex differences in the rates of depression. In contrast, unlike depression, a variation was found in gender ratios for prevalence of general anxiety which supports the influence of local factors in the genesis of this condition.

Lastly, there is evidence that the higher prevalence of depression in women is attributable to increased frequency of comorbidity of depression and anxiety in female subjects. When pure cases are examined the sex ratio is approximately equal for both anxiety and depression (Angst *et al.*, 1997).

Psychosocial factors

What determines the gender differences in prevalence remains unclear. Both biological and psychosocial factors have been considered. The psychosocial hypothesis is based on an assumption that (a) females are psychologically more dependent and have the tendency to internalize pain and stress and (b) the role of women in most societies is of relatively lower value. The combination of a tendency to internalize and self-blame and being in a position of lower status with less power over their environment renders women more vulnerable to depression when under stress (Pajer, 1995). The validity of such hypotheses is unclear.

Early childhood experiences including disturbed mother–child relationships and neurotic symptoms (Veijola *et al.*, 1998) and childhood sexual abuse (Cheasty *et al.*, 1998) have been linked to adult depression; most studies were carried out in females. However, other less remote risk factors may be more important in males than females. A primary care study in Finland (Salokangas and Putanen, 1998) found a stronger connection between risk factors such as negative life events, poor physical health, poor marital/ other relationships, work situation and alcohol abuse (these often accumulating in the same subjects) and depression in males than females. In women there is no difference in response to family or work stress irrespective of whether they are married or single mothers, while unmarried fathers cope worse than married ones to the above stressors. Claims that females are more vulnerable to stress than males is not supported by these findings although there may be sex differences in vulnerability which are highly specific to the type of stressor and situation.

Influence of female physiology

It is of note that the gender differences in the rates of depression appear to exist mainly for the duration of the female reproductive years. They emerge in puberty and disappear after the menopause. Pubertal status rather than age predicts the gender differences in the prevalence of depression (Angold et al., 1998). The disappearance of sex differences in the prevalence rates of depression over the age of 55 is not explained by differential effects of marital status, child care or employment (Bebbington, 1998). These findings indicate the importance of biological factors and, in particular, that of female physiology in the genesis of depressive symptoms in women. It is likely that two mechanisms may be operating in increasing the rates of depression in women:

(a) female reproductive physiology may render women more vulnerable to depression and
(b) the presence of certain forms of mood abnormalities specific to the female gender during the reproductive years, more specifically premenstrual dysphoric disorder, may be contaminating the data in prevalence studies, inflating the rates of depression in women.

COURSE OF DEPRESSIVE DISORDER

It is now recognized that depressive illness is a long-term, recurring disorder. The risk of recurrence increases with each new episode irrespective of gender, age or type of disorder (Kessing, 1998). Earlier in the course of the illness, in both unipolar and bipolar sufferers, females are at higher risk of recurrence than males. After the first episode middle-aged and older females with unipolar disorder are at higher risk of relapse than younger women. However, a first episode occurring below the age of 20 increases the risk in later life.

The Baltimore site of the ECA study repeat interviews in 1993–6 found an incidence rate of 3 per 1000 per year and suggested that the gender differences in prevalence are due to differences in incidence and not chronicity of the disorder (Eaton *et al.*, 1997). They noted that incidence rates for depressive disorder peaked in the 30s age group and were smaller in the 50s. Although females were at higher risk for new cases, the average duration of episode (12 weeks) and the risk of recurrence were no different between the genders. These findings are supported by the NIMH Collaboration Progress on Psychobiology of Depression-Clinical studies (Simpson *et al.*, 1987) which showed no significant gender differences in the course of major depressive disorder, i.e. time to recovery, time to first recurrence and the number or the severity of the recurrence.

Although the prevalence of *bipolar disorder* is the same in males and females, there are gender differences in its course and presentation. Women have more depressive and fewer manic episodes and are more likely to suffer from mixed mania. Rapid cycling is more common in women and this may result from possibly higher rates of hypothyroidism, higher use of antidepressants or gonadal steroid effects (Leibenluft, 1996). There has been little systematic review of the effects of reproductive system events including puberty, menstrual cycle, pregnancy, menopause, use of oral contraceptives or hormone replacement therapy on the course of bipolar disorder.

PREMENSTRUAL DYSPHORIC DISORDER (PMDD)

About 75 per cent of women report minor premenstrual changes. These occur most commonly for the first time in the teens to late 20s and remit with the menopause. 'Premenstrual Syndrome (PMS)' was the term used previously to describe troublesome premenstrual symptoms and although less specific and with variable definition this is thought to occur in 20–50 per cent of women.

PMDD as defined by the DSM-IV occurs in 3–5 per cent of women. It differs from the PMS by its characteristic symptom pattern, symptom severity and associated impairment. For the diagnosis to be made the symptoms must occur in most menstrual cycles in the past year during the last week of the luteal phase and remit within a few days of the follicular phase (for diagnostic criteria see Table 5.1).

Table 5.1 Diagnostic criteria of PMDD

Five or more of the following symptoms with at least one being of the first four:

1 feeling sad, hopeless or self-deprecating
2 feeling tense, anxious or 'on edge'
3 marked lability of mood with frequent tearfulness
4 persistent irritability, anger and increased interpersonal conflict
5 decreased interest in usual activities which may be associated with withdrawal from social relationships
6 difficulty concentrating
7 feeling fatigued, lethargic or lacking in energy
8 marked changes in appetite which may be associated with binge eating or craving certain foods
9 hypersomnia or insomnia
10 a subjective feeling of being overwhelmed or out of control and
11 physical symptoms such as breast tenderness or swelling, headache, sensation of 'bloating' or weight gain, There may be muscle/joint pain.

Suicidal thoughts may be present. Typically the symptoms are of severity and impairment in functioning, comparable to those of Major Depressive Episode. Both physical and mood related symptoms show remarkable stability across cycles.

Lifetime psychiatric disorder is common in women with PMDD; mood disorders predominate, although anxiety disorders, in particular panic attacks, are also common (Steiner, 1997). It is important, therefore, for PMDD to be distinguished from a premenstrual exacerbation of a current mental disorder. The criteria for PMDD must be confirmed by prospective daily ratings during two or more symptomatic cycles.

Pathophysiology

Much of the research literature refers to the premenstrual syndrome, PMS, rather than PMDD and this may cause some difficulties in making comparisons between studies and in generalizing the findings, considering that PMDD has a narrower and stricter definition.

Serotonin

The precise pathophysiology of PMDD is not known but a dysregulation of the serotonergic neurotransmitter system is thought to be involved, influenced by the fluctuation in gonadal hormones. Evidence of dysregulated sensitivity at the GABA-A/ benzodiazepine-receptor complex has also been shown in PMS (Sundstrom *et al.*, 1997). The superior response of this syndrome to treatment with selective serotonin re-uptake inhibitors compared to selective noradrenergic (maprotiline) or dopaminergic (bupropion) antidepressant agents (Ericksson *et al.*, 1995; Steiner *et al.*, 1997) and the blunted prolactin response to the serotonergic agent, dl-fenfluramine, shown during the luteal phase of women with PMDD (Fitzgerald *et al.*, 1997) support the hypothesis that impaired serotonin neurotransmission may be involved in the pathogenesis of this disorder.

Oestrogens

Low oestrogen levels are thought to be associated with pathological mental states in relation to female physiology in PMS and postnatal depression. Symptom severity correlates positively with increased concentrations of oestradiol and luteinizing hormone during the luteal phase (Seippel *et al.*, 1998). Oestrogen affects many central monoamine systems implicated in the pathogenesis of depressive symptomatology. The density of 5-HT2A receptors, in areas of the brain concerned with mood control, is increased by oestrogens (Fink *et al.*, 1996).

Women suffering with premenstrual syndrome, post-partum blues and perimenopausal transition symptoms share common features: depressed mood, irritability, anxiety, panic, sleep disturbance, memory and cognitive dysfunction, and decreased sense of well-being. These same symptoms can be elicited by antioestrogenic agents such as progesterone, progestin and tamoxifen. On the basis of this observation, Arpels (1996) proposes that the female brain is an oestrogen target and whenever brain oestrogen levels fall below a certain threshold, brain dysfunction ensues.

Non-gonadal hormones

Other, non-gonadal, hormonal changes have also been reported, such as circadian disturbances of prolactin and thyroid stimulating hormone found in PMDD sufferers compared to normals (Parry *et al.*, 1996), mid-cycle elevations of parathyroid hormone in PMS with transient secondary hyperparathyroidism (Thys-Jacobs and

Alvir, 1995) and low arginin-vasopressin concentrations through-out the menstrual cycle in PMS (Rosenstein, 1996).

Biological rhythms

Because of the similarities in clinical picture between PMDD and Seasonal Affective Disorder (SAD), both presenting with 'atypical' depressive features, and their cyclicity, it has been suggested that a disturbance in the biological clock (the circadian pacemaker located in the suprachiasmatic nucleus in the hypothalamus) function may be responsible. Indeed, patients with PMDD have blunted circadian rhythms of melatonin and appear to respond therapeutically to sleep deprivation and phototherapy; the latter failed to advance melatonin offset time in PMDD subjects (Parry *et al.*, 1997). PMDD subjects have a higher score on seasonality of mood and vegetative symptoms and a higher rate of SAD (Maskall *et al.*, 1997).

MENOPAUSE AND DEPRESSION

Studies of depressive symptomatology in menopausal women indicate that the menopause is not associated with increased rates of depression. Mild mood changes and symptoms of anxiety which do not amount to psychiatric disorder may be present for a few years prior to the onset of the natural menopause and occur following surgical menopause (Pearce *et al.*, 1995). There is no consistent symptom-complex of psychological features in associa-tion with this stage of a woman's life. Robinson *et al.* (1996) in a review of five cross-cultural studies found enormous differences in the experience of the menopause not only among women from different cultures but also within the same culture. Reported menopausal symptoms were influenced by a combination of physi-cal changes, cultural factors and individual perceptions and expec-tations. Nicol-Smith (1996) in a critical review of the research, published in the preceding thirty years, concluded that there is not sufficient evidence at the present to support the view that the menopause causes depression. However, women with a previous history of mood disorder that is cyclic in nature or associated with reproductive events may be at risk of depression in the menopause (Pearlstein *et al.*, 1997).

The beneficial role of hormone replacement therapy (HRT), in particular the oestrogen component, has been established in the treatment of psychological and physical symptoms after surgical menopause; in natural menopause, however, their value in treating psychological symptoms is questionable, although they are effective in controlling vasomotor symptoms (hot flushes) and probably reducing the risk of osteoporosis and ischaemic heart disease. There is also evidence that oestrogens improve vigilance and memory in women with early Alzheimer's dementia (Backstrom, 1995).

TREATMENT OF DEPRESSION IN WOMEN

There appear to be differences in response to treatment between males and females, although the research literature available in this area is still quite limited. The gender differences are apparent both in the response to pharmacotherapy and the response to psychotherapy. Women respond better to more focused forms of psychological treatment and 'problem-solving', such as cognitive/behavioural therapy, and work better in a group therapy setting (Pajer *et al.*, 1995).

Pharmacological antidepressant treatment

Four decades have elapsed since the first effective antidepressant drugs, iproniazid (a monoamine oxidase inhibitor) and imipramine (a tricyclic), were discovered in the late 1950s. During this time major progress has been made in the understanding of the pathogenesis of depressive illness, including major developments in the unravelling of biochemical brain mechanisms and the function of central neurotransmitter systems involved in depression and this has guided the design of new antidepressants. The aims have been to improved efficacy, minimized side effects, safety in overdose and earlier onset of action.

Despite the development of pharmacologically more sophisticated drugs, so far, no single antidepressant has demonstrated proven superiority in efficacy compared to others. Between 50–70 per cent of depressed people respond to the first antidepressant drug they receive, irrespective of the class to which it belongs. However, progress has been made in producing drugs with higher selectivity of action and hence reduced adverse effect profile, with better tolerability and particularly increased safety in overdose. As far as earlier onset of action is concerned little progress has been made.

Antidepressant drugs licensed in the UK

A list (not exhaustive) of the general antidepressant drug groups currently used in the UK is shown in Table 5.2. Irrespective of what group they belong to, all licensed antidepressant drugs licensed in the UK, so far, act by increasing central adrenergic and/or serotonergic activity. This is effected either by blocking the re-uptake of the monoamine into the neuronal terminal or by preventing its breakdown in the neuron, hence increasing 5-HT and/or NA availability at postsynaptic receptor sites. Some newer antidepressants have a different mode of action targeting receptors directly but again causing an increase in serotonergic and noradrenergic activity. After 2–3 weeks of drug treatment, various changes occur in the density of receptors and signal transduction systems both within and outside the noradrenergic and serotonergic systems which probably have major significance in the mode of action of antidepressants.

Tricyclic antidepressants (TCAs)

The clinically relevant, direct, pharmacological actions of the TCAs are the blockade of re-uptake of 5-HT and NA, some being more powerful NA re-uptake inhibitors (i.e. desipramine) and others more powerful 5-HT re-uptake inhibitors (i.e. clomipramine). The other pharmacological properties they possess, such as anticholinergic, antihistaminic, alpha1 adrenoceptor blockade and cardiac membrane stabilization, are clinically irrelevant and are responsible for the multitude of side effects this group of antidepressants is associated with. There are some differences between the side effects of the tertiary amines (amitriptyline, imipramine) and their derivatives, the secondary amines (nortriptyline, desipramine), the latter being less sedative and causing less anticholinergic side effects.

A major criticism of the tricyclic antidepressant treatment in primary care has been the use of sub-therapeutic doses. Doses below 75mg per day have no antidepressant efficacy in depressive illness; the established therapeutic dose is 125–150mg/day in the average patient. Tentative therapeutic plasma concentrations for

Table 5.2 Pharmacological actions of antidepressants

Antidepressant	Presumed mechanism of action	Undesirable pharmacological actions
Tricyclics (TCAs)	NA and 5-HT re-uptake inhibition	anticholinergic, antihistaminic, Alpha1, adrenergic antagonism, direct membrane stabilization
SSRIs	5-HT re-uptake inhibition	stimulation of 5-HT receptor subtypes probably not relevant to antidepressant action (e.g. 5-HT3)
SNRIs	NA and 5-HT re-uptake inhibition	
MAOIs	inhibition of monoamine oxidase (MAO)	interaction with tyramine ('cheese reaction') and sympathomimetics; irreversible and non-selective inhibition of both MAO iso-enzymes (MAO-A and MAO-B)
RIMAs (moclobemide)	selective and reversible inhibition of MAO-A	
Other		
Nefazodone	5-HT re-uptake inhibition and 5-HT2 receptor antagonism	
Mirtazapine	Alpha2 adrenoceptor and 5-HT2 and 5-HT3 receptor antagonism	
Tianeptine*	5-HT re-uptake enhancer	

Note: * not licensed in the UK

TCAs have been suggested, although monitoring of these is useful in preventing toxicity and checking compliance rather than of therapeutic value. TCAs have a narrow therapeutic index and doses only ten times the therapeutic dose can be cardiotoxic. In slow metabolizers toxicity can occur even at therapeutic doses and it has been argued that the plasma concentrations of TCAs should be more widely used (Preskorn and Jerkovich, 1990). Lofepramine is the only TCA not to be associated with cardiotoxicity and is relatively safe in overdose.

Dawkins and Potter's review (1991) cites reports on gender differences in relation to treatment with tricyclics. There seems to be preferential response to imipramine in men compared to women. Oestrogens may affect the response to tricyclic antidepressant drug treatment and variable imipramine responses in depressed women on oral contraceptives have been suggested (imipramine response impaired on high oestrogen doses and possibly increased on low oestrogen doses). Gender differences in the metabolism of TCAs have also been suggested but the evidence is inconsistent.

Selective serotonin re-uptake inhibitors (SSRIs)

The SSRIs have largely replaced the TCAs as first choice antidepressants in recent years, despite their greater costs. Their more favourable side effect profile and reduced drop-out rates (Anderson and Tomenson, 1994) as well as safety in overdose are probably the reasons for this, although effective marketing by the pharmaceutical companies may have contributed to the increase in their popularity.

Unlike the TCAs, the SSRIs have very dissimilar chemical structure although they share the same pharmacological action (5-HT re-uptake inhibition). Because of their selectivity for the serotonergic neurotransmitter system the side effects with which they are associated are a product of their serotonergic actions. It is thought that the antidepressant effect of the SSRIs is mediated via the post-synaptic 5-HT1A receptor and therefore stimulation of other receptors, i.e. 5-HT1D, 5-HT3 and possibly 5-HT2, are therapeutically redundant and responsible for undesirable side effects.

Pharmacokinetic and pharmacodynamic considerations

Some SSRIs interact with tricyclic antidepressants and some antipsychotics, increasing their plasma concentrations, as they are metabolized by the same cytochrome P450 subtype (2D6 and 3A). Such combinations can be used, with caution, to avoid dangerous toxic TCA or antipsychotic concentrations. It is essential to note that SSRIs should never be combined with monoamine oxidase inhibitors (MAOIs) as the additive effect of their different pharmacological actions on the serotonergic system can cause excessive serotonergic activation resulting in the potentially lethal 'Serotonin Syndrome'. Care should be taken also to allow an adequate washout period when changing from one of these two drug groups to the other, taking into account their respective half-lives and duration of action. The wide differences in the half-lives of the different SSRIs should be noted. Fluoxetine, for example, has an active metabolite, norfluoxetine, with a long half-life requiring a washout period of 5 weeks after fluoxetine discontinuation before safely starting treatment with an MAOI. In contrast, paroxetine has a short half-life and is therefore likely to be associated with withdrawal symptoms on abrupt drug discontinuation.

The SSRIs have been used in the treatment not only of depressive illness but also of eating disorders (bulimia), anxiety disorders, impulsive and aggressive behaviour and premenstrual dysphoric syndrome. The most common side effects are nausea, headache and sexual dysfunction in particular anorgasmia, in women.

Monoamine oxidase inhibitors (MAOIs)

The MAOIs are thought to exert their antidepressant effects by binding on to brain monoamine oxidase (MAO), the enzyme responsible for breaking down monoamines in the neuronal terminals, blocking its effect and increasing the availability of noradrenaline and serotonin at synaptic level. This action is non-selective, blocking both iso-enzymes (MAO-A and MAO-B), therefore interfering also with the breakdown of other substances and causing potentially dangerous interactions with other agents such as tyramine (hence the requirement for a tyramine-free diet), indirectly acting sympathomimetics, some narcotic analgesics and tricyclics. A further problem encountered in the use of these antidepressants is their irreversible binding on the MAO, requiring a washout period of a minimum two weeks after discontinuation of treatment, to allow adequate time for new enzyme synthesis. For these reasons, despite their recognized efficacy, use of the old MAOIs (phenelzine, tranylcypromine and isocarboxazid) has decreased significantly in recent years.

Reversible monoamine oxidase inhibitors (RIMAs)

RIMAs are a new group of MAOIs which are devoid of the undesirable effects of their predecessors because of their selectivity (bind only to MAO-A, the iso-enzyme which breaks down 5-HT and NA, the neurotransmitters relevant to antidepressant action) and their reversible action (the MAO-A is freed when drug levels drop following discontinuation of drug treatment). Moclobemide is the only RIMA licensed in the UK at the present but others are likely to be available in the near future.

Selective serotonin and noradrenaline re-uptake inhibitors (SNRIs)

The SNRIs are dual action antidepressants (stimulating both adrenergic and serotonergic activity in the brain) but unlike the TCAs they do not have anticholinergic, antihistaminic or cardio-toxic effects. Venlafaxine is the only SNRI currently licensed in the UK. It has good bioavailability and it has been claimed that it has an earlier onset of action compared to some other antidepressants. Milnacipran, another SNRI already available in some European countries, is likely to be licensed in the UK shortly.

Novel antidepressants

The improved understanding of the antidepressant mechanisms of action on the neurotransmitter systems led to the design of drugs with higher selectivity and specific receptor effects that reduce the possibility of side effects.

Nefazodone is a novel antidepressant related chemically to trazodone but has a different pharmacological profile; it is a relatively weak 5-HT re-uptake inhibitor and a potent 5-HT2 receptor antagonist. The latter property is thought not only to enhance its antidepressant action (facilitates 5-HT transmission via 5-HT1A receptors) but is also thought to reduce the likelihood of sexual dysfunction, a relatively common side effect of other antidepressants.

Mirtazapine is another novel antidepressant with a distinct pharmacological profile. It has dual action increasing both adrenergic and serotonergic activity; this is achieved by blocking alpha2 adrenoceptors which are located on both adrenergic and serotonergic (heteroreceptors) neuronal terminals. It also has 5-HT2 and 5-HT3 receptor antagonist properties which enhance 5-HT1A receptor transmission and reduce the incidence of side effects such as nausea, insomnia and sexual problems.

ANTIDEPRESSANT DRUGS IN WOMEN

Despite the major progress made in the psychopharmacology of depression, little research has been produced to examine the gender differences in the pharmacology of antidepressants. Although large numbers of women do take part in clinical trials of new anti-depressant drugs, in general the data on males and females are lumped together with no attempt to look at possible differences between the genders. We do not know whether women's response or experience of side effects, are the same or different from those of men, in relation to the drugs under investigation. Large, multi-centre clinical trials which are required by the regulatory bodies for the licensing of new medicines (Food and Drugs Administration (FDA) in the US or Committe of Safety of Medicines (CSM) in the UK offer possibilities of studying not only whether there are differential effects between the genders but also the possible effects of oral contraception, HRT, or menstrual cycle on the pharma-cokinetics and pharmacodynamics of the drug under investigation.

However, these have not been systematically examined although there is some evidence suggesting the presence of pharmacokinetic differences involving absorption, distribution and metabolism in women. Gastric acid secretion is lower and gastrointestinal transit time slower in women and these fluctuate in relation to hormonal changes during the menstrual cycle. The proportion of body fat to muscle is higher in women (this increases further with age) and this may affect drug distribution volume. Whether there are differences in hepatic metabolism and the activity of the enzymes within the cytochrome P450 system is unclear. However, the gonadal female hormones may affect the activity of some P450 iso-enzymes and that of monoamine oxidase (MAO) as well as altering GI tract motility (Dawkins et al., 1991). These effects may alter antidepressant plasma concentrations, and produce fluctuations of these during the menstrual cycle, influence the incidence of side effects, possibly increase drug half-lives. Animal research suggests that oestrogens affect the sensitivity of receptors within neurotransmitter systems relevant to depression and there may be pharmacodynamic effects on the action of the antidepressants.

During pregnancy, because of changes in protein binding capacity, decreased absorption, progesterone-induced decreased GI motility and increased hepatic metabolism, the doses of antidepressants may need to be changed, particularly in the last trimester.

Drug prescribing for women of childbearing potential

The thalidomide scare in the 1950s illustrated the major adverse effects a seemingly harmless drug can have on the normal development of the unborn foetus and led to extreme caution in prescribing for women of reproductive potential. In fact, until recently, in the US such women were not included in clinical trials involving new drugs. In accordance with the ABPI (Association of British Pharmaceutical Industry) guidelines, women of reproductive potential are required to use adequate contraception during clinical trials and pregnancy tests are carried out prior to study entry. Although the teratogenicity of new drugs is tested on animals this does not preclude possible teratogenic effects on the human foetus. None of the licensed antidepressants, therefore, have been subjected to controlled clinical trials in pregnancy. Information on their potential effects on the foetus or newborn baby is gathered through case reports or retrospective surveys. The general principle in clinical practice is to prescribe drugs that have been used clinically for a long time where more information is available about their safety.

Antidepressant drugs during pregnancy – practical considerations

It should be noted that the British National Formulary (BNF) warns 'no drug is safe beyond all doubt in early pregnancy'. The prescriber, therefore, has the difficult task of making a decision which should ensure that the risk to the foetus is minimized while the woman of childbearing potential is not denied effective treatment. A frank discussion should be held between doctor and patient and a decision regarding treatment made with the active participation of the patient. It is also essential that the prescriber is familiar with the pharmacology of the antidepressants and their potential for teratogenicity or other adverse effects on the foetus/newborn. Information can be obtained if needed from the National Drug Information Service which is part of the European Network of Teratology Information Services.

Considering that in the UK almost 50 per cent of pregnancies are unplanned, often it is not possible to plan ahead and agree in advance an optimal treatment plan in women with depressive illness. Also, in many cases, unfortunately, by the time pregnancy is discovered, organogenesis has started or been completed (embryonic phase: 6–8 weeks post conception; foetal phase: up to 13–14 weeks). The pharmaceutical companies for their own protection do not recommend the use of their products during pregnancy. Many recommend that the drugs should be discontinued prior to conception or as soon as pregnancy is detected. Such action, however, may be associated with:

1   risk of relapse,
2   possible harm to the baby as well as the mother through attempted suicide, in particular drug overdose, and
3   sudden discontinuation (particularly of tricyclics and SSRIs with short half-life) may cause withdrawal symptoms with the potential of harm to the foetus.

If a decision is made for the antidepressant to continue for the duration of the pregnancy the possible risk of neonatal withdrawal symptoms needs to be considered and anticipated.

ELECTROCONVULSIVE TREATMENT (ECT)

ECT, a much maligned and misunderstood treatment, is an effective alternative to pharmacological therapy in some patients with severe depression or when emergency treatment is required. ECT delivery and the equipment used has improved considerably in the last few years. The Royal College of Psychiatrists has issued clear guidelines which are regularly updated and monitored by a working group and yearly workshops are held for those involved in administering this treatment (including psychiatrists and anaesthetists).

Stimulus titration and determining of seizure threshold on an individual basis ensures maximum therapeutic efficacy by delivering an adequate electrical stimulus for the patient. The initial seizure threshold is highly variable and gender in addition to age and pre-ECT pharmacotherapy influence this. Twice weekly administration appears to be a reasonable frequency of treatment and this is the schedule generally used in the UK.

Although seizure duration is thought to be important in the efficacy of ECT, this is not always shown to be the case. Many of the new ECT machines have EEG equipment attached and this may facilitate further research into the role of various EEG parameters, such as the frequency of epileptic discharges, their slowing during the spike-wave phase, the pattern of rhythmic spike-wave, sharp wave complexes or others produced during ECT, in clinical improvement.

Concerns about cognitive impairment from neuronal damage in relation to ECT are not substantiated; serum neuron-specific enolase, a sensitive marker of neuronal damage, does not change after individual sessions or at the end of a course of ECT (Berrouschot et al., 1997). Retrograde amnesia has been described in some patients and strong predictors of its magnitude post-ECT were pre-ECT global cognitive status and the duration of post-ictal disorientation (Sobin et al., 1995).

The mode of action of ECT is not clear although it seems to be related to the induction of changes within the neurotransmitter systems implicated in the pathogenesis of depression. This is an action similar to the antidepressant drugs but less selective and with more acute and possibly more powerful effects. The assumption that response to ECT is independent of the adequacy of previous pharmacological treatment has been challenged by recent research showing that the clinical outcome of medication-resistant depressed patients was inferior to those without established medication resistance (Prudic et al., 1996). It is, however, better than a selective serotonin re-uptake inhibitor and this is in keeping with evidence suggesting that dual action antidepressants may be more effective than the more selective ones in the treatment of more severe depressive illness (Anderson and Tomenson, 1994).

CONCLUSIONS

At present it appears that women may be at higher risk of depression. This issue needs to be examined further, perhaps, with more sophisticated approaches. More studies are needed making comparisons between as well as within cultures. The role of both biological and psychosocial factors in determining gender differences requires further investigation.

Finally, both psychological and pharmacological treatments need to be compared between males and females. Significantly more research is required into the pharmacokinetics and pharmacodynamics of antidepressant drugs in women.

REFERENCES

Anderson, I.M. and Tomenson, B.M. (1994) 'The efficacy of selective serotonin re-uptake inhibitors in depression: a meta-analysis of studies against tricyclic antidepressants', *Journal of Psychopharmacology* 8: 238–49.

Andrew, M., McGuffin, P. and Katz, R. (1998) 'Genetic and non-genetic subtypes of major depressive disorder', *British Journal of Psychiatry* 173: 523–26.

Angold, A., Costello, E.J. and Worthman, C.M. (1998) 'Puberty and depression: the roles of age, pubertal status and pubertal timing', *Psychological Medicine* 28(1): 51–61.

Angst, J., Merikangas, K.R. and Preisig, M. (1997) 'Subthreshold syndromes of depression and anxiety in the community', *Journal of Clinical Psychiatry* 58 (suppl. 8): 6–10.

Angst, J. (1998) 'The prevalence of depression', in: M. Briley and S. Montgomery (eds) *Antidepressant Therapy at the Dawn of the Millenium*, London: Martin Dunitz Ltd., pp. 191–212.

Arpels, J.C. (1996) 'The female brain hypoestrogenic continuum from the premenstrual syndrome to menopause. A hypothesis and review of the data', *Journal of Reproductive Medicine* 41 (9): 633–9.

Backstrom, T. (1995) 'Symptoms related to the menopause and sex steroid treatments', in: G.R. Bock and J.A. Goode (eds) *Non-reproductive Actions of Sex Steroids, Ciba Foundation Symposium 191*, Chichester: John Wiley & Sons, 171–80.

Bebbington, P., Katz, R. and McGuffin, P. *et al.* (1989) 'The risk of minor depression before age 65: results from a community survey', *Psychological Medicine* 19: 393–400.

Bebbington, P.E., Dunn, G., Jenkins, R., Lewis, G., Brugha, T., Farrell, M. and Meltzer, H. (1998) 'The influence of age and sex on the prevalence of depressive conditions: report from the National Survey of Psychiatric Morbidity', *Psychological Medicine* 28 (1): 9–19.

Berrouschot, J., Rolle, K., Kuhn, H.J. and Schneider, D. (1997) 'Serum neuron-specific enolase levels do not increase after elctroconvulsive therapy', *Journal of Neurological Science* 150 (2): 173–6.

Blazer, D.G., Kessler, R.C., McGonagle, K.A. and Swartz, M.S. (1994) 'The prevalence and distribution of major depression in a national community sample: the National comorbidity Survey', *American Journal of Psychiatry* 38: 1039–46.

Canetto, S.S. and Safinofsky, I. (1998) 'The gender paradox in suicide', *Suicide Life Threat Behaviour* 28(1): 1–23.

Cheasty, M., Clare, A.W. and Collins, C. (1998) 'Relation between sexual abuse in childhood and adult depression: case control study', *British Medical Journal* 316(7126): 198–201.

Dawkins, K. and Potter, W.Z. (1991) 'Gender differences in pharmaco-kinetics and pharmacodynamics of psychotropics: focus on women', *Psychopharmacology Bulletin* 27(4): 417–26.

Dube, K.C. (1970) 'A study of prevalence and biosocial variables in mental illness in a rural and an urban community in Uttar Pradesh, India', *Acta Psychiatrica Scandinavica* 46: 327–59.

Eaton, W.W., Kramer, M. and Anthony, J.C. *et al.* (1989) 'The incidence of specific DIS/DSM-III mental disorders: data from the NIMH Epidemiologic Catchment Area Program', *Acta Psychiatrica Scandinavica* 79: 163–78.

Eaton, W.W., Anthony, J.C., Gallo, J., Cai, G., Tien, A., Romanoski, A., Lyketsos, C. and Chen, L.S. (1997) 'Natural history of Diagnostic Interview Schedule/DSM-IV major depression. The Baltimore Epidemiologic Catchment Area follow-up', *Archives of General Psychiatry* 54(11): 993–9.

Ericksson, E., Hedberg, M.A., Andersch, B. and Sundblad, C. (1995) 'The serotonin reuptake inhibitor, paroxetine is superior to the noradrenaline reuptake inhibitor maprotiline in the treatment of premenstrual syndrome', *Neuropsychopharmacology* 12(2): 167–76.

Ernst, C. and Angst, J. (1992) 'The Zurich Study XII. Sex differences in depression. Evidence from longitudinal epidemiological data', *European Archives of Psychiatry Clinical Neuroscience* 241: 222–30.

Fink, G., Sumner, B.E., Rosie, R., Grace, O. and Quinn, J.P. (1996) 'Estrogen control of central neurotransmission: effect on mood, mental state and memory', *Cellular and Molecular Neurobiology* 16(3): 325–44.

Fitzgerald, M., Malone, K.M., Li, S., Harrison, W.M., McBride, P.A., Endicott, J., Cooper, T. and Mann, J.J. (1997) 'Blunted serotonin response to fenfluramine challenge in premenstrual dysphoric disorder', *American Journal of Psychiatry* 154(4): 556–8.

Gater, R., Tansella, M., Korten, A., Tiemens, B.G., Mavreas, V.G. and Olatawura, M.O. (1998) 'Sex differences in the prevalence and detection of depressive and anxiety disorders in general health care settings: report from the World Health Organization Collaborative Study on Psychological Problems in General Health Care', *Archives of General Psychiatry* 55(5): 405–13.

Hankin, B.L., Abramson, L.Y., Moffitt, T.E., Silva, P.A., McGee, R. and Angell, K.E. (1998) 'Development of depression from preadolescence to young adulthood: emerging gender differences in a 10-year longitudinal study', *Journal of Abnormal Psychology* 107(1): 128–40.

Harlow, B.L., Cramer, D.W. and Annis, K.M. (1995) 'Association of medically treated depression and age at natural menopause', *American Journal of Epidemiology* 141(12): 1170–6.

Kendler, K.S., Eaves, L.J., Walters, E.E., Neale, M.C., Heath, A.C. and Kessler, R.C. (1996) 'The identification and validation of distinct depressive syndromes in a population based sample of female twins', *Archives of General Psychiatry* 53(5): 391–9.

Kessing, L.V. (1998) 'Recurrence in affective disorder, II: Effect of age and gender', *British Journal of Psychiatry* 172: 29–34.

Kroenke, K. and Spitzer, R.L. (1998) 'Gender differences in the reporting of physical and somatoform symptoms', *Psychosomatic Medicine* 60(2): 150–5.

Leibenluft, E. (1996) 'Women with bipolar illness: clinical and research issues', *American Journal of Psychiatry* 153(2): 163–73.

Lepine, J.P. for the DEPRES Steering Committee (1997) 'European perspective on depression', *Primary Care Psychiatry* 3 (suppl. 1): S3–S6.

Lewinsohn, P.M., Gotlib, I.H., Lewinsohn, M., Seeley Jr and Allen, N.B. (1998) 'Gender differences in anxiety disorders and anxiety symptoms in adolescents', *Journal of Abnormal Psychology* 107(1): 109–17

Maskall, D.D., Lam, R.W., Misri, S., Carter, D., Kuan, A.J., Yatham, L.N. and Zis, A.P. (1997) 'Seasonality of symptoms in women with luteal phase dysphoric disorder', *American Journal of Psychiatry* 154(10): 1436–41.

Nicol-Smith, L. (1996) 'Causality, menopause and depression: a critical review of the literature', *British Medical Journal* 313(7067): 1229–32.

Orley, J. and Wing, J.K. (1979) 'Psychiatric disorder in two African villages', *Archives of General Psychiatry* 36: 513–20.

Pajer, K. (1995) 'New strategies in the treatment of depression in women', *Journal of Clinical Psychiatry* 56 (suppl. 2): 30–7.

Parry, B.L., Udell, C., Elliott, J.A., Berga, S.L., Klauber, M.R., Mostofi, N., LeVeau, B. and Gillin, J.C. (1997) 'Blunted phase-shift responses to morning bright light in premenstrual dysphoric disorder', *Journal of Biological Rhythms* 12(5): 443–56.

Parry, B.L., Hauger, R., LeVeaw, B., Mostofi, N., Cover, H., Clopton, B. and Gillin, J.C. (1996) 'Circadian rhythms of prolactin and thyroid-stimulating hormone during the menstrual cycle and early versus late sleep deprivation in premenstrual dysphoric disorder', *Psychiatry Research* 62(2): 147–60.

Pearce, J., Hawton, K. and Blake, F. (1995) 'Psychological and sexual symptoms associated with the menopause and the effects of hormone replacement therapy', *British Journal of Psychiatry* 167(2): 163–73.

Pearlstein, T., Rosen, K. and Stone, A.B. (1997) 'Mood disorders and menopause', *Endocrinology and Metabolism Clinics of North America* 26(2): 279–94.

Preskorn, S.H. and Jerkovich, G.S. (1990) 'Central nervous system toxicity of tricyclic antidepressants: Phenomenology, course, risk factors and role of therapeutic drug monitoring', *Journal of Clinical Pharmacology* 10: 88–95.

Prudic, J., Haskett, R.F., Mulsant, B. and Malone, K. (1996) 'Resistance to antidepressant medications and short-term clinical response to ECT', *American Journal of Psychiatry* 153(8): 985–92.

Robinson, G. (1996) 'Cross-cultural perspectives on menopause', *Journal of Nervous and Mental Disease* 184(8): 453–8.

Rosenstein, D.L., Kalogeras, K.T., Kalafut, M., Malley, J. and Rubinow, D.R. (1996) 'Peripheral measures of arginine-vasopressin, atrial natriuretic peptide and adrenocorticotropic hormone in premenstrual syndrome', *Psychoneuroendocrinology* 21(3): 347–59.

Salokangas, R.K. and Putanen, O. (1998) 'Risk factors for depression in primary care. Findings of the TADEP project', *Journal of Affective Disorder* 48(2–3): 171–80.

Schmidt, P.J., Nieman, L.K., Danaceau, M.A., Adams, L.F. and Rubinow, D.R. (1998) 'Differential behavioural effects of gonadal steroids in women with and in those without premenstrual syndrome', *New England Journal of Medicine* 338(4): 209–16.

Seippel, L. and Backstrom, T. (1998) 'Luteal-phase oestradiol relates to symptom severity in patients with premenstrual syndrome', *Journal of Clinical Endocrinology and Metabolism* 83(6): 1988–92.

Simon, G.E. and von Korf, M. (1995) 'Reevaluation of secular trends in depression rates', *American Journal of Epidemiology* 135: 1411–22.

Simon, R.W. (1998) 'Assessing sex differences in vulnerability among employed parents: the importance of marital status', *Journal of Health and Social Behaviour* 39(1): 38–54.

Simpson, H.B., Nee, J.C. and Endicott, J. (1987) 'First-episode major depression. Few sex differences in course', *Archives of General Psychiatry* 54(7): 633–9.

Sobin, C., Sackeim, H.A., Prudic, J., Devanand, D.P., Moody, B.J. and McElhiney, M.C. (1995) 'Predictors of retrograde amnesia following ECT', *American Journal of Psychiatry* 152(7): 995–1001.

Steiner, M. (1997) 'Premenstrual syndromes', *Annual Reviews in Medicine* 48: 447–55.

Sundstrom, I., Ashbrook, D. and Backstrom, T. (1997) 'Reduced benzodiazepine sensitivity in patients with premenstrual syndrome: a pilot study', *Psychoneuroendocrinology* 22(1): 25–38.

Thys-Jacobs, S. and Alvir, M.J. (1995) 'Calcium-regulating hormones across the menstrual cycle: evidence of a secondary hyperparathyroidism in women with PMS', *Journal of Clinical Endocrinology and Metabolism* 80(7): 2227–32.

Tylee, A. (1991) 'Recognising depression', *Practitioner* 235: 669–72.

Veijola, J., Puukka, P., Lehtinen, V., Moring, J., Lindholm, T. and Vaisanen, E. (1998) 'Sex differences in the association between childhood experiences and adult depression', *Psychological Medicine* 28(1): 21–7.

Weissman, M.M. and Klerman, G.L. (1977) 'Sex differences and the epidemiology of depression', *Archives of General Psychiatry* 34: 98–111.

Weissman, M.M., Bruce, L.M. and Leaf, P.J. *et al.* (1990) 'Affective disorders', in: L.N. Robins and D.A. Regier (eds) *Psychiatric Disorders in America. The Epidemiologic Catchment Area Study*, New York: The Free Press, pp. 53–80.

Wilhelm, K. and Parker, G. (1989) 'Is sex necessarily a risk factor to depression?', *Psychological Medicine* 19: 401–13.

Yonkers, K.A., Zlotnick, C., Allsworth, J., Warshaw, M., Shea, T. and Keller, M.B. (1998) 'Is the course of panic disorder the same in women and men?', *American Journal of Psychiatry* 155(5): 596–602.

Chapter 6

Women and schizophrenia

Gabriella Zolese

INTRODUCTION

Schizophrenia affects women in different ways. Despite gender differences being described by Kraeplin as early as 1896, it is only in recent years that more research has been focused in this area. The differences in gender were regarded as confounding variables in schizophrenia research but are now rightly considered a constant variable. Bleuler himself in 'Dementia Praecox or the group of schizophrenias' (1950) described schizophrenia as a disease of young men characterized by social withdrawal, poor premorbid adjustment, negative symptoms and blunted affect.

In a recent review article Kulkarni (1997) outlined reasons for the lack of interest in the schizophrenia of women. Researchers have frequently lumped together all presentations of schizophrenia so that little attention was paid to symptom differences. Women were often excluded from studies because of the belief that those who suffer from schizophrenia were unable to report reliably their menstrual histories. Studies were also conducted using samples selected from hospital populations, which therefore included mostly men who have now been shown to have a poorer outcome for the disorder and therefore fill the hospital wards much more than women.

Recent research has now outlined major differences between the sexes. There is consensus that schizophrenia is a neurodevelopmental disorder which appears in men at a younger age than women (Murray, 1994). Brain imaging studies have confirmed that it is a disease that actually changes the morphology of the brain (Harvey *et al.*, 1993). Obstetric complications and perinatal insults are also associated with this type of schizophrenia and seem to affect men more than women (O'Callaghan *et al.*, 1992). Premorbid functioning, harbouring of the 'prodromal' signs of this devastating disorder, is better in women. Gonadal hormones appear to have a protective effect, which might explain some of the differences. The illness itself is characterized by more 'negative' symptoms in men and more 'affective' symptoms in women which in turn contribute to a better outcome. Response to antipsychotic drugs and susceptibility to their side effects has also been researched. The importance of these differences is obvious as they should influence the prognosis, treatment and service provisions for women who suffer from schizophrenia.

In this chapter research evidence for epidemiological, clinical and neurobiological factors in schizophrenia in women will be reviewed. The implications for treatment and service provisions will also be discussed.

EPIDEMIOLOGY

Incidence

Incidence rates for schizophrenia are similar throughout the world. It is generally accepted that the incidence in men and women is equal; however, this is difficult to ascertain. Recent studies suggest that the rates might be higher in men (Seeman, 1998). This phenomenon could be explained by a number of factors: women access psychiatric services in a different way, which would influence ascertainment. They present often with more prominent affective symptoms, which introduce recruitment bias and therefore different pick up rates.

Nearly thirty years ago Rosenthal (1970) examined the admission records for 'dementia praecox' in the US mental hospitals for the year 1933. He found admission rates of 30 in 100,000 for male and 15 in 100,000 for female. The development of strict diagnostic criteria and generally more rigorous methodology has led to evidence that women are less likely to suffer from schizophrenia. In the 1980s, Lewine *et al.*, using the Diagnostic and Statistical Manual for Mental Disorders 3rd edition (DSM-III), demonstrated a lower incidence of schizophrenia in women (Lewine *et al.*, 1984). The possibility that a number of patients had been left out by the upper age limit of 45 years imposed by the diagnostic criteria was pointed out. However, using the diagnostic criteria of the revised version (DSM-III-R) which removed this age limit, the difference in incidence between the sexes still persisted (Castle et al., 1993b).

Two main points have to be made about these findings: one is that women tend to present with more affective symptoms and therefore might not be included in the initial recruitment in studies with a stringent case definition; second, the later age at onset would also influence recruitment because of possible comorbidity. For example, physical diseases are more likely to be present in older age. As schizophrenia affects women in later life there is an increased chance that they would not be included in studies that generally exclude comorbid physical illness.

Age of onset

Clinicians have been aware of gender differences in age of onset of schizophrenia. Rosenthal (1970) looked at first admissions over one year to the New York state hospitals and found that at the age of 25 years 70 per cent were male and 30 per cent were female. At the age of 35 years, however, the rates became equal and by 50 years of age there was a reverse trend so that two to three females to one male needed admission for schizophrenia. McCabe (1975) confirmed age–sex differences using the Danish psychiatric register and Forrest and Hay (1972) showed that of 100 consecutive first admissions for schizophrenia, 33 per cent of males and of 5 per cent females had been admitted before the age of 20 years.

A number of these studies were criticized for their methodology; they had used highly selected populations, diagnostic criteria which included age-limit and age at first hospitalization rather than age at first psychiatric contact. Nevertheless the differences between age at onset were confirmed once studies with better designs were conducted (Lewine et al., 1984). In 100 female and 100 male patients using DSM-III criteria for schizophrenia, Loranger (1984) found that 90 per cent of males became ill before age 30 but this was only true of 20-30 per cent of females; however, after 35 years of age 17 per cent of females and only 2 per cent of the males suffered from schizophrenia. Lewis (1992) more recently looked at first admission before 25 years of age and found that 50–60 per cent of male admissions had occurred before this age but only 30 per cent of females. Hafner et al., (1993) confirmed the finding that women fall ill three to five years later than males.

Recently Faraone *et al.* (1994), in an elegant study, analysed data correcting for age distribution of the population. If age distribution of males and females differs, then observed differences in age of onset could be artefactual. In the general population females tend to live longer, and schizophrenic males tend to die earlier. Therefore females might suffer the onset of disease at a later age. The authors also re-diagnosed the patients using DSM-III-R which eliminates the age limit of 45 to diagnose schizophrenia. Their results confirmed a true gender difference of age at onset in schizophrenia.

Jablensky and Cole (1997) re-analysed data from the 10 countries WHO study of schizophrenia. Data from 778 men and 653 women showed that marital status had an independent effect on age at onset. i.e. being married was associated with a delayed onset of schizophrenia.

One other possible explanation for this difference is the readiness by which men are referred to psychiatric services when compared to women. Beiser *et al.*, (1993) found a larger delay between onset of symptoms and hospital admission in women than in men. This might be explained by the fact that women with psychotic symptoms cause less 'problems' to those around them. They are less likely to be threatening and less likely to fulfil criteria for compulsory admission.

The incidence of schizophrenia therefore is unequal in the sexes; when the 'late adolescence/early adulthood' form is looked at this is more common in males. However, epidemiologists have identified a second peak of age of onset for schizophrenia which occurs mostly in women in older age (Castle and Murray, 1993a). This late onset psychosis appears to be very similar to the early onset male schizophrenia.

Ethnicity

The incidence of schizophrenia is overall similar in most cultures and races. The World Health Organization study of ten countries found similar rates (Jablensky *et al.*, 1992).

In Ghana (Sikarnartey and Eaton, 1984) the point prevalence of schizophrenia for ages 25–44 is 1.68/1000 for males and 0.26/1000 for females. After 45 this ratio is inverted. Studies from Poland found similar rates (Flor-Henry, 1990). Sartorius *et al.* (1978) reanalysed data from a cohort of 306 patients suffering from schizophrenia who had participated in the WHO study of 1973.

The authors found that male gender correlated with chronicity, and it was the best single predictor of outcome. In Nigeria (Ohaeri, 1992) a cohort of 340 (199 men, 141 women) patients with DSM-III-R diagnosis of schizophrenia were studied. Men had a significant earlier age of onset than women (24 ± 6 years and 27 ± 8 years respectively). By the age of 30, 83 per cent of men had become ill compared to 66 per cent of women.

NEUROBIOLOGY

Genetics

As early as 1934 Rosanoff and colleagues found a lower concordance for schizophrenia in male than in female monozygotic twins. This led to the hypothesis that schizophrenia is aetiologically a different disease in women as compared to men. Researchers have since tested this hypothesis but the findings are controversial. Some authors have found that the risk of developing schizophrenia is significantly lower in relatives of males than female schizophrenic probands (Goldstein et al., 1990a; Bellodi et al., 1986). Goldstein and colleagues, in particular, analysed the data from the IOWA-500 cohort of 332 patients with schizophrenia according to DSM-III criteria. The authors found that the age-corrected lifetime risk of the relatives of male patients was 2.2 per cent compared with that of relatives of females which was 5.2 per cent. When schizophrenia spectrum disorders were included in the analysis the difference was attenuated. In fact male relatives were at a higher risk of developing schizotypal personality disorder. However, relatives of female probands were at a higher risk of developing the more severe forms of the spectrum disorders, i.e. schizophrenia. Both male and female relatives of the female patients were at the same risk of developing schizophrenia (Goldstein et al., 1990a). However, the opposite findings have also been reported (Onstad et al., 1991; Kendler et al., 1995). These discrepancies in findings might either reflect methodological flaws or they might just be the results of differences between populations. Kendler (1995) comments that in Ireland where drug abuse is relatively rare there might be a reduction of 'sporadic' cases.

Despite the contradictory results, attempts at looking at mode of transmission have recently taken new momentum for an explanatory model based on the sex chromosomes. De Lisi and Crow (1989) particularly have put forward the hypothesis that there might be a locus for psychosis in the pseudoautosomal region of the short arm of the X and Y chromosomes. This hypothesis is backed up by the findings that individuals who have extra X chromosomes are more likely to suffer from psychoses and also that siblings with psychosis are more likely to be the same gender, and that relatives of female probands are at greater risk of developing schizophrenia (De Lisi *et al.*, 1993). Although this hypothesis has been criticized (Kulkarni, 1997), nevertheless the sex differences for this disorder continue to spur genetic research.

Brain imaging studies

The discovery of non-invasive brain imaging (Computerized Axial Tomography) opened a new era of research for psychiatry and especially for schizophrenia. In 1976 Johnstone and her colleagues (1976) showed that the brains of those suffering from chronic schizophrenia had enlarged ventricles on Computerized Tomography (CT-scan). A number of studies since then have shown differences in CT-scan and Magnetic Resonance Imaging (MRI) in the appearances of the brains of patients who suffer from schizophrenia (Turner *et al.*, 1986; Harvey *et al.*, 1993). Andreasen and colleagues (1990) using CT- and MRI-scans reported greater frequency of structural abnormalities in men with schizophrenia rather than women. Men had larger ventricles, the thalamus appeared significantly smaller in men and patients who exhibited mostly negative symptoms had significantly larger ventricles than those who had more positive ones. These abnormalities were confirmed by Lewine *et al.* (1990); male patients had the highest frequencies of abnormalities on MRI; these included smaller corpus callosum areas and a rounded bulbous splenium. More recently Flaum *et al.* (1995) did not find any associations between brain abnormalities and gender. Contrary to the findings described above, Gur *et al.* (1991) and Nasrallah *et al.* (1990) showed that female patients had smaller brains and larger lateral and third ventricles on MRI-scans. These different findings have been attributed to small sample sizes, and the different methods used by investigators to correct for normal variation in head size. Overall there seems to be a strong suggestion that brain dysmorphology is more apparent in those with a more severe illness and similar in both genders. Lauriello and co-authors

(1997) selected a group of female patients who had suffered schizophrenia at early onset and were severely symptomatic; many of the patients were compulsorily admitted to hospital and resided there. They were compared to a similar group of male patients and all compared to a group of healthy men and women in the same age range. All patients underwent MRI-scans. These showed the same deficit in cortical grey matter in women and men with schizophrenia when compared to the healthy controls. Similarly ventricular enlargement was prominent in the experimental subjects.

Cowell *et al.* (1996) studied a group of 91 patients and 114 healthy controls. The authors found sex differences such as smaller frontal lobe in men associated with more clinical 'disorganization'. Overall studies on the differences in the morphology of the brain between the sexes remain controversial and inconclusive; however, there is some consensus that men more often than women show structural brain abnormalities that are more clearly of neurodevelopmental origin (Lewis, 1989).

Neurodevelopmental theory

Obstetric complications

There is now very strong evidence of the association between obstetric complications at birth, or perinatal insults, and brain abnormalities found in patients with schizophrenia. These are confined essentially to males with an early onset of schizophrenia. It is further compounded by the association between other neurodevelopmental brain disorders, such as autism, and males (Murray and Lewis, 1987). Obstetric complications are associated with early onset schizophrenia and more often with males (O'Callaghan *et al.*, 1992). Such associations are not found in female patients, in those with a late onset illness and in those with a more acute presentation (O'Callaghan *et al.*, 1991; Owen *et al.*, 1988).

The controversial evidence for a male neurodevelopmental schizophrenia continues to puzzle researchers. Explanation as to why males should be more vulnerable to early brain insults have been put forward. The nervous system matures more slowly in males. Female brains show an earlier myelinization, earlier neuronal connections and a faster bilateral distribution of cerebral function (Seeman and Lang, 1990). Male brains could therefore be more vulnerable to obstetric complications (Lewis, 1992).

Maternal influenza

The observation that schizophrenia is associated with being born in winter or in early spring has given momentum to the 'viral hypothesis'. A number of studies have reported an association between influenza exposure in pregnancy and schizophrenia in the offspring (Murray, 1994). The elegant study of O'Callaghan *et al.*, in 1991 investigated the effect of the influenza A2 epidemic in England and Wales in 1957. Their results showed an association between infection of the mothers in the second trimester of pregnancy and an increased risk of developing schizophrenia in later life. In addition this increase was more striking for women. This does not necessarily suggest that the female foetus is more susceptible to gestational viral infection; the male foetus could be at greater risk of more severe brain insults and therefore more spontaneous abortions.

Neuroendocrine differences

There is fairly robust evidence that schizophrenia in women at early onset is more benign, has more affective symptoms and a better clinical course, with less hospitalization and better social outcome. This seems to be linked to the lack of association with brain insults intrafoetally and perinatally. However, when the illness develops in later life it is as devastating as the 'early onset type' in men. Because of the association between age at onset, outcome and menopause, research has been directed by the hypothesis that the expression of schizophrenia might be modulated by sex hormones.

Oestrogen receptors are distributed throughout the brain. When the oestrogen levels fall premenstrually or in the menopause, psychotic symptoms have been shown to worsen (Gerada and Reveley, 1988; Seeman and Lang, 1990). Indeed oestrogen replacement therapy has also been used to improve positive symptoms of schizophrenia in a single case report of a post-menopausal woman (Lindamer *et al.*, 1997). Further evidence comes from the role of hormones in puerperal psychosis (Wieck *et al.*, 1991; Gitlin and Pasnau, 1989). The theory that oestrogens might be playing a protective role in women would explain some of the gender differences in this disorder.

Measurements of oestradiol levels in 32 women who suffered an acute episode of schizophrenia showed that when the oestradiol levels were high, symptoms as measured by the Brief Psychiatric Rating Scale (BPRS, Overall and Gorham, 1962) improved (Riecher-Rossler *et al.*, 1994). This finding is linked with the evidence that oestrogens have a neuroleptic-like effect; it has been shown that lower doses of neuroleptics are needed when oestrogens rise (Gattaz *et al.*, 1994). (See Chapter 2, 'A physiological perspective' by Dr Scott.)

The protecting effect of oestrogen might be expressed as early as intrafoetally when maturation occurs (see above) or it might be an effect expressed in adolescence. At this time there is a rapid and dramatic increase in hormone levels with an increased risk of schizophrenia. Women might be more protected by oestrogens and consequently men more vulnerable to early onset disease (Seeman and Lang, 1990). The cyclical nature of symptomatology at the premenstrual, menopausal and postpartum periods, discussed earlier in the chapter, compound the evidence that high levels of oestrogen might have an antipsychotic-like effect.

In an open clinical trial adjunctive administration of oestrogen to neuroleptics in a sample of 11 women who suffered from schizophrenia, compared to 7 who were only receiving neuroleptics, improved positive psychotic symptoms significantly (Kulkarni, 1996). Understandably there are other social factors contributing to the development of schizophrenia which might protect women. Risk behaviours such as drug taking are more typical of males. Traditionally occupational stress is known to be more pronounced in men, although this is a trend that is changing for women. In addition, strong family ties and engagement in a more supportive social network is more typical for women.

SYMPTOMATOLOGY AND CLINICAL VARIABLES

Premorbid function

Premorbid functioning has been shown to be a strong predictive variable of better outcome of schizophrenia in both genders (Goldstein *et al.*, 1990b). Premorbid deficits are found more prominently in males than in females who go on to develop schizophrenia. A number of retrospective studies have described women with schizophrenia having had better premorbid social, sexual and marital adjustments (McGlashan and Bardenstein, 1990). In a population of children at high risk, Foerster *et al.* (1991) found that interview with mothers identified premorbid deficits in boys rather than girls. In particular early schizoid traits were reported more frequently, and these were also reliable predictors of early onset schizophrenia. Torrey and colleagues (1991) reviewed childhood histories of 23 pairs of non-concordant identical twins. Within pairs the ill twin began to change behaviourally earlier for 14 males in comparison to 9 females. This seems to suggest that the effect of gender exists well before the age of onset of psychotic symptoms.

Retrospective studies are always vulnerable to flaws: the methodological difficulties of retrospectively assessing personality in childhood from informants carry especially a great risk of confounding. Research that has been carried out using informants such as parents or spouses of patients has to be considered very cautiously because of potential for bias. Parents of patients who have been ill a long time might have a very distorted recall of their sons and daughters before the illness. Dalkin *et al.* (1994), using the data from the Study on Determinants of Outcome of Severe Mental Disorders, examined premorbid personality in first-onset psychosis. The authors reported no differences between male and female patients in schizoid traits, but explosive traits were significantly more common in women. This finding, however, might be influenced by the fact that mothers were more often the informants of male patients. The reporting might also have been biased by the length of contact between the mothers and the male patients.

Done *et al.* (1994), using data from the National Child development study, analysed teachers' ratings at age 7 and 11 years in a randomly selected sample of a cohort who had developed mental illness. The children, all born in 1958, had been followed up prospectively and the patients identified using the mental health enquiry. Results showed that by age 7 those who later developed schizophrenia were already more likely to be rated as overreactive, hostile and engaging in inconsequential behaviour. Instead, girls by age 11 were more likely to be rated as withdrawn, unforthcoming and depressed. The authors comment how changes were more striking in boys and social maladjustment showed a progression in girls but not in the boys: 'Changes overtime that differ between the two sexes may be relevant in further understanding the origins of psychosis'. Similar antecedents to schizophrenia have been identified in High Risk children with boys being more disruptive, anxious and rejected by peers and girls more withdrawn and nervous (Olin and Mednick, 1996).

Type of psychosis

If age of onset is different in women does this mean the symptoms of illness are different as well? Researchers have suggested that there are two main types of illness, one affecting men with earlier age of onset, and one with a later age of onset affecting women (McGlashan and Bardenstein, 1990; Mayer *et al.*, 1993). Women appear to have better premorbid adjustment, a more prominent affective component and frequent delusions (Goldstein *et al.*, 1990b). Castle *et al.* (1994), in a latent class analysis of a large sample of 447 patients with non-affective functional psychosis, confirmed these results. These authors found three subtypes of schizophrenia: an early onset 'neurodevelopmental' type with a male : female ratio of 7 : 3; a 'paranoid' type with an equal ratio; and a third subtype idenitified as 'schizoaffective', mostly affected women and carried a negligible familial risk. However, when women develop schizophrenia in late life negative symptoms appear to be more prominent. Hafner *et al.* (1993) found that the symptoms did not differ greatly between sexes; however, when males with early onset and females with late onset schizophrenia were compared, the females had a higher frequency of negative symptoms and a worse course of illness. The authors explain this as due to the 'protective' action of the female hormones, which disappears at menopause. A family study conducted in Ireland confirmed these findings (Kendler *et al.*, 1995).

Course of illness and outcome

The age of onset therefore is later, the type of illness appears more 'benign' with more affective symptoms and its course appears to be different. Schizophrenia in women tends to have a more remitting course and more favourable outcome (Flor-Henry, 1990). Despite methodological flaws in some of the studies, in a careful review of 102 studies, Angermeyer and colleagues (1990) found consensus that the outcome of schizophrenia for women was better. Of course some of the differences shown in the past studies could be due to self selection by the way that the two genders make use of psychiatric services.

Goldstein and co-authors (1990b) in their retrospective study from case notes examined the first and second admission of 90 patients (F=32, M=58). The authors found no differences in age of onset, education, marital status, race, religion and socio-economic status. However, results of univariate analysis strongly showed that women had a significantly lower mean number of rehospitalizations and shorter length of stay in hospital at 5 and 10 years of follow-up. In male patients premorbid functioning was worse. When entered in a multiple regression analysis, premorbid functioning contributed to 13 per cent of the variance but gender remained a significant variable.

A better course of illness was found also in a large sample of patients followed up after 15 years from their initial hospitalization. Women had a higher employment rate, better general social competence and were more likely to be married (McGlashan and Bardenstein, 1990). In a group of patients with schizophrenia with a 'chronic course', researchers found that, although symptoms were equal in the two sexes, women had a significantly better quality of social interaction and generally 'more fullness of life' (Breier et al., 1992). From the point of view of the patient this is a very good outcome.

Angemeyer et al. (1989), in an 8-year follow-up study of patients admitted with schizophrenia, confirmed these findings. The male patients were more likely to be readmitted and spent twice as long in hospital. However, there was an attenuation of gender differences over the years. Other studies have demonstrated the attenuation of the gender effect over a longer period of follow-up (Jonsson and Nyman, 1991; Nyman, 1989). However, as women do better in the initial years following their breakdown, they might be later followed up less intensely, receive fewer services and when older are left more disadvantaged.

Better outcome overall for women has also been described by Breier and Astrachan (1984). In this paper, more male than female schizophrenia patients committed suicide. In a prospective study of 153 patients with schizophrenia, the death rate for men was twice that of women and their readmission rate was double at 12 years' follow-up (Affleck et al., 1976). It must be noted, however, that in the general population men commit suicide more often than women. In patients with schizophrenia the ratio of suicide in men to women is smaller. This might be due to affective symptoms being more commonly present in women with this illness (Goldstein et al., 1993).

Better outcome is therefore explained by a more benign form of the disorder in women, better response to drug treatment as women tend to be more compliant (Seeman and Lang, 1990) and better engagement in other psychosocial treatments (Haas et al., 1990).

Expressed emotions and family environment

Social psychiatry research emphasized the importance of the social interaction between patients and their family on the course of the illness. These interactions are 'expressed emotions' (EE). A large number of studies identified higher relapse rates with higher expressed emotions. Gender differences have also been found in family studies: Vaughn and colleagues (1984) found higher rates of sensitivity in males of high EE families than females. However, in a very thorough review of aggregate data from 25 studies on EE and schizophrenia, Bebbington and Kuipers (1994) found that the predictive value of relapse of EE was very similar in men and women.

TREATMENT

Antipsychotic drugs

Since the discovery of Chlorpromazine in 1952, antipsychotic drugs have represented the first line of treatment for both the acute phase of schizophrenia and to prevent relapse. Their mechanism of action is to block the dopamine receptors, in particular the D_2 receptor, which reduce hallucinations, delusions and the psychomotor arousal typical of this disorder. However, in different degrees, the antipsychotics also effect other receptors, mainly the D_1 in the basal ganglia, and cholinergic and adrenergic receptors.

This side effect profile is particularly important for women. Female patients are more likely to develop pseudoparkinsonism and akathisia. Tardive dyskinesia has been reported more frequently in menopausal women (Yassa and Jeste, 1992). The more severe side effect profile for women might be explained by the fact that oestrogens appear to enhance dopamine blockade.

Oestrogens have been shown to increase the density of Dopamine type 2 receptors in animals and this might explain their neuroleptic-like effects in women. Premenstrual exacerbations of psychosis (low oestrogens), postpartum psychosis (low oestrogens) and increased number of late onset schizophrenia (low oestrogens) in women are all linked to female hormonal changes (Seeman and Lang, 1990). It is not surprising therefore that women of reproductive age respond to lower doses of neuroleptic medication during the acute phases of the illness (Seeman, 1989). However, after the menopause the reverse is true.

It is important to bear in mind that women, who might be more compliant, also have different absorption, storage and metabolism from male patients (Yonkers *et al.*, 1992). Oestrogens have antidopaminergic properties, therefore, although the dose required in pre-menopausal women is lower than men, the likelihood of developing unwanted effects is higher.

Women tend to suffer from less acute dystonias following neuroleptics administration (Swett, 1975) and therefore subsequent compliance is better in women than men (Zito *et al.*, 1985). This might be due to slower gastric emptying in women which in turn delays absorption and gives rise to less side effects. Seeman and Lang (1990) suggest, however, that this might be a direct effect of oestrogens on the homeostasis between acethylcholine and dopamine. The monthly fluctuation of dopamine blockade mediated by oestrogens has somehow prepared the brain to adjust to a sudden dopamine blockade. (See Chapter 2, 'A physiological perspective' by Dr Scott.)

Cerebral blood flow has also been shown to be 15 per cent higher in women which might lead to a better distribution of neuroleptics in the brain (Gur *et al.*, 1982). Higher percentage of body fat might also explain why women have a longer delay in relapse as compared to men. Neuroleptics are lipophilic and therefore more neuroleptics are stored in women.

Dopamine blockade causes an increase in the production of prolactin which is mediated by dopamine. Women often report galactorrhea, amenorrhoea and infertility. Weight gain and skin problems are also frequent side effects which are obviously more important for women. Therefore, in the longer term, the administration of neuroleptic drugs and the consequent decrease in oestrogens increases the risk of developing osteoporosis and heart disease. These side effects are particularly significant not just when considering how to improve compliance but also to ensure a normal reproductive life for our patients.

Recently, the introduction of the atypical antipsychotics has reduced the incidence of these unwanted effects. Clozapine and to some degree other, newer drugs have a very different mode of action from the traditional neuroleptics. Clozapine has a weak dopamine blocking action (about 20 per cent versus 80 per cent for haloperidol) and a high affinity for 5-HT receptors. Extrapyramidal side effects are rare and so is the development of hyperprolactinaemia.

The drugs of choice for schizophrenia in women are now atypical antipsychotics which reduce the risk of long-term extrapyramidal side effects and do not alter the reproductive cycle. If it is true that oestrogens are protective against psychosis then there is an even better case for not interfering with prolactin production.

Drug treatment with the traditional antipsychotics could be titrated according to the luteal phase; however, this is only feasible in more specialized units. Another important adjunct to treatment should be hormone replacement therapy which would counteract some of the unwanted side effects.

Psychosocial treatment

In spite of the differences in age at presentation, in psychopathology and in outcome there is surprisingly very little research in the social and psychological therapies for women. Some work has been done on family therapy and psychosocial interventions. In the New York Hospital, Haas and colleagues (1990) randomized 92 inpatients of both sexes to a brief inpatient family intervention. This consisted mostly of education regarding schizophrenia. Their results showed that women did better in terms of a 'superior family and occupational functioning' at 18 months' follow-up. The reasons for the better outcome in women can be seen as reflecting the normal social differences between the two sexes. Families and society have higher expectations of men than of women. It is possible that the families of male patients were more demanding of their relative. Women are generally more compliant to dependency on their families, therefore more readily accepting treatment that involves more intervention from family members. A further factor that might explain the better outcome is the better premorbid social adjustment in women.

The presence of mood symptoms which put women with schizophrenia more at risk of suicide (see above) should be addressed routinely in the management of schizophrenia in women.

Psychological interventions addressing, for example, the loss associated with the separation from children and family, and may be the fear of losing custody of their children, should be considered. Mothers with schizophrenia are monitored more closely and scrutinized by social services. Even the common practice of sending patients home for the week-end might be seen in a different light when the patient could have been the main carer before hospitalization and therefore expectations on the part of the family might be higher. Whilst ill, women are potentially vulnerable to sexual harassment and assault. Thomas, Bartlett and Mezey (1995) found that 39 per cent of women had experienced unwanted sexual comments, 32 per cent had experienced sexual molestation and 4 per cent had been sexually assaulted whilst in hospital. It is clear that women need services that not only protect them but also provide a sensitive environment. In the UK the government has recently legislated on the establishment of single-sex wards in hospitals.

CONCLUSIONS

The need to recognize differences in schizophrenia in women is increasingly more apparent. Focusing research on schizophrenia in women will improve treatment for female patients and also contribute to a better understanding of this disease in both sexes. These gender differences have repercussion for services and a need for more specialized units that pay particular attention to women is long overdue.

REFERENCES

Affleck, J.W., Burns, J. and Forrest A.D. (1976) 'Long-term follow up of schizophrenic patients in Edinburgh', *Acta Psychiatrica Scandinavica* 53: 227–37.

American Psychiatric Association (1980) *Diagnostic and Statistical Manual of Mental Disorders (3rd edn)* (DSM-III), Washington, DC: APA.

American Psychiatric Association (1987) *Diagnostic and Statistical Manual of Mental Disorders (3rd edn, revised)* (DSM-III-R), Washington, DC: APA.

Andreasen, N.C., Ehrhardt, J.C., Swayze II, V.W., Alliger, R.J., Yuh,

W.T.C., Cohen G. and Ziebell, S. (1990) 'Magnetic resonance imaging of the brain in schizophrenia', *Archives of General Psychiatry* 47: 35–44.

Angermeyer, M.C., Kuhn, L. and Goldstein, J.M. (1990) 'Gender and the course of schizophrenia', *Schizophrenia Bulletin* 16: 293–307.

Angermeyer, M.C., Goldstein, J.M. and Kuhn, L. (1989) 'Gender differences in schizophrenia: rehospitalization and community survival', *Psychological Medicine* 19: 365–82.

Bebbington, P. and Kuipers, L. (1994) 'The predictive utility of expressed emotion in schizophrenia: an aggregate analysis', *Psychological Medicine* 24(3): 707–18.

Beiser, M., Erickson, D. and Fleming, J.A.E., *et al.* (1993) 'Establishing the onset of psychiatric illness', *American Journal of Psychiatry* 150: 1349–54.

Bellodi, L., Bussoleni C. and Scorza-Smeraldi R., *et al.* (1986) 'Family study of schizophrenia: exploratory analysis for relevant factors', *Schizophrenia Bulletin* 12: 120–8.

Bleuler, E. (1950) *Dementia Praecox or the Group of Schizophrenias*, trans J. Zinken, New York: International University Press.

Breier, A., Schreiber, J., Dyer, J. and Pickar, D. (1992) 'Course of illness and predictors of outcome in chronic schizophrenia: implications for pathophysiology', *British Journal of Psychiatry* 161 (suppl. 18): 38–43.

Breier, A. and Astrachan, B.M. (1984) 'Characterisation of schizophrenic patients who commit suicide', *American Journal of Psychiatry* 141: 2, 206–9.

Castle, D.J. and Murray, R.M. (1993a) 'The epidemiology of late-onset schizophrenia', *Schizophrenia Bulletin* 19(4): 691–700.

Castle, D.J., Wessely, S. and Murray, R.M. (1993b) 'Sex and schizophrenia: effects of diagnostic stringency, and associations with and premorbid variables', *British Journal of Psychiatry* 162: 658–64.

Castle, D.J., Sham, P.C. and Wessely, S., *et al.* (1994) 'The subtyping of schizophrenia in men and women: a latent class analysis', *Psychological Medicine* 24(1): 41–51.

Cowell, P.E., Kostianovsky, D.J. and Gur, R.C., *et al.* (1996) 'Sex differences in neuroanatomical and clinical correlations in schizophrenia', *American Journal of Psychiatry* 153(6): 799–805.

Dalkin, T., Murphy, P., Glazebrook, C., Medley, I. and Harrison, G. (1994) 'Premorbid personality in first-onset psychosis', *British Journal Psychiatry* 164: 202–7.

De Lisi, L.E., Lehner, T. and Bass, N. *et al.* (1993) 'Evidence for a sex chromosome locus for schizophrenia', *Schizophrenia Research* 9: 117.

De Lisi, L.E. and Crow, T.J. (1989) 'Evidence for a sex chromosome locus for schizophrenia', *Schizophrenia Bulletin* 15: 431–40.

Done, D.J., Crow, T.J., Johnstone, E.C. and Sacker, A. (1994) 'Childhood antecendents of schizophrenia and affective illness: social adjustment at ages 7 and 11', *British Medical Journal* 309: 699–703.

Faraone, S.V., Chen, W.J. and Goldstein, J.M., *et al.* (1994) 'Gender differences in age at onset in schizophrenia', *British Journal of Psychiatry* 164: 625–9.

Flaum, M., Swayze, V.W. II and O'Leary D.S. (1995) 'Effects of diagnosis, laterality, and gender on brain morphology in schizophrenia', *American Journal Psychiatry* 152(5): 704–14.

Flor-Henry, P. (1990) 'Influence of gender in schizophrenia as related to other psychopathological syndromes', *Schizophrenia Bulletin* 16: 2, 211–27.

Foerster, A., Lewis, S.W. and, Owen, M.J. (1991) 'Premorbid personality in psychosis: effects of sex and diagnosis', *British Journal of Psychiatry* 158: 171–6.

Forrest, A.D. and Hay, A.J. (1972) 'The influence of sex on schizophrenia', *Acta Psychiatrica Scandinavica* 48: 49–58.

Gattaz, W.F., Vogel, P. and Riecher-Rossler, A. *et al.* (1994) 'Influence of the menstrual cycle phase on the therapeutic response in schizophrenia', *Biological Psychiatry* 36: 137–9.

Gerada, C. and Reveley, A.M. (1988) 'Schizophreniform psychosis associated with the menstrual cycle', *British Journal of Psychiatry* 152: 700–2.

Gitlin, M.J. and Pasnau, R.O. (1989) 'Psychiatric syndromes linked to reproductive function in women: a review of current knowledge', *American Journal of Psychiatry* 146: 1413–22.

Goldstein, J.M., Santangelo, S.L., Simpson, J. and Tsuang, M.T. (1993) 'Gender and mortality in schizophrenia: do women act like men?', *Psychological Medicine* 23: 941–8.

Goldstein, J.M., Faraone, S.V. and Chen, N.J. *et al.* (1990a) 'Sex differences in the familial transmission of schizophrenia', *British Journal Psychiatry* 156: 819–26.

Goldstein, J.M., Santangelo, S.L., Simpson, J.C. and Tsuang, M.T. (1990b) 'The role of gender in identifying subtypes of schizophrenia', *Schizophrenia Bulletin* 16: 263–75.

Gur, R.E., Mozley, P.D. and Resnick, S.M. *et al.* (1991) 'Magnetic resonance imaging in schizophrenia. 1. Volumetric analysis of brain and cerebrospinal fluid', *Archives of General Psychiatry* 48: 407–12.

Gur, R.C., Gur, R.E. and Obrist, W.D. *et al.* (1982) 'Sex and handiness differences in cerebral blood flow during rest and cognitive activity', *Science* 217: 659–61.

Haas, G.L., Glick, I.D. and Clarkin, J.F. *et al.* (1990) 'Gender and schizophrenia outcome: a clinical trial of an inpatient family intervention', *Schizophrenia Bulletin* 16: 277–92.

Hafner, H., Maurer, K. and Loffler, W. *et al.* (1993) 'The influence of age and sex on the onset and early course of schizophrenia', *British Journal Psychiatry* 162: 80–6.

Harvey, I., Ron, M. and Du Boulay, G. *et al.* (1993) 'Diffuse reduction of cortical volume in schizophrenia on magnetic resonance imaging', *Psychological Medicine* 23: 591–604.

Jablensky, A. and Cole, S.W. (1997) 'Is the earlier age at onset of schizophrenia in males a confounded finding? Results from a cross-cultural investigation', *British Journal Psychiatry* 170: 234–40.

Jablensky, A., Sartorius, N. and Ernberg, G. *et al.* (1992) 'Schizophrenia: manifestations, incidence and course in different cultures. A World Health Organization 10-country study', *Psychological Medicine*, Monograph (suppl. 20).

Johnstone, E.C., Crow, T.C. and Frith, C.D. *et al.* (1976) 'Cerebral ventricular size and cognitive impairment in chronic schizophrenia', *Lancet* ii: 924–6.

Jonsson, H. and Nyman, A.K. (1991) 'Predicting long-term outcome in schizophrenia', *Acta Psychiatrica Scandinavica* 83: 342–6.

Kendler, K.S. and Walsh, D. (1995) 'Gender and schizophrenia. Results of an epidemiologically-based family study', *British Journal of Psychiatry* 167: 184–92.

Kraeplin, E. (1896) 'Dementia praecox' Psychiatrie Barth: Leipzig (5th ed.) 426–441, in *The Clinical Roots of the Schizophrenia Concept* (trans. 1987 by J. Cutting and M. Sheperd), Cambridge: Cambridge University Press.

Kulkarni, J. (1997) 'Women and schizophrenia: a review', *Australian and New Zealand Journal of Psychiatry* 31(1): 46–56.

Kulkarni, J., de Castella, A., Smith D., Taffe, J. and Keks, N. (1996) 'A clinical trial of the effects of oestrogen in acutely psychotic women', *Schizophrenia Research* 20: 247–52.

Lauriello, J., Hoff, A., Wieneke, M.H., Blankfeld, H., Faustman, W.O., Rosenbloom, M., DeMent, S., Sullivan, E.V., Lim, K.O. and Pfefferbaum, A. (1997) 'Similar extent of brain dysmorphology in severely ill women and men with schizophrenia', *American Journal of Psychiatry* 154(6): 819–25.

Lewine, R.J., Gulley, L.R., Risch, S.C., Jewart R. and Houpt, J.L. (1990) 'Sexual dimorphism, brain morphology and schizophrenia', *Schizophrenia Bulletin* 16: 195–203.

Lewine, R.J., Burbach, D. and Meltzer, H.Y. (1984) 'Effect of diagnostic criteria on the ratio of male to female schizophrenic patients', *American Journal of Psychiatry* 141: 84–7.

Lewis, S. (1992) 'Sex and schizophrenia: vive la difference', *British Journal of Psychiatry* 161: 445–50.

Lewis, S. (1989) 'Congenital risk factors for schizophrenia', *Psychological Medicine* 19: 5–13.

Lindamer, L.A., Lohr, J.B., Harris M.J. *et al.* (1997) 'Gender, oestrogen, and schizophrenia', *Psychopharmacological Bulletin* 33: 221–8.

Loranger, A.W. (1984) 'Sex differences in age at onset of schizophrenia', *Archives of General Psychiatry* 41: 157–61.

Mayer, C., Kelterborn, G. and Naber D. (1993) 'Age of onset in schizophrenia: relations to psychopathology and gender', *British Journal of Psychiatry* 162: 665–71.

McCabe, M.S. (1975) 'Demographic differences in functional psychoses', *British Journal of Psychiatry* 127: 571–6.

McGlashan, T.H. and Bardenstein, K.K. (1990) 'Gender differences in affective, schizoaffective and schizophrenic disorders', *Schizophrenia Bulletin* 16: 319–26.

Murray, R.M. (1994) 'Neurodevelopmental schizophrenia: the rediscovery of Dementia Praecox', *British Journal of Psychiatry* 165 (suppl. 25): 6–12.

Murray, R.W. and Lewis, S.W. (1987) 'Is schizophrenia a neurodevelopmental disorder?', *British Medical Journal* 295: 681–2.

Nasrallah, H.A., Schwarzkopf, S.B., Olson, S.C. and Coffman, J.A. (1990) 'Gender differences in schizophrenia on MRI brain scans', *Schizophrenia Bulletin* 16: 205–10.

Nyman, A.K. (1989) 'Nonregressive schizophrenia – a long-term comparative follow up investigation', *Acta Psychiatrica Scandinavica* 79: 59–73.

O'Callaghan, E., Gibson, T. and Colohan, H., *et al.* (1992) 'Risk of schizophrenia in adults born after obstetric complications and their association with early onset of illness: a controlled study', *British Medical Journal* 305: 1256–9.

O'Callaghan, E., Sham P., Takei N. *et al.* (1991) 'Schizophrenia after prenatal exposure to 1957 A2 influenza epidemic', *Lancet* 337: 1248–50.

Ohaeri, J.U. (1992) 'Age at onset in a cohort of schizophrenia in Nigeria', *Acta Psychiatrica Scandinavica* 86(5): 332–4.

Olin, S.S. and Mednick, S.A. (1996) 'Psychosis: identifying vulnerable populations premorbidly', *Schizophrenia Bulletin* 22(2): 223–40.

Onstad, S., Skre, I. and Tongersen, S. *et al.* (1991) 'Twin concordance for DSM-III schizophrenia', *Acta Psychiatrica Scandinavica* 83: 395–401.

Overall, J.E. and Gorham, D.R. (1962) 'The brief psychiatric rating scale', *Psychology Reports* 10: 799–812.

Owen, M.J., Lewis, S.W. and Murray, R.M. (1988) 'Obstetric complications and schizophrenia', *Psychological Medicine* 18: 331–9.

Riecher-Rossler, A., Hafner, H. and Stumbalum, M. *et al.* (1994) 'Can oestradiol modulate schizophrenic symptomatology?', *Schizophrenia Bulletin* 20: 203–13.

Rosanoff, A.J., Handy, L.M. and Plesset, I.R. (1934) 'The aetiology of so-called schizophrenic psychosis: with special references to their occurrence in twins', *American Journal of Psychiatry* 91: 247–86.

Rosenthal, D. (1970) *Genetic Theory and Abnormal Behaviour*, New York: McGraw-Hill.

Sartorius, N., Jablensky, A. and Shapiro, R. (1978) 'Cross-cultural differences in the short-term prognosis of schizophrenic psychoses', *Schizophrenia Bulletin* 4: 102–13.

Seeman, M.V. (1998) 'Schizophrenia and other psychotic disorders', in L.A. Wallis (ed.) *Textbook of Women's Health*, Philadelphia: Lippincott-Raven.

Seeman, M.V. (1996) 'The role of oestrogen in schizophrenia', *Journal of Psychiatry and Neuroscience* 21: 123–7.

Seeman, M.V. and Lang, M. (1990) 'The role of estrogens in schizophrenia gender differences', *Schizophrenia Bulletin* 16: 185–95.

Seeman, M.V. (1989) 'Neuroleptic prescription for men and women', *Social Pharmacology* 3: 219–36.

Sikarnartey, T. and Eaton, W.W. (1984) 'Prevalence of schizophrenia in the Labadi district of Ghana', *Acta Psychiatrica Scandinavica* 69: 156–61.

Swett, C. (1975) 'Drug-induced dystonia', *American Journal of Psychiatry* 132: 532–4.

Thomas, C., Bartlett, A. and Mezey, G.C. (1995) 'The extent and effects of violence among psychiatric inpatients', *Psychiatric Bulletin* 19: 600–4.

Torrey. E.F., Taylor. E. and Bowler, A. *et al.* (1991) 'Evidence of early brain changes in subgroups of twins with schizophrenia', *Schizophrenia Research* 4: 285.

Turner, S.W., Toone, B.K. and Brett-Jones, J.R. (1986) 'Computerised tomographic scan changes in early schizophrenia – preliminary findings', *Psychological Medicine* 16: 219–25.

Vaughn, C.E., Snyder, K.S., Jones, S., Freeman, W.B. and Falloon I.R. (1984) 'Family factors in schizophrenia relapse. Replication in California of British research on expressed emotions', *Archives of General Psychiatry* 41(12): 1169–77.

World Health Organization (1973) *Report of the International Pilot Study of Schizophrenia*, vol. 1, Geneva: World Health Organization.

Wieck, A., Kumar R. and Hirst, A.D. *et al.* (1991) 'Increased sensitivity of dopamine receptors and recurrence of affective psychosis after childbirth', *British Medical Journal* 303: 613–16.

Yassa, R. and Jeste, D.V. (1992) 'Gender differences in tardive dyskinesia: a critical review of the literature', *Schizophrenia Bulletin* 18(4): 701–15.

Yonkers, K.A., Kando, J.C. and Cole, J.O. *et al.* (1992) 'Gender differences in pharmacokinetics and pharmacodynamics of psychotropic medication', *American Journal of Psychiatry* 149: 587–95.

Zito, J.M., Routt, W.W. and Mitchell, J.E. *et al.* (1985) 'Clinical characteristics of hospitalised psychotic patients who refuse antipsychotic drug therapy', *American Journal of Psychiatry* 142: 822–6.

Chapter 7

Perinatal psychiatry

Dora Kohen

Perinatal psychiatry deals with a large constellation of clinical and psychosocial problems starting in the early days of pregnancy and continuing a year after the delivery period.

These wide-ranging problems include past history of social, personal, psychological and psychiatric problems that may be exacerbated in pregnancy and minor to severe psychological and psychiatric problems that appear following delivery. The wide-ranging spectrum of different diagnosis and disorders seen in this period makes it difficult to discuss a unified theory of the role different variable. Variables that are associated with perinatal psychiatric problems range from the hormonal changes taking place in the woman and her genetic make up to demographic variables and social support. We know that different perinatal psychiatric problems are associated with various acute or long-standing social, psychological, personal and psychiatric problems.

PRE-EXISTING PSYCHIATRIC DISORDERS AND PREGNANCY

For women with pre-existing psychiatric disorders little is known of how pregnancy exacerbates the situation and if it has an effect on the course of the illness. Available data suggests that pregnancy is a time of emotional instability. The woman's social, personal and psychological needs increase. This is the time when the woman will need input and information into her medication usage and the possible effects on the foetus. The woman will need reassurance and support and regular psychiatric input.

Patients with pre-existing, severe, enduring mental illness and a dual diagnosis of severe mental illness and substance abuse are at a very vulnerable stage of their lives. These are usually women who have been reasonably manageable with the help of neuroleptic medication. Their lifestyles may not be the most appropriate for pregnancy or the newborn. They may have scanty accommodation, irregular food intake, unplanned life style and may abuse large quantities of drugs or alcohol. It is expected that family, partners if any, their general practitioners, key worker or the antenatal clinic will spot their needs and will usually alert the primary care and the psychiatric services.

Schizophrenia and pregnancy

The fertility of women with schizophrenia is rising and may not be different from that of the general population today. This may be due to the increased male fertility as much as the use of the novel antipsychotics and other factors (Lane et al., 1992 and Oates, 1997). In the past the classical neuroleptics raised prolactin levels to the extent that ovulation was suppressed or stopped completely. Institutional care provided segregation. Today care in the community, psychological treatments and novel pharmacological agents provide a normalized lifestyle and fertility.

Although it is very difficult to discuss epidemiology, one can say that one third of pregnant women with schizophrenia get pregnant while psychiatrically very unwell and not really carrying the responsibility of their action, whereas two-thirds are in remission and get pregnant willingly. The first group do not contact the psychiatric or antenatal services. The second group are those who are in remission but well known to the services and contact services after getting pregnant. The clinical picture is usually a mixture of anxiety from their part, concern from the family or community services, inability to cope with the new demand imposed on them and social problems usually led by inadequate accommodation and financial difficulties. Where the patient has no family and the father of the foetus is not available, obstetric services raise the alarm via the child and family services of the hospital.

Assessment of needs

If the mother is keen to bring up the baby, a period of mental state assessment together with the evaluation of parenting abilities takes place. The assessment of parenting abilities is done in a hospital-based mother and baby unit or in social services-led mother–baby centres according to the psychiatric needs of the mother. The assessment is followed by a case conference led by child and family services. If the mother has shown to be involved with the newborn and safe in feeding, bathing and caring, they usually go home to be seen regularly by the community services. If the mother has shown signs of possible neglect then the baby is put on the 'at risk register' for regular monitoring and reassessment of the situation. If the mother is not keen to continue to care for the newborn there is usually an immediate case conference and the baby is sent to foster care. Although foster care can seem to be an uncaring way of solving the problem, with recent stories of neglect and abuse, this is becoming a usual path to follow.

The most difficult situation arises when the mother is very keen to care for the baby but the services and authorities do not believe she has the credentials to do so. That is when case conferences are followed by the involvement of the legal system. This is a long and arduous process and may be quite painful for the mother and the families.

A pregnant woman who is psychotic but refuses treatment presents complicated legal and ethical issues. If the patient's mental illness interferes with the capacity to make decisions about her treatment, and she may become a danger to herself or to others, her psychiatric condition is treated under the Mental Health Act (MHA) 1983.

Management

A partnership between the community mental health teams and primary care should manage the specific needs of these patients. Usually they need appropriate accommodation suitable for the newborn, a key worker to monitor the patient's mental health and establish appropriate psychiatric treatment, health visitors and child and family services to monitor the wellbeing of the newborn. Voluntary organizations can play a role in the management.

During pregnancy, anti-psychotic medication should be monitored and given regularly. There are sources that prefer to decrease medication at the last two weeks before pregnancy. Following the case conference, child and family services should be involved to establish the future needs of the unborn baby and to decide whether there is a need to keep the child on the at risk register.

Parenting abilities of the mother need to be reassessed. Parenting abilities of all adults that plan to be in the same household as the baby should have general assessment by social services.

A regular key worker for the mother and a social worker for the baby should meet as necessary to look at the arising needs of the family. Voluntary organizations such as Homestart or NewPin should be involved.

PSYCHIATRIC MORBIDITY ARISING IN PREGNANCY

There are different types of minor psychiatric morbidity such as generalized anxiety disorders, panic attacks, phobias and obsessional disorders that appear during pregnancy in conjunction with, or without, any mood disorder. Concerns about changing social, professional and personal roles, new responsibilities and the effect of the child on family life contribute to the situation.

Women should be assessed and made part of a treatment programme. It is well known that if problems are tackled efficiently, the woman will be more confident in responding to the needs of the baby. Patients will need support to prevent any reoccurrence of a previous episode of affective disorders. Depression during pregnancy is a common occurrence. Women with a previous episode of depression may have an exacerbation at any trimester of the pregnancy period. It is also common to see a first episode of depression starting during pregnancy. Depression can be accompanied by experiences of major anxiety, panic attacks, phobias and disturbing obsessional thoughts.

MANAGEMENT OF PSYCHIATRIC PROBLEMS DURING PREGNANCY

Management of psychiatric problems during pregnancy involves complex issues, such as the need for medical treatment and its effects on the foetus, and also the therapeutic management of associated social and personal issues which may complicate the situation in relation to pregnancy.

Medication during pregnancy is a very loaded issue not only because of the implications of teratogenesis but also because many of the mental health problems are exacerbated due to unmet social, financial and personal needs of the pregnant women.

Antidepressant medication

Tricyclic antidepressants have been used extensively in pregnancy in the last three to four decades. The literature shows that they do not appear to increase the risk of teratogenesis even when used in the first trimester (Althuser *et al.*, 1996). Data is starting to emerge on the use of selective serotonin re-uptake inhibitors (SSRI) in pregnancy (Pastuszak *et al.*, 1993; Goldstein, 1995; Cohen and Rosenbaum, 1997). There is also prospective controlled multicentre data on sertraline, paroxetine and citalopram showing that those SSRIs are not risk factors for congenital abnormalities when used in the first trimester in recommended doses (Kulin *et al.*, 1998).

Selective serotonin re-uptake inhibitors (SSRIs) are a specific class of antidepressants where the depressant treatment does not have debilitating side effects. They have been carefully studied as pre-partum treatment option. Birth outcomes in pregnant women taking fluoxetine have been studied and it is generally accepted that there is no increase in teratology (Goldstein, 1995; Chambers *et al.*, 1996; Cohen and Rosenbaum, 1997). Althuser *et al.* (1995) have analysed newborns breastfed by mothers on Sertraline and noted no adverse effects. The European Network of the Teratology Information Services (ENTIS) has collected and evaluated data on almost 700 pregnancies in which exposure to tricyclic and non-tricyclic antidepressants occurred. Approximately two thirds of mothers were on multidrug therapy and of those half took a benzodiazepine and about 95 per cent of those were exposed to the drug in the first trimester. The most striking feature of the pregnancy outcomes is that 97 per cent of babies were morphologically normal. There was no increase in either a particular type of malformation or a specific pattern of defects. Overall no causal relationship could be established between *in utero* exposure to antidepressants and adverse pregnancy outcome (McElhatton *et al.*, 1996).

There are also longitudinal studies looking at neurological and behavioural milestones of children born to mothers who have used SSRI in pregnancy and no difference has been established (Nulman *et al.*, 1997). The investigations and assessment of those children indicate that there were no differences in IQ, temperament, mood or general and global behaviour in any of the children.

MAOIs are usually avoided in pregnancy because they have been associated with higher congenital anomalies in animal studies.

Mood stabilizers

Mood stabilizers such as lithium salts, carbamazepine and valproic acid are used in bipolar affective disorder and in affective disorders such as depression. All three of those drugs are associated with increased rates of foetal abnormalities when used in the first trimester. Lithium salts, especially when used in the first trimester, are associated with several-fold increase in cardiac anomalies (Schou et al., 1973). Lithium use in pregnancy has been associated with hypotonia, hypoglycaemia and cyanosis in the infant.

Valproic acid and carbamazepine, which are potent anti-epileptics, have been studied in relation to epilepsy which in itself carries a risk of congenital anomalies. The first trimester exposure to valproic acid is associated with a 15-fold risk of spina bifida and facial abnormalities. Carbamazepine increases the risk of spina bifida and neural tube defect (Althuser et al., 1996).

But with women who decompensate easily when not medicated, the treatment should continue during pregnancy. Lithium should be given several doses per day to avoid peaking, and lithium levels should be repeated four-weekly to keep the patients within therapeutic limits. Two to four weeks before delivery the lithium dose should be tapered to one half to avoid toxicity in the mother following the fluid changes after delivery.

Neuroleptic medication

Women with schizophrenia require close follow-up and treatment during pregnancy. The classical neuroleptics, which have been used for several decades, are not associated with any congenital anomalies (Althuser, 1996). There have been several novel anti-psychotics in the market in the last several years but there is insufficient information on their use in pregnancy. There are single case reports on the novel anti-psychotics but they do not seem to be a risk factor with any form of anomalies.

When possible, neuroleptics should be avoided during pregnancy but when neuroleptics are needed doses should be maintained at lower levels. The transient perinatal syndrome in infants is characterized by tremor, hypotonia and poor feeding and is seen in newborn babies exposed to any classical neuroleptics near term. The condition generally improves within the first to second week.

Obviously it will be very difficult to assess the multidimensional and multifactorial qualities such as psychological development in children who might possibly have undefined forms of genetic predisposition to psychiatric illness and deprived social and psychological background. Nevertheless there has not been any neurodevelopmental or behavioural anomalies in follow-up longitudinal study of these infants (Slone et al., 1977). Informal naturalistic information forms the basis for the general understanding that there are no behavioural or physical abnormalities attached to intrauterine exposure to maternal antipsychotic usage.

Anticholinergic agents have been held responsible for transient perinatal syndrome as well as some cardiovascular malformations in the infants. With the decrease of neuroleptic dosage in pregnancy, anticholinergics should be monitored and decreased appropriately.

Although occasional use of benzodiazepines in pregnancy does not cause any neonatal difficulties if they are used regularly in the first trimester of pregnancy, the risk of oral clefts and possibly developmental delays emerges. If used near delivery hypotonia, apnoea and inability to feed can be seen (Althuser, 1996; McElhatton et al., 1996).

A study was carried out to investigate the outcome of pregnancy in 115 women who had been exposed to paracetamol overdose. Exposures occurred in all trimesters; however, it is important to note that the majority of pregnancy outcomes were normal. There were only two spontaneous abortions occurring two weeks following the overdose which may be related to the paracetamol. The overall conclusion was that paracetamol overdose was not an indication for termination of pregnancy (McElhatton, 1990).

There are three points that would summarize the general guidelines of drug treatment during pregnancy. A useful drug, whether a neuroleptic or antidepressant, should never be stopped without a good reason because there is only limited evidence that those drugs may be associated with any form of teratogenesis, even in the first trimester. The lowest possible therapeutic dose should be prescribed and the patient should be monitored for symptoms of toxicity.

Electroconvulsive therapy

Electroconvulsive therapy (ECT) has been used in psychotic depression, mania and some acute confusional state successfully in different stages of pregnancy. It is now accepted that if administered and monitored appropriately it would not cause any risks or side effects either to the patient or to the foetus (Althuser et al., 1996; Miller, 1994).

Non-medical interventions are of paramount importance in tackling any form of mental health problem in pregnancy. Support, counselling and the different forms of therapy, such as generalized anxiety treatment programmes, cognitive behavioural therapies, supportive psychotherapy and the input from voluntary groups, are crucial in solving the problem.

POSTPARTUM PSYCHIATRIC DISORDERS

The time following delivery is a period of vulnerability and emergence of psychiatric disorders. It is well established that there is a relative risk of psychiatric disorders that is associated with childbirth. This fact has been known since the time of Hippocrates. French and German writers of the eighteenth century all mention puerperal insanity. In the early nineteenth century, Esquirol provided quantitative data on puerperal insanity following childbirth. He noted that some had melancholia and some had mania and that it generally had a good prognosis. In 1856 Marcé wrote his famous article on the 'folie of pregnant women, the newly delivered and the breastfeeding women'. Following articles elaborated on different aspects of the clinical presentation of this entity and its relationship to different puerperal sepsis, infections and eclampsia, in 1961, Paffenbarger's investigation provided evidence about risk factors.

Perris in 1974 described cycloid psychoses as an acute psychotic episode with hereditary background of confusion, perplexity, affective features, transient delusions and thought disorder. He noted the full recovery but a tendency to recurrence. Puerperal psychosis has similarities with cycloid psychosis and has been used interchangeably.

The relationship between childbirth and psychiatric admissions was found to be extremely high in the first thirty days following childbirth (Kendell *et al.*, 1987). Mental and behavioural disorders associated with puerperium are accepted as a diagnostic entity and are part of the ICD-10 diagnosis criteria. Postpartum mood disorders are classified according to the duration and severity of the condition. But it is well established that clinical symptomatology of postpartum illness is affective in nature and therefore DSM-1V has not granted the postpartum disorders diagnostic category but has classified them with affective disorders and it has a section entitled 'postpartum onset specifier' where the onset is within four weeks of delivery.

Neuroses and adjustment reactions

In the first two weeks following delivery there are several major changes in the life of a mother. On one side there are the needs and the continuous demands of the infant. On the other side there may be exhaustion, sleep deprivation, physical discomfort in the pelvis, perineum and mamilliary pain. There may be the psychological and personal elements ranging from recovery of the figure to changes in family dynamics and jealousy of older siblings or the partner. All the above may contribute to the emergence of generalized anxiety, panic disorders, phobias and obsessional neurosis.

Generalized anxiety is seen in the form of vigilance, scanning and apprehensive expectation, autonomic symptomatology and motor irritability. It may involve simple tasks such as bathing the baby and more complex issues such as fear of sudden infant death. Puerperal panic and phobias about the infant can lead to insomnia, irritability and avoidance of the baby.

Obsessional features can involve impulses of rejection, infanticide and of child abuse. Rejection can be a powerful feeling in women who are unable to bond with their babies. Rejection when not overtly discussed can be poorly recognized by professionals and may lead to further problems. It is usually associated with depression; however, neglect and child abuse may follow. This may start in the form of shouting and may lead to serious assault such as starvation, suffocation and strangulation of the baby.

It is accepted that 3–6 per 1000 children are severely abused (Baldwin and Oliver, 1975) but more recent information leads us to accept that this may be much higher and many sudden infant death syndrome cases may be the result of physical abuse by the mother.

Postpartum blues (maternity or baby blues)

This is a transitory state beginning the first week following delivery and lasting 10–15 days. It occurs in 50–70 per cent of all mothers after delivery. Lability of mood, anxiety and distress are the main symptoms. A history of depression or PMDD are risk factors for this condition. This transient condition does not need any treatment except support and counselling and the appropriate information given to the family to help them cope with it. It never comes to the attention of the psychiatrist and it would very rarely come to the attention of the general practitioner but it is usually observed by the health visitor and the relatives. It is very useful to alert the health visitors who in turn will keep the general practioner informed of the possibility of a depressive disorder that may follow.

Postnatal depression

Non-psychotic postnatal depression starts 2–4 weeks following the birth of the baby and it is an established fact that it is seen in 10–15 per cent of women postpartum. Previous history of depression, especially previous postpartum depression, social and personal problems, lack of support and stressful life events, contribute to the condition. A history of depression previous to pregnancy or childbirth is associated with 24 per cent risk of postpartum depression and depression starting during pregnancy is associated with 35 per cent risk of postpartum depression (O'Hara, 1995). A previous episode of postpartum depression increases the risk for depression on the following pregnancies up to 50 per cent.

The clinical symptoms that lead to the diagnosis and proper management can be masked. Mothers usually find it difficult to contradict well-established expectations of fulfilment and contentment following the birth of the child. It is possible to attribute symptoms such as poor sleep, loss of appetite and loss of weight, fatigue and lack of energy and even low mood to the demands of the newborn rather than the mood disorder of the mother.

If not diagnosed, treated and managed on time this clinical picture can lead to problems in the emotional, cognitive and future intellectual development of the child. The condition can even become quite dramatic when the mother cannot cope with the newborn and elements of neglect, different levels of abuse and, rarely, infanticide become the issue.

The best treatment and management of such cases should be multidisciplinary. The patient with postpartum depression should receive various levels of support. Antidepressant medication has been shown to be effective; both tricyclics and SSRIs are widely used in the treatment of postpartum depression.

Counselling is an additional, valuable method of contributing to the management of such cases. A controlled study of fluoxetine and cognitive behavioural counselling has shown that both methods are effective treatment; after an initial session of counselling, additional benefits results from either fluoxetine or further counselling but there seems to be no advantage in receiving both (Appleby *et al.*, 1997).

Breastfeeding and antidepressant treatment is a contentious issue. There is a lot of sensitivity among professionals, relatives and patients themselves to the question whether the breast milk of the medicated mother would affect the child. It is well known that there is no known barrier between mother blood and breast milk. But still there is a great interpersonal variability in antidepressant levels in the breast milk and in the breast milk to maternal plasma. There is a large amount of information in the form of case reports and review data from publication on the serum levels of mothers treated with antidepressants. There are no known adverse effects on the infant and there is no evidence of accumulation in the infant (Wisner *et al.*, 1996). To date there is no known effect on the breastfed infants' growth and the following development but we still need further data on this important issue (Misri and Sivertz, 1991; Wisner *et al.*, 1995; Yoshida *et al.*, 1998).

Benzodiazepines accumulate in breast milk and are not generally recommended in breastfeeding women. Although regular usage is not recommended, occasional dose is not known to have side effects on breastfed newborns (Buist *et al.*, 1990). Antipsychotic drugs are widely used in breastfeeding women and no major specific side effects have been noted with newborns. Nevertheless it is well known that chlorpromazine causes drowsiness in the infant. Both classical and novel neuroleptics need further research and assessment before their safety is established.

Lithium in breast milk reaches almost two-thirds of maternal plasma levels. The neonatal kidney cannot process lithium salts and it results in accumulation and toxicity. Lithium is not compatible with breastfeeding and it is contraindicated in breast-feeding women (Tunnessen and Hertz, 1972; Kacew, 1993).

Carbamazepine as a mood stabilizer does not accumulate and therefore does not cause any side effects or toxicity in newborns; therefore carbamazepine is accepted as compatible with breast-feeding. Valproic acid is a mood stabilizer that can be used in breastfeeding mothers because no toxicity has been recorded. Nevertheless there is a risk of hepatotoxicity and it should be used with caution (Beeley, 1986).

Oestradiol patches have been used to treat women with post-partum depression (Gregoire *et al.*, 1996); however, this is not an established form of treatment pattern and we need further research on the subject.

The ethical issues of the medical treatment of a breastfeeding woman have been widely discussed. But the critical issue is the untreated depressed mother and the possible detrimental effects on the newborn. Low birth weight, neonatal distress, prematurity, and later listlessness followed by problems in reaching milestones and developmental retardation are some expected effects of depression on the children of depressed mothers.

Puerperal (postpartum) psychosis

This is a severe, dramatic, potentially dangerous clinical picture which occurs in 0.1–0.2 per cent of women following delivery. It can start the day following delivery or can be seen up to 2–3 weeks after delivery. There is a general understanding that the earlier it starts the better the prognosis. It is an affective disorder with usually psychotic symptomatology in the form of severe agitation, fluctuation of mood and confusion, poor concentration and attention, loss of sleep and appetite, and thought disorder with possible disorientation, delusions and hallucinations. The patient may show signs of acute confusion, may wander away and even put the newborn in danger of neglect. The patient may have delusions in relation to the existence or purpose of the newborn or may refuse to accept that it is her baby or that she has been pregnant at all.

Episodes of puerperal psychosis meet the criteria of affective illness and are basically the same as affective illnesses occurring following childbirth, which acts as a precipitant (Dean and Kendell, 1981; Platz and Kendell, 1988). Due to the fact that epidemiological studies do not support this as a separate entity, it is classified with affective disorders in DSM-IV.

Women with a history of bipolar affective disorder and a previous episode of puerperal psychosis have a 50 per cent risk of developing a new episode following delivery (Dean *et al.*, 1989). Primiparity and a family history of bipolar affective disorder increase the risk but there is the understanding that a history of schizophrenia does not increase the risk of puerperal psychosis if the woman is appropriately managed. Very few cases of puerperal psychosis end up having a diagnosis of schizophrenia but if the patient has psychotic symptomatology the prognosis is worst and antipsychotic medication should be used for longer periods of time and sometimes prophylactically.

There is an increased risk of subsequent episodes if the patient has had her first episode at the postpartum period. Postpartum psychosis presents with a dramatic clinical picture and carries the risk of child neglect and infanticide. Hospitalization and psychotropics such as mood stabilizers and neuroleptics need to be used soon. If the patient does not respond to psychotropics, electroconvulsive therapy (ECT) has been used successfully. Medication is usually tapered off and stopped within a year of recovery but the patient should be informed of the risk and the signs of relapse. If there is a subsequent pregnancy the mood stabilizers can be started prophylactically in the third trimester or sometimes at delivery. This may decrease the risk of relapse (Stewart *et al.*, 1991).

Prophylactic lithium usage in puerperal psychosis after delivery in women who are not breastfeeding seems to be an acceptable treatment (Stewart *et al.*, 1991). The mother should receive social and personal support during her stay in hospital and as a preparation for return to the community. She should also have an assessment of her mothering abilities and should be prepared to collaborate with community agencies such as the primary care system, health visitors, voluntary and statutory organizations, and mother and baby groups. These can be of paramount importance in the follow-up and wellbeing of the mother and the newborn.

Breast feeding and puerperal psychosis

This is an important component of the management of puerperal psychosis. More and more women now opt for breastfeeding and it is an established fact that there are great benefits to the physical health and development of the child. Therefore most psychiatric units and mother–baby units now would encourage the patient to breastfeed.

Breastfeeding should be organized according to the individual needs and set guidelines. Before the infant has been exposed to medication a number of safeguards should be in place. A thorough paediatric assessment would determine the infant's baseline clinical status and level of alertness; sleeping and feeding patterns should be recorded. Doses should be kept low to reduce exposure to the child. Breast feeding should be discontinued if infant serum levels are higher than negligible. Infant exposure may be minimized by mixed bottle and breastfeeding and by taking the medication immediately after the feeding.

Antipsychotic treatment is essential for the wellbeing of psychotic mothers. Chlorpromazine can cause drowsiness and phenothiazines can cause galactorrhoea but no other adverse effects have been reported. Clozapine theoretically can accumulate in breast milk and this may result in the fatal effect of agranulocytosis. Therefore it is contraindicated in breastfeeding mothers.

There are no reports on breastfeeding and the novel antipsychotics and therefore these should be avoided for the time being.

Short-acting medications should always be preferred to long-acting ones as long-acting ones accumulate. The newborn should receive a supplemented feeding programme with the bottle as well as the breast. This will reduce exposure to drugs while it will offer the benefits of breast milk. There are many centres, mainly in the US, that measure the breast milk-levels of psychotropic medication across a 24-hour period and determine the time of the day when medication peaks in the breast milk. The newborn's serum levels should be assayed at different times of the day to establish levels of drugs and metabolites.

Postpartum anxiety disorders

These disorders, including postpartum panic disorder and postpartum obsessive compulsive disorder, have been described in the last decade. They need to be differentiated from postpartum depression and comorbid states such as the mixed anxiety depression state if possible. These can be an exacerbation of pre-existing disorders or they can be first-onset episodes. Treatment methods should include counselling and support, cognitive-behavioural approaches and SSRI treatment when necessary.

UNTREATED PSYCHIATRIC DISORDERS IN THE MOTHER AND ITS EFFECTS ON THE CHILD

Maternal mental illness affects the child's behaviour and development through mother-and-child relationship at all stages of its growth. Untreated psychiatric disorders have detrimental effects on the development and wellbeing of the child, such as lower levels of engagement with the mother. These effects may range from simple indifference to a wide-ranging spectrum up to infanticide.

In socially disadvantaged populations, maternal depression is associated with disturbance in early infant behaviour. Untreated maternal depression has negative effects on the child (Rutter and Quinton, 1984; Cox et al., 1987). There is also good evidence that links emotional disturbance of children to depressive episodes in the mother. Depressed mothers express more dislike toward their 3-month-old babies and at age 9 months babies of depressed mothers perform less well on different tasks. Stein et al. (1991) studied 19-month-old babies of depressed mothers who were less responsive, less interactive and showed less positive affect than the control group. It is also known that insecure attachments are more frequent in children who have mothers with a history of depression. Foreman (1998) summarizes the information on child development and mothers with disorders such as substance misuse, personality disorder, somatization disorder and neurotic depression and how they affect children at least as much as do psychotic disorders.

Avoidance of and resistance to the mother, behavioural problems and difficulties in expressive language have been established in children with depressive mothers (Cox et al., 1987).

Beck et al. (1996) completed a meta-analysis of 17 studies of the association between maternal depression and infant temperament and found a moderate correlation between postpartum depression and disturbance of infant temperament as rated by the mother.

Children of depressed parents may themselves be at higher risk of depression (O'Hara, 1995). Murray and Cooper (1997) have linked maternal depression and cognitive development of the child through the effects of the quality of mother–child interaction. The association between depressed mother and reduced quality of interaction although very important is still very dependent on many other factors, such as the presence of a father and the social and marital difficulties which have a separate effect on the capacity of the mother to interact.

On the other hand there are studies looking at psychiatric disorders of a child-abusing population. Taylor (1991), in his study on parents convicted of child abuse, found that more than half of the parents had received psychiatric treatment and almost a third had hospital admission. Of the convicted mothers 42 per cent were diagnosed with major depression or schizophrenia.

D'Orban (1979), in his study on women who kill their children, found that 27 per cent had severe mental illness and half had attempted suicide during the time of the murder. The study by the Department of Health in the UK on parental psychiatric disorder and fatal child abuse reveals that 23 per cent of the perpetrators and 10 per cent of the partners have a mental illness (Falcov, 1996).

When it comes to mothers who physically abuse their children, the commonest diagnosis would be anxiety, depression and personality problems. Hawton *et al.* (1985) has shown that deliberate self-harm in mothers is associated with child abuse. The majority of parents who injure their children are young, deprived and with long-standing social and personal problems.

The general understanding today is that women with depression and anxiety together with social deprivation, personality problems and substance abuse are at higher risk of harming their children. These all stem from mainly social issues that need to be managed longitudinally in the community. Voluntary organizations, pressure groups and mental health professionals should share their efforts to underline the importance of psychiatric morbidity in the mother and its link to the future of society.

CONCLUSION

Pregnancy and the postpartum period are a time of vulnerability for different types of psychiatric problem. It is very important to educate women and alert the family and services to any risk of destabilization of the psychological wellbeing and the emergence of mental health problems.

Since mothers are usually discharged from hospital within a couple of days after delivery any change in mood, anxiety or other mental health problem will emerge at home. The family, the general practitioners and especially health visitors should be alerted to any past history of PMDD, depression or psychiatric problems and the clinical significance of minor symptomatology. Appropriate treatment and management of the problem will decrease the risk of further relapses, personal and social dysfunction and the emergence of irreversible problems.

REFERENCES

Althuser, L.L., Burt, V.K. and McMullen, M. *et al.* (1995) 'Breastfeeding and sertraline; a 24-hour analysis', *Journal of Clinical Psychiatry* 56: 243–5.

Althuser, L., Cohen, L. and Szuba, M.P. *et al.* (1996) 'Pharmacological management of psychiatric illness in pregnancy: dilemmas and guidelines', *American Journal of Psychiatry* 153: 592–606.

American Psychiatric Association; *Diagnostic and Statistical Manual of Mental Disorders*, 4th ed. (1995), Washington DC: American Psychiatric Association.

Appleby, L., Warner, R., Whitton, A. and Faragher, B. (1997) 'A controlled study of fluoxetine and cognitive-behavioural counselling in the treatment of postnatal depression', *British Medical Journal* 314: 932–6.

Baldwin, J.A. and Oliver, J.E. (1975) 'Epidemiology and family characteristics of severely abused children', *British Journal of Preventive and Social Medicine* 29: 205–21.

Beck, C.T. (1996) 'A meta-analysis of the relationship between postpartum depression and infant temperament', *New Research* 45: 225–30.

Beeley, L. (1986) 'Drugs and breastfeeding', *Clinincs in Obstetrics and Gynaecology* 13: 247–51.

Brockington, I. (1996) *Motherhood and Mental Health*, Oxford: Oxford University Press.

Buist, A., Norman, T.R. and Dennerstein, L. (1990) 'Breastfeeding and the use of psychotropic medication; a review', *Journal of Affective Disorder* 19: 197–206.

Chambers, C.D., Johnson, K.A. and Dick, L.M. *et al.* (1996) 'Birth outcome in pregnant women taking fluoxetine', *New England Journal of Medicine* 335: 1010–15.

Cohen, L.S. and Rosenbaum, J.F. (1997) 'Birth outcomes in pregnant women taking fluoxetine', *New England Journal of Medicine* 336: 872.

Cox, A.D., Puckering, C. and Pound, D. *et al.* (1987) 'The impact of maternal depression on young children', *Journal of Child Psychology and Psychiatry* 18: 917–28.

Dean, C. and Kendell, R.E. (1991) 'The symptomatology of puerperal illnesses', *British Journal of Psychiatry* 139: 128–33.

Dean, C., Williams, R.J. and Brockington, I. (1989) 'Is puerperal psychosis the same as bipolar manic-depressive disorder? A family study', *Psychological Medicine* 19: 637–47.

D'Orban, P.T. (1979) 'Women who kill their children', *British Journal of Psychiatry* 134: 560–71.

Falcov, A. (1996) *Fatal child abuse and Parental Psychiatric Disorder*, Working together Part 8 reports, Department of Health ACPC Series No. 1, London: HMSO.

Foreman, D.M. (1998) 'Maternal mental Illness and mother–child relations', *Advances in Psychiatric Treatment* 4: 135–43.

Goldstein, D.J. (1995) 'Effects of third trimester fluoxetine exposure on the newborn', *Journal of Clinical Psychopharmacology* 15: 417–20.

Gregoire, A.J.P., Kumar, R. and Everitt, B. *et al.* (1996) 'Transdermal oestrogen for treatment of severe depression', *Lancet* 347: 930–3.

Hawton, K., Roberts, J. and Goodwin, G. (1985) 'The risk of child abuse among mothers who attempt suicide', *British Journal of Psychiatry* 146: 486–9.

Kacew, S. (1993) 'Adverse effects of drugs and chemicals in breast milk on the nursing infant', *Journal of Clinical Pharmacology* 33: 213–21.

Kendell, R.E., Chalmers, J.C. and Platz, C. (1987) 'Epidemiology of puerperal psychoses', *British Journal of Psychiatry* 150: 662–73.

Kendell, R.E., Rennie, D., Clarke, J.A. and Dean, C. (1981) 'The social and obstetric correlates of psychiatric admission in the puerperium', *Psychological Medicine* 11: 341–50.

Kulin, N.A., Pastuszak, A. and Sage, S.R. *et al.* (1998) 'Pregnancy outcome following maternal use of the new selective serotonin reuptake inhibitors', *Journal of American Medical Association* 279: 609–10.

Lane, A., Mulvany, M. and Kinsella, A. *et al.* (1992) 'Evidence for increased fertility in married male schizophrenics', *Schizophrenia Research* 6: 94–7.

Marcé, L.V. (1856) 'Manie hysterique intermittente á la suite de sevrage; acces revenant á chaque epoque menstruelle; traitement infructueux par les toniques; guerison par la diete lacté', *Gazette des Hopitaux Paris* 29: 526.

McElhatton, P.R., Garbis, H.M. and Elefant, E. *et al.* (1996) 'The outcome of pregnancy in 689 women exposed to therapeutic doses of antidepressants. A collaborative study of European Network of teratology Information Services (ENTIS)', *Reproductive Toxicology* 10: 285–94.

McElhatton, P.R., Sullivan, F.M. and Volans, G.N. (1990) 'Paracetamol poisoning in pregnancy: an analysis of cases referred to the Teratology Information Service of the National Poisons Information Service', *Human and Experimental Toxicology* 9: 147–53.

Miller, L.J. (1994) 'Use of electroconvulsive therapy during pregnancy', *Hospital and Community Psychiatry* 45: 444–50.

Misri, S. and Sivertz, K. (1991) 'Tricyclic drugs in Pregnancy and lactation: a preliminary report', *International Journal of Psychological Medicine* 21: 157–71.

Murray, L. and Cooper, P. (1997) 'Postpartum depression and child development', *Psychological Medicine* 27: 253–60.

Nulman, I., Rovet, J. and Stewart, D.E. (1997) 'Neurodevelopment of children exposed in utero to antidepressant drugs', *New England Journal of Medicine* 336: 258–62.

O'Hara, M.W. (1995) *Postpartum Depression: Causes and Consequences*, New York: Springer-Verlag.

Oates, M. (1997) 'Patients as parents; risk to children', *British Journal of Psychiatry* 170: 22–7 (suppl.).

Paffebarger, R.S. (1961) 'The picture puzzle of postpartum psychosis', *Journal of Chronic Diseases* 13: 161–73.

Pastuszak, A., Schick-Boschetto, B. and Zuber, C. *et al.* (1993) 'Pregnancy outcome following first trimester exposure to fluoxetine', *Journal of American Medical Association* 269: 2246–8.

Perris, C. (1974) 'A study of cycloid psychoses', *Acta Psychiatrica Scandinavica* suppl. 253.

Platz, C. and Kendell, R.E. (1988) 'A matched control Follow-up and family study of "Puerperal Psychoses"', *British Journal of Psychiatry* 153: 90–4.

Rutter, M. and Quinton, D. (1994) 'Parental psychiatric disorders; effects on children', *Psychological Medicine* 14: 853–80.

Schou, M., Goldfield, M.D. and Weinstein, M.R. *et al.* (1973) 'Lithium and pregnancy 1: Report from the register of lithium babies', *British Medical Journal* 2: 135–6.

Slone, D., Siskind, V. and Heinoman, O.P. *et al.* (1977) 'Antenatal exposure to the phenothiazines in relation to congenital malformations, perinatal mortality rate, birth weight and intelligence quotient score', *American Journal of Obstetrics and Gynaecology* 128: 485–8.

Stein, A., Gath, D., Bucher, J., Bond, A., Day, A. and Cooper, P. (1991) 'The relationship between postnatal depression and mother child interaction', *British Journal of Psychiatry* 158: 46–52.

Stewart, D.E., Klompenhouwer, J.L., Kendell, R.E. and Van Hulst, A.M. (1991) 'Prophylactic lithium in puerperal psychosis: the experience in three centres', *British Journal of Psychiatry* 158: 393–7.

Taylor, C.G., Norman, J. and Murphy, M. *et al.* (1991) 'Diagnosed intellectual and emotional impairment among parents who seriously mistreat their children', *Child Abuse and Neglect* 15: 389–401.

Tunnessen, W.W. and Hertz, C.G. (1972) 'Toxic effects of lithium in newborn infants: a commentary', *Journal of Paediatrics* 81: 804–7.

Wisner, K.L., Perel, J.M. and Findling, R.L. (1996) 'Antidepressant treatment during breast-feeding', *American Journal of Psychiatry* 153: 1132–7.

Wisner, K.L., Perel, J.M. and Foglia, J.P. (1995) 'Serum clomipramine and metabolite levels in four nursing mother–infant pairs', *Journal of Clinical Psychiatry* 56: 17–20.

Yoshida, K., Smith, B., Craggs, M. and Kumar, C. (1998) 'Fluoxetine in breast milk and developmental outcome of breast-fed infants', *British Journal of Psychiatry* 172: 175–9.

Chapter 8

Eating disorders

Ulrike Schmidt

INTRODUCTION

Eating disorders are quintessentially women's disorders. Not only is the vast majority of sufferers of anorexia nervosa and bulimia nervosa female, but feminist scholars have suggested that the development of eating disorders in adolescents in contemporary Western society is intrinsically linked with female sex-role development. Others have suggested that across cultures and across the centuries female self-starvation is a means of negotiating the transition, disconnection and oppression that women uniformly endure (for review see Fallon *et al.*, 1994).

The extraordinary recent media interest in eating disorders has lead to multiple public misconceptions about eating disorders. On the one hand these are trivialized as slimmers' diseases, affecting only vacuous, fashion-conscious young women and on the other hand afflicted individuals are seen as 'manipulative', 'personality disordered' or 'freaks'. The reality of these often chronic, severe disorders, which are associated with considerable psychological and physical comorbidity, is a far cry from these hyped-up public perceptions.

Recent research suggests considerable differences in the aetiology, course and treatment response of the three disorders anorexia nervosa, bulimia nervosa and binge-eating disorder. However, there are also important similarities and overlaps. In order to facilitate the reader in being able to compare and contrast these different conditions, I will discuss all three disorders under each of the section headings, rather than discuss them all separately.

HISTORY AND CLASSIFICATION

The nineteenth century physicians Lashgue (1873) and Gull (1874) are often credited with the first medical descriptions of anorexia nervosa. However, far earlier descriptions of anorexia nervosa exist, including the thirteenth-century case of St Catherine of Siena, recorded meticulously by her confessor Raymond of Capua. St Catherine starved to purify herself and to expiate her sins and she used a fine straw, which she inserted into her throat to bring up food she had eaten. Despite the insistence by her Church elders, including intervention from the pope, that she had taken her fasting too far, she continued and she probably died from starvation.

Two subtypes of anorexia nervosa have been defined in the American system of classification (DSM-IV; APA, 1994) (see Table 8.1). The classical form of anorexia nervosa is now termed 'restricting subtype' which is distinguished from anorexia nervosa 'binge purge subtype', where in addition to the weight loss the individual concerned regularly binge eats and/or purges (i.e. uses self-induced vomiting or misuses laxatives, diuretics or enemas). In the WHO classification (ICD-10; WHO, 1992) there are no such subgroups.

There has been widespread concern about the fact that the diagnostic criteria for anorexia nervosa include weight and shape concerns as there are many anorexics – especially those from non-Western cultures – who do not fulfil these criteria. These individuals may justify their weight loss in terms of persistent stomach pain or lack of appetite. Body image distortion is no longer regarded as one of the necessary criteria for anorexia nervosa.

The first cases of bulimia nervosa were noted by the French physician Janet who, at the turn of the nineteenth century, described several cases in which the avoidance of food alternated with overeating. The term bulimia nervosa was coined by Russell (1979) who saw the condition as 'an ominous variant of anorexia nervosa'. However, it is now clear that the majority of cases of bulimia nervosa do not have a history of anorexia nervosa.

DSM-IV (APA, 1994) (see Table 8.2) has introduced two subtypes of bulimia nervosa, a purging and a non-purging subtype. Another important difference between the DSM and ICD definitions of bulimia nervosa is the absence of a frequency criterion for bingeing in the ICD classification. A relatively new diagnostic concept is that of binge eating disorder (BED; see Table 8.3), which

Table 8.1 Diagnostic criteria of anorexia nervosa

DSM-IV criteria (APA, 1994) for anorexia nervosa

A Refusal to maintain body weight at or above a minimally normal weight for age and height, (e.g. weight loss leading to maintenance of body weight less than 85 per cent of that expected; or failure to make expected weight gain during period of growth, leading to body weight less than 85 per cent of that expected).

B Intense fear of gaining weight or becoming fat, even though underweight.

C Disturbance in the way in which one's body or shape is experienced, undue influence of body shape and weight on self-evaluation, or denial of the seriousness of current low body weight.

D In post-menarchal females, amenorrhoea, i.e. the absence of at least three consecutive menstrual cycles (a woman is considered to have amenorrhoea if her periods occur only following hormone, e.g. oestrogen, administration).

Specify type:

Restricting Type
    during the episode of anorexia nervosa, the person does not regularly engage in binge eating or purging behaviour (i.e. self-induced vomiting or the misuse of laxatives, diuretics or enemas).

Binge-Eating/Purging Type
    during the episode of anorexia nervosa, the person has regularly engaged in binge-eating or purging behaviour (i.e. self-induced vomiting or the misuse of laxatives, diuretics, or enemas).

appears in the appendix of DSM-IV (1994) as a category deserving further study. As in bulimia nervosa the main feature is binge eating; however, in contrast to bulimia nervosa binge eating is not compensated for by behaviours such as purging, fasting or excessive exercise. In the ICD-classification these cases are subsumed under atypical bulimia nervosa.

EPIDEMIOLOGY

Anorexia nervosa

Anorexia nervosa typically affects young women (male to female ratio 1:10) within a few years of their menarche (median age of onset of 17). Whilst there is an association with educational achievement, anorexia nervosa is not – as used to be thought –

Table 8.1 Continued

ICD-10 (WHO, 1992) for anorexia nervosa

For a definite diagnosis, all the following are required:

(a) Body weight is maintained at least 15 per cent below that expected (either lost or never achieved), or Quetelet's body-mass index* is 17.5 or less. Prepubertal patients may show failure to make the expected weight gain during the period of growth.

(b) The weight loss is self-induced by avoidance of 'fattening foods'. One or more of the following may also be present: self-induced vomiting; self-induced purging; excessive exercise; use of appetite suppressants and/or diuretics.

(c) There is body-image distortion in the form of a specific psychopathology whereby a dread of fatness persists as an intrusive, overvalued idea and the patient imposes a low weight threshold on himself or herself.

(d) A widespread endocrine disorder involving the hypothalamic–pituitary–gonadal axis is manifest in women as amenorrhoea and in men as a loss of sexual interest and potency. (An apparent exception is the persistence of vaginal bleeds in anorexic women who are receiving replacement hormonal therapy, most commonly taken as a contraceptive pill.) There may also be elevated levels of growth hormone, raised levels of cortisol, changes in the peripheral metabolism of the thyroid hormone, and abnormalities of insulin secretion.

(e) If onset is prepubertal, the sequence of pubertal events is delayed or even arrested (growth ceases; in girls the breasts do not develop and there is a primary amenorrhoea; in boys the genitals remain juvenile). With recovery, puberty is often completed normally, but the menarche is late.

Note: * Quetelet's body-mass index = weight (kg)/height (m^2) to be used for age 16 or above.

more common in women of high social class (Turnbull *et al.*, 1996). In Britain, the incidence of this disorder is 7 per 100,000 population (Turnbull *et al.*, 1996), which translates into 4000 new cases per year. The prevalence in young women ranges from 0.1–1 per cent (for review see Van Hoeken *et al.*, 1998). Although earlier research suggested that anorexia nervosa might recently have increased in frequency we now know that this is not the case (Turnbull *et al.*, 1996).

Bulimia nervosa

Ninety per cent of those suffering with bulimia nervosa are female. The typical age of onset of bulimia nervosa is 18. All social classes

Table 8.2 Diagnostic criteria of bulimia nervosa

DSM-IV (APA, 1994) criteria of bulimia nervosa

A   Recurrent episodes of binge-eating. An episode of binge-eating is characterized by both of the following:

    1 eating, in a discrete period of time (e.g. in any two-hour period), an amount of food that is definitely larger than most people would eat in a similar period of time and under similar circumstances.

    2 a sense of lack of control over eating during the episodes (e.g. a feeling that one cannot stop eating or control what or how much one is eating).

B   Recurrent inappropriate compensatory behaviour in order to prevent weight gain, such as self-induced vomiting; misuse of laxatives, diuretics, enemas, or other medications; fasting; or excessive exercise.

C   The binge eating and inappropriate compensatory behaviours both occur on average, at least twice a week for 3 months.

D   Self-evaluation is unduly influenced by body shape and weight.

E   The disturbance does not occur exclusively during episodes of anorexia nervosa.

Specify type

Purging type
    during the current episode of bulimia nervosa, the person has regularly engaged in self-induced vomiting or the abuse of laxatives, diuretics, or enemas.

Non-purging type
    during the current episode of bulimia nervosa, the person has used other inappropriate compensatory behaviours, such as fasting or excessive exercise, but has not regularly engaged in self-induced vomiting or the misuse of laxatives, diuretics, or enemas.

are affected, with a preponderance in those of lower socio-economic status. In Western countries the incidence of bulimia nervosa in the general population is at least 13 per 100,000 (for review see Van Hoeken *et al.*, 1998). The incidence in young women is 52 per 100,000 (Turnbull *et al.*, 1996). In the UK, there has been a three-fold increase in the incidence of cases presenting to primary care between 1988 and 1993 (Turnbull *et al.*, 1996). The incidence of bulimia nervosa is lowest in rural areas, intermediate in urbanized areas, and highest in large cities. The prevalence of bulimia nervosa in Western women is approximately 1–3 per cent (Van Hoeken *et al.*, 1998); if partial syndromes are included the prevalence rate increases to over 5 per cent. General practitioners detect only about 12–50 per cent of cases of bulimia nervosa.

Table 8.2 Continued

ICD-10 (WHO, 1992) criteria for bulimia nervosa

For a definite diagnosis, all the following are required:

(a) There is a persistent preoccupation with eating, and an irresistible craving for food; the patient succumbs to episodes of overeating in which large amounts of food are consumed in short periods of time.

(b) The patient attempts to counteract the 'fattening' effects of food by one or more of the following: self-induced vomiting; purgative abuse; alternating periods of starvation; use of drugs such as appetite suppressants, thyroid preparations or diuretics. When bulimia occurs in diabetic patients they may choose to neglect their insulin treatment.

(c) The psychopathology consists of a morbid dread of fatness and the patient sets herself or himself a sharply defined weight threshold, well below the premorbid weight that constitutes the optimum or healthy weight in the opinion of the physician. There is often, but not always, a history of an earlier episode of anorexia nervosa, the interval between the two disorders ranging from a few months to several years. This earlier episode may have been fully expressed, or may have assumed a minor cryptic form with a moderate loss of weight and/or a transient phase of amenorrhoea.

Binge eating disorder

Two per cent of individuals in the community meet criteria for BED. The ratio of female to male cases is approximately 3 : 2. Binge eating disorder commonly co-occurs with obesity and 25–30 per cent of individuals seeking treatment for obesity meet BED criteria (for review see Levine and Marcus, 1998).

CLINICAL FEATURES AND COMORBIDITY

Anorexia nervosa

Typically there is marked avoidance of high calorie, especially fatty, foods. Affected individuals usually are very preoccupied with food and meal preparation (reading of recipes, cooking for others), whilst at the same time eating little themselves. In the early stages of the illness, friends and family may congratulate the sufferer on having lost her 'puppy fat' and may admire her self-control and discipline, thereby reinforcing her self-starvation further. Often the individual becomes very particular about the cooking utensils used and the way a meal is prepared. She may cut up her food into tiny

Table 8.3 Research criteria for binge-eating disorder (Appendix B, DSM-IV)

A   Recurrent episodes of binge eating. An episode of binge eating is characterized by both of the following.

1   Eating, in a discrete period of time (e.g. within any 2-hour period) an amount of food that is definitely larger than most people would eat in a similar period of time under similar circumstances

2   A sense of lack of control over eating during the episode (e.g. a feeling that one cannot stop eating or control what or how much one is eating).

B   The binge-eating episodes are associated with three (or more) of the following:

1   Eating much more rapidly than normal;
2   Eating until feeling uncomfortably full;
3   Eating large amounts of food when not feeling physically hungry;
4   Eating alone because of being embarrassed by how much one is eating;
5   Feeling disgusted with oneself, depressed, or very guilty after overeating.

C   Marked distress regarding binge eating is present.
D   The binge eating occurs, on average, at least 2 days a week for 6 months.
E   The binge eating is not associated with the regular use of inappropriate compensatory behaviours (e.g. purging, fasting, excessive exercise) and does not occur exclusively during the course of anorexia nervosa or bulimia nervosa.

morsels. Some vomit, or use laxatives, others will chew and spit their food if they feel they have overeaten. As mentioned above, overvalued ideas about shape and weight are not expressed by all patients with anorexia nervosa.

Despite severe emaciation the affected individual may continue to feel well and relentlessly pursue her various activities. Over-activity and obsessionality are common, leading to perfectionist attention to detail at work and to obsessional exercise routines. In some cases symptoms typical of a major affective disorder like anhedonia, lack of motivation and concentration, sadness, irritability, or poor sleep may be present.

Comorbidity with other psychiatric disorders and personality disturbance is common. Some of the comorbid conditions are the result of starvation and these are improved by weight gain. Depression (50 per cent), obsessive compulsive disorder (25 per cent) and social phobia (33 per cent) are particularly common

Table 8.4 Physical complications of eating disorders

Skin/hair	Dry skin
	Lanugo hair
	Loss of head hair
	Russell's sign (finger callusess on the dorsum of the hand)
Teeth	Tooth surface loss
	caries
Muscles	Proximal myopathy
Bones	Osteoporosis
Cardiovascular problems	Low heart rate
	Hypotension
	Blue peripheries, chilblains, gangrene
	Cardiac valvular problems
	Arrythmia and sudden death
	QT-prolongation
	Cardiomyopathy
Pulmonary complications	Aspiration pneumonitis
CNS	Decreased brain substance with increased ventricular spaces and sulci
	Persistent brain structural abnormalities
	Dendrites show evidence of stunting of growth and neuronal repair
	Cognitive impairment with deficits in memory, flexibility and inhibitory tasks
Fertility and reproductive function	Fertility reduced
	Perinatal mortality raised
	Low birth weight
Renal function	Pre-renal failure
	Impaired concentration
	Renal stones
Endocrine system	Ovarian size reduced, small follicles, reduced production of oestrogens or progesterone
	Excess CRF and high levels of cortisol
Gastrointestinal complications	Salivary gland hypertrophy
	Increased levels of amylase
	Oesophagitis
	Irritable bowel syndrome post-recovery
	Delayed gastric emptying and poor motility
	Ulcers
	Gastric dilatation
	Pancreatitis
	Steatorrhoea and protein-losing gastroenteropathy
	Constipation
	Ileus
	Rectal prolapse
Liver	Fatty infiltration of the liver and raised liver enzymes

continues overleaf

Table 8.4 Continued

Haematological complications	Bone marrow dysfunction with reduction in white cells, red cells and platelets Decreased CD8 T-cells
Fluid and electrolyte imbalance	Dehydration Rebound peripheral oedema Low sodium, potassium, chloride, magnesium, phosphate, Metabolic alkalosis Metabolic acidosis

(Herzog *et al.*, 1996). The binge–purge subtype of anorexia nervosa is associated with higher levels of depression (80 per cent) and alcohol and substance misuse (10–20 per cent).

A quarter of the group with restricting anorexia nervosa have avoidant, dependent or obsessive compulsive personality types, whereas 40 per cent of those with the binge-purge subtype have a borderline or histrionic type of personality (Herzog *et al.*, 1996).

Bulimia nervosa

Weight loss prior to onset is typical. Usually this is the result of strenuous dieting, often with periods of fasting. Sometimes the weight loss may be the result of a physical illness. Up to one third of cases have a past history of anorexia nervosa. Another third have a history of obesity. Episodes of binge-eating are a physiological response to sustained under-eating. Restrained eating leads to the mainly cognitive factor of 'counter-regulation', i.e. the tendency to abandon restraint when something has been eaten. Bingeing reinforces dietary restraint. Binges usually consist of large amounts of sweet or savoury high calorie foods. Some individuals may experience a sense of loss of control after only small amounts of food have been eaten and may subjectively describe these as binges. Often episodes of binge-eating are precipitated by feelings of depression, anxiety, loneliness and boredom or by violations of self-imposed dietary rules. Most individuals with bulimia nervosa experience their binges as shameful and distressing and may try to keep this activity a secret. As binges set in, efforts to eat little are re-doubled. The individual may calorie-count everything she eats and weigh herself several times a day. Eating in the presence of others may become increasingly difficult or even impossible. A variety of weight control strategies may be used. The most common is self-induced vomiting. Preoccupation with weight and shape is intense. Body image problems are thought to reflect cognitive-emotional difficulties rather than sensory perceptional deficits. Self-worth is often exclusively defined in terms of dietary or weight-and-shape goals. Low self-esteem and poor self-confidence are an integral part of the bulimic syndrome. In some cases there may be extreme self-loathing or self-disgust. Occasionally, weight-and-shape concerns are not the driving force for the disorder and BN develops as a result of exaggerated fears of food allergies or in the context of religious beliefs about the value of fasting.

Lifetime rates of major depression are high and range from 36 to 70 per cent (Herzog *et al.*, 1996 for review). Major depression can precede, occur simultaneously with or start after the onset of bulimia nervosa. Likewise, anxiety disorders frequently occur, the onset of these often precedes the onset of the bulimia. Just over a third of cases of bulimia nervosa have a lifetime history of post-traumatic stress disorder.

In clinical samples of women with bulimia nervosa, alcohol and substance misuse is common; however, this is not the case in community-based samples (Welch and Fairburn, 1996).

Deliberate self-harm occurs in a substantial proportion of individuals with bulimia nervosa. Eighteen to 23 per cent report having taken an overdose and cutting or burning is reported by 15–26 per cent (e.g. Lacey, 1993). Stealing is reported by approximately half of the cases seen in clinical practice (Lacey, 1993). Some authors have suggested that there may be a subgroup of bulimia nervosa characterized by the co-occurrence of impulsive behaviours, the so-called 'multi-impulsive bulimia' (cf. Lacey, 1993), yet other studies do not find such clustering of impulsive behaviours in bulimic individuals (Welch and Fairburn, 1996).

Comorbid personality disorder is frequently found (for review see Herzog *et al.*, 1996), with Cluster B and cluster C personality disorders occurring equally commonly.

Binge-eating disorder

This shares some features with non-bingeing obese individuals and some with individuals with bulimia nervosa. In contrast to non-bingeing obese individuals, obese binge-eaters have an earlier onset of obesity; tend to eat more; have more frequent weight fluctuations and more weight-related distress and have more psychopathology (e.g. depression).

In contrast to individuals with bulimia nervosa those with BED often start bingeing first and later begin to diet and they also show less dietary restraint (for review see Levine and Marcus, 1998). The disorder is often highly distressing to those affected.

MEDICAL COMPLICATIONS

The medical complications of anorexia nervosa and bulimia nervosa usually result from either nutritional deficits and self-starvation or from the after-effects of vomiting or laxative misuse (see Table 8.3). More detailed information is contained in the review by Sharpe and Freeman (1993). It is beyond the scope of this chapter to discuss the medical risks of obesity that are often observed in sufferers of binge eating disorders.

AETIOLOGY

Social factors

Slimness is highly valued in Western culture, whereas obesity is highly stigmatized. As a result, dieting to lose weight is highly prevalent in young Western women. However, despite the increased prevalence of dieting there has been no increase in the incidence of anorexia nervosa (Turnbull et al., 1996). Thus a 'culture of slimness' is not a necessary precondition for the development of this disorder. Certainly, this cultural emphasis of slimness has coloured contemporary Western presentations of anorexia nervosa, in that concerns about weight and fatness as a justification for weight loss now predominate. However, it must be borne in mind that in non-Western societies and throughout history there were many anorexics without 'fat phobia'. Additionally, a cultural focus on slimness and weight control is an important maintaining factor for the illness and may cause the course to be more severe, as evidenced by a recent trend for a higher mortality (Sullivan, 1995) and increased readmission rates (Nielsen, 1990).

In contrast, in bulimia nervosa dieting – which usually precedes bingeing – is a very clear risk factor, which increases the risk of developing the disorder eight-fold (Patton et al., 1990). Groups under particularly strong pressure to be slim, such as female dancers and models, have an increased risk of developing bulimia nervosa. Likewise, male performers and sportsmen like jockeys and wrestlers may also be at increased risk of developing bulimia-like symptoms. Young women from non-Western cultures experiencing rapid culture change have high rates of bulimia nervosa.

Binge eating disorder seems to affect a group of individuals who are biologically prone to obesity, yet who are trying to push their weight below their biological set point, to fit in with current cultural requirements.

Biological factors

Anorexia nervosa is often linked to leanness within the family (Hebebrand and Remschmidt, 1995). Female relatives of an affected individual have a ten-fold increase in their risk of developing the disorder. Twin studies suggest that anorexic traits and the full syndrome have a significant genetic component (Treasure and Holland, 1995).

One hypothesis is that anorexia nervosa is caused by a dysfunction in the control of body composition. Leptin, a hormone produced by fat cells which signals to the brain that energy stores are sufficient, is one of the key components in the control of body composition. However, so far no abnormality in leptin function in anorexia nervosa has been found, with levels being low in underweight patients, increased with weight gain and returning to the normal range on recovery (Treasure et al., 1997).

An alternative hypothesis is that anorexia nervosa is the result of an abnormality in the hypothalamic pituitary adrenal system which leads to a catabolic response to chronic stress (Connan, personal communication).

Yet others have suggested that the vulnerability to develop anorexia nervosa is related to abnormal 5HT function. In support of this, recent research found an abnormality on one of the genes controlling one of the subtypes of serotonin receptors to be more common in women with anorexia nervosa (Enoch et al., 1998).

In bulimia nervosa family studies have shown a raised lifetime risk of eating disorders (3.4 per cent to 19.8 per cent), affective disorders (9–37.1 per cent), substance misuse disorders (8–40 per cent) and cluster B personality disorders (12 per cent) amongst first-degree relatives (for review see Lilenfeld et al., 1998).

Evidence from twin studies suggests an estimated heritability of 32–63 per cent for bingeing, of 50-84 per cent for vomiting and of 50–55 per cent for bulimia nervosa (e.g. Sullivan *et al.*, 1998). Some of the genetic liability may be non-specific and shared with the liability to develop phobia and panic disorder (Kendler *et al.*, 1995). It has also been thought that the degree of heritability may be an overestimate, as – in contrast to other psychiatric disorders – the equal environments assumption on which twin studies are predicated is not fulfilled in BN.

Unlike in anorexia nervosa there is no 5-HT2A promoter polymorphism (Enoch *et al.*, 1998).

Studies of the neurobiology of BN are marred by difficulties in assessing which abnormalities predate the symptoms and which are the results of the disorder. Dieting may contribute to neurobiological disturbances. Much of the neurobiological research has focused on serotonin, because of its well-known role in appetite control. Several studies have found evidence of lowered central 5-HT in bulimic women. In addition, research has focused on the role of norepinephrine, endogenous opates and the neuropeptides including peptide YY and their role in the causation or maintenance of BN (for review see Mayer and Walsh, 1998).

Family factors

In anorexia nervosa there is little evidence to support any gross disturbance in family functioning (Schmidt *et al.*, 1993). Minuchin and colleagues (1978) suggested that families of patients with anorexia nervosa are characterized by: enmeshment and overinvolvement, rigidity and poor conflict resolution. Most of these features probably are a consequence of having a sick child in the family. For example, enmeshment and overinvolvement are equally common in families with a child with cystic fibrosis (Blair *et al.*, 1995), with the main difference between anorexia nervosa families and cystic fibrosis families being that families with a child with anorexia nervosa are weaker at problem solving.

Parental depression and parental obesity are risk factors for bulimia nervosa and binge-eating disorder. This could either be a genetic effect or result from their impact on childhood environment. Childhood adversity with parental neglect and physical or sexual abuse are common but are non-specific risk factors for both bulimia nervosa and binge eating disorder (Fairburn *et al.*, 1997).

A family environment where other family members diet and make critical comments about weight, shape and eating also contributes to the risk of developing BN or BED (Fairburn *et al.*, 1997; 1998).

Psychological factors

Personality and core beliefs

Anorexics often have a helpless, avoidant coping style which is present from childhood (Troop and Treasure, 1997). Obsessional personality traits, perfectionism and a tendency to please others are also common.

The personality traits that have been thought to increase the risk for the development of BN include perfectionism; a ruminative coping style; impulsivity and mood lability; thrill seeking, excitability and a marked tendency to dysphoria in response to rejection and non-reward. The core beliefs of individuals with bulimia nervosa are characterized by feelings of defectiveness and shame, vulnerability, and fears of abandonment. There is good evidence to suggest that these beliefs are very similar in quality and quantity to those experienced by individuals with depression.

Childhood factors

Picky eating and digestive problems in childhood increase the risk of later anorexia nervosa, whereas pica and problem meals increase the risk of bulimia nervosa. Other childhood factors that have been identified as risk factors for bulimia nervosa include negative self-evaluation, childhood shyness, absence from school through anxiety, lack of childhood friends (Fairburn *et al.*, 1997) and childhood feelings of helplessness (Troop and Treasure, 1997).

Individuals with BED also have more negative self-evaluation than normal controls during childhood (Fairburn *et al.*, 1998).

Factors precipitating onset

Approximately 70 per cent of cases of anorexia nervosa and bulimia nervosa are precipitated by a severe life event or difficulty (Schmidt *et al.*, 1998). There is, however, some difference in the types of problem that are experienced. In bulimia nervosa interpersonal

problems often trigger onset, whereas in a subgroup of individuals with anorexia nervosa so-called pudicity problems, i.e. events
and difficulties which are perceived by the individual as sexually
shaming, precede the onset.

TREATMENT

Anorexia nervosa

Depending on the patient's age, the medical severity and duration of
their disorder, different types of treatment may be appropriate. In
young patients (aged ≤ 16), and in those where the onset of the
illness is in early adolescence, irrespective of their chronological age,
it is usually helpful to involve the family in treatment (Russell *et al.*,
1987). Parental counselling, i.e. working separately with the parents
to understand the illness and to deal with the problems it causes, is
as effective as, and more acceptable than, a traditional form of
family therapy which involves all family members including the
patient.

Different forms of brief focused outpatient psychotherapy have
been evaluated in less severe older cases (weight loss less than 25
per cent of total body weight). Frequently, the therapy has to be
continued long term (≥ 1 year). It is vital that psychological treatment is supplemented by regular medical monitoring. Brief focused
forms of psychotherapy, such as cognitive analytical therapy or
brief dynamic therapy, are more effective than supportive therapy
(Troop and Treasure, 1997). New models of cognitive behavioural therapy are being developed, as are techniques to prevent
relapse.

Those with severe weight loss will require inpatient treatment. In
the past this involved strict behaviour modification programmes
with bed-rest and isolation, with a reintroduction of 'privileges'
contingent on weight gain. Such regimes are now thought to be
obsolete. At best they lead to patients 'eating their way out of
hospital' and at worst they are deeply traumatic and compound the
sufferers' psychological difficulties by increasing their sense of self-
loathing and personal ineffectiveness.

Modern inpatient treatment in specialized units with an expertise
in the management of eating disorders will focus on building up
a good working alliance with the patient. Treatment involves a

combined focus on nutritional rehabilitation and psychotherapy. Day hospital treatment may be an effective alternative to inpatient treatment in anorexia nervosa, but this treatment modality has as yet not been fully evaluated.

In those rare situations where a patient's life is at risk through her anorexia nervosa and she is unwilling or unable to co-operate with a life-saving treatment plan, she may need to be detained under Section III of the Mental Health Act to facilitate life-saving treatment. If at all possible this should be carried out within a specialist unit.

There is no role for the use of medication in the treatment of acute anorexia nervosa whilst the patient is severely emaciated. However, recent research has shown that, if given after weight rehabilitation, fluoxetine may reduce relapse rates.

Bulimia nervosa

Cognitive behaviour therapy (CBT) is the best evaluated and most widely used treatment for bulimia nervosa and should be considered as the first line treatment (for review see Schmidt, 1998). In studies comparing it to other psychological treatments it performs at least as well as if not better than, the comparison treatment. It can be used individually or be applied to groups. About 40–60 per cent of patients become symptom-free following a course of CBT and maintain these gains in the long-term (Fairburn et al., 1995). The approach is based on the cognitive model of bulimia nervosa in which concerns about shape and weight are seen as both causative and maintaining factors. It is thought that underlying these shape and weight concerns are long-standing feelings of ineffectiveness and low self-esteem. Weight-and-shape concerns are thought to trigger dieting, which in turn triggers bingeing, which leads to compensatory vomiting or purging in a cascade of interlocking vicious circles. Treatment is collaborative and is usually given as a package of 16–20 sessions. In milder cases, manualized forms of CBT can be applied. Pure self-care without any therapist interventions leads to abstinence rates from bulimic behaviour of 20 per cent. Guided self-help, where the manual is delivered with a small amount of therapist support, is as effective as full CBT, but requires less therapist time (e.g. Thiels et al., 1998).

An interesting alternative to CBT is interpersonal therapy, developed originally at NIMH for the treatment of depression. This treatment, which does not systematically address pathological eating habits or weight-and-shape concerns, has shown considerable promise, with long-term results as good as those of CBT (Fairburn et al., 1995).

Exposure treatments have also been used in the treatment of bulimia nervosa, either as exposure to and prevention of vomiting, or as cue exposure to small amounts of binge-food, which the patient looks at, smells and tastes followed by prevention of binge-ing. The results of these treatments have been inconclusive and their value in the treatment of bulimia nervosa remains uncertain.

As mentioned above with the best existing treatments only 40–60 per cent of bulimic patients become symptom-free. For patients with severe comorbidity (e.g. personality disorder, depression or substance misuse) and those with severe childhood trauma more intensive and prolonged forms of psychological treatment may be necessary. Suggested treatment options for these more complex cases include broadening the focus of CBT to cover motivational (Treasure et al., in press) and interpersonal issues, more intensive body image work or schema-work. Alternatively, different psychological treatments like dialectical behaviour therapy or cognitive analytical therapy might be used or day- or inpatient treatment in specialized units (for review see Wilson, 1996; Schmidt, 1998). However, our knowledge about how best to help these more complex patients is as yet limited.

A wide range of different medications has been used in the treatment of bulimia nervosa in over twenty randomized controlled studies. These include mood stabilizers, appetite suppressants, opioid antagonists and antidepressants. The latter have shown the most consistently positive results. Virtually all classes of antidepressant have been found to reduce bingeing and /or purging in the short term. However, the observed abstinence rates from bulimic behaviours are extremely variable. Antidepressant medication is effective in bulimia nervosa irrespective of the presence and/ or severity of depressive symptoms. Fluoxetine, an SSRI, is widely used as an antibulimic agent. It is most effective if used at a dose of 60 mg/day rather than at the usual antidepressant dose of 20 mg/ day. However, even at a dose of 60 mg/day only 20 per cent of patients become symptom-free (for review see Mayer and Walsh, 1998; Schmidt, 1998).

Combinations of CBT and an antidepressant are superior to antidepressant treatment alone and to placebo. There is, however, no clear superiority of CBT used in combination with an anti-depressant compared to CBT alone or CBT plus placebo (for review see Schmidt, 1998).

Binge-eating disorder

Treatments for binge-eating disorder have been adapted from those that have effectively reduced binge-eating in bulimia nervosa or from those that have produced weight loss in obese individuals. Both psychological and pharmacological interventions have been evaluated.

Cognitive behavioural therapy is effective in normalizing eating and reducing binge frequency, but this intervention does not lead to significant weight loss. Only those who remain abstinent from binge-eating beyond the end of treatment are likely to experience sustained weight loss. Pure self-help and guided self-help formats of CBT are as effective as therapist-aided CBT. Likewise, there is also preliminary evidence that interpersonal psychotherapy may be useful in reducing bingeing in BED patients (for review see Levine and Marcus, 1998). Lastly, behavioural weight loss programmes are also helpful.

Different pharmacological agents have been evaluated in the treatment of binge-eating disorder. These include: antidepressants (fluoxetine, desipramine); anorectic agents (d-fenfluramine); and opiate antagonists (naltrexone). All of these lead to moderate short-term reductions in binge-eating (for review see Levine and Marcus, 1998).

COURSE AND OUTCOME

Anorexia nervosa

The median duration of the illness is 6 years (Herzog *et al.*, 1997b). Even patients who fall into the good outcome category often have residual problems such as abnormal attitudes to food and eating. A third of patients have a poor prognosis. Anorexia nervosa has the highest mortality of any psychiatric illness (Sullivan, 1995). Roughly half of the deaths result from medical complications, the other half result from suicide. Predictors of a lethal course are an abnormally low serum albumin level and a low weight ($\leqslant 60$ per cent average body weight) (Herzog *et al.*, 1997a). Specialist treatment improves the outcome, as the mortality rate in areas without a specialized treatment service is higher than in areas where specialist treatment centres are available (Crisp *et al.*, 1992).

Bulimia nervosa

The median duration of bulimia nervosa is between 3 and 6 years. Without treatment the disorder runs a fluctuating, chronic course. Of those receiving treatment 50 per cent to 70 per cent are symptom-free 5–10 years after presentation, while 9–20 per cent continue to meet full criteria of the disorder and 3–4 per cent develop anorexia nervosa (Keel and Mitchell, 1997). Mortality from all causes is 0.3–1.1 per cent. The remainder develop a range of milder eating disorders including non-purging bulimia nervosa, binge-eating disorder, eating disorder not otherwise specified or obesity. The risk of relapse is substantial. Nearly one-third of women who had been in remission experience relapse during the first four years following presentation. Thereafter, risk of relapse lessens. Predictors of poor treatment outcome include greater severity of bulimic symptoms, premorbid obesity, low self-esteem, comorbid depression, personality disorder, multi-impulsive bulimia and a discordant family environment (for review see Schmidt, 1998).

Binge-eating disorder

Very little is known about outcome. One study examined treatment outcome after six years and found that the majority of patients no longer had a major DSM-IV eating disorder; 6 per cent had BED; 7 per cent had shifted to bulimia nervosa; and a further 7 per cent fell into the category of eating disorder not otherwise specified (Fichter *et al.*, 1998).

CONCLUSION

Eating disorders are chronic, severe and common disorders, which afflict mainly young women. Major scientific advances have been made in the genetic, neurobiological and psychosocial aspects of these disorders over the last few years. We also have excellent epidemiological data about the community levels of morbidity and the demand for services (Turnbull *et al.*, 1996). Moreover, we have solid research information about the efficacy of psychotherapy and pharmacotherapy, especially in bulimia nervosa. However, other areas of our knowledge are far more patchy, for example the number of randomized controlled trials into the treatment of anorexia nervosa are few and far between.

So what are the challenges lying ahead? Certainly, in terms of aetiological research, paradigms that allow us to investigate simultaneously biological/genetic and psychosocial/environmental factors, and tease out their relative contributions and interactions, are called for and are currently in progress (Karwautz *et al.*, submitted). From the point of view of the clinician and service planner we need much better information about effective treatments for anorexia nervosa. Despite the abundance of studies into the treatment of bulimia nervosa these consist mostly of short- to medium-term interventions in research settings and there is much less evidence about the clinical effectiveness of treatments in non-specialist settings. From the point of view of the sufferer easier access to high quality services is essential. Two successive reports commissioned by the Royal College of Psychiatrists (1992; Robinson, 1999) identified patchy, poor provision of services with unplanned proliferation of private services in many areas. Lastly, from the point of view of everyone concerned, the public image of eating disorders still leaves a lot to be desired. Perhaps changing the public perception of eating disorders – as is the intention of the latest Royal College of Psychiatrists' Campaign on fighting stigma in mental illness – is the biggest challenge of all.

REFERENCES

American Psychiatric Association (1994) *Diagnostic and Statistical Manual of Mental Disorders (DSM-III-R)*, 4th ed. revised, Washington DC: APA.

Blair, C., Freeman, C. and Cull, A. (1995) 'The families of anorexia nervosa and cystic fibrosis patients', *Psychological Medicine* 25: 985–93.

Crisp, A.H., Callender, J. S., Halek, C. and Hsu, L.K.G. (1992) 'Long-term mortality in anorexia nervosa: a 20-year follow-up of the St George's and Aberdeen cohorts', *British Medical Journal* 161: 104–7.

Enoch, M.A., Kaye, W.H., Rotondo, A., Greenberg, B.D., Murphy, D.L. and Goldman, D. (1998) '5-HT$_{2A}$ promoter polymorphism – 1438/A, anorexia nervosa, and obsessive-compulsive disorder', *Lancet* 351: 1785–6.

Fairburn, C.G., Doll, H.A., Welch, S.L., Hay, P.J., Davies, B.A. and O'Connor, M.E. (1998) 'Risk factors for binge eating disorder', *Archives of General Psychiatry* 55: 1998.

Fairburn, C.G., Welch, S.L., Doll, H.A., Davies, B.A. and O'Connor, M.E. (1997) 'Risk factors for bulimia nervosa: a community based case control study', *Archives of General Psychiatry* 54: 509–17.

Fairburn, C.G., Norman, P.A., Welch, S.L., O'Connor, M.E., Doll, H.A. and Peveler, R.C. (1995) 'A prospective study of outcome in bulimia nervosa and the long-term effects of three psychological treatments', *Archives of General Psychiatry* 52: 304–12.

Fallon, P., Katzman, M. and Wooley, S. (eds) (1994) *Feminist Perspectives in Eating Disorders*, New York: The Guilford Press.

Fichter, M.M., Quadflieg, N. and Gnutzmann, A. (1998) 'Binge eating disorder: treatment outcome over a 6-year course', *Journal of Psychosomatic Research* 44: 385–405.

Hebebrand, J. and Remschmidt, H. (1995) 'Anorexia nervosa viewed as an extreme weight condition: genetic implications', *Human Genetics* 95: 1–11.

Herzog, W., Deter, H.C., Fiehn, W. and Petzold, E. (1997a) 'Medical findings and predictors of long term physical outcome in anorexia nervosa – a prospective 12 year follow-up study', *Psychological Medicine* 27: 269–79.

Herzog, W., Schellberg, D. and Deter, H.C. (1997b) 'First recovery in anorexia nervosa patients in the long term course: a discrete time survival analysis', *Journal of Consulting and Clinical Psychology* 65: 169–77.

Herzog, D.B., Nussbaum, K.M. and Marmor, A.K. (1996) 'Comorbidity and outcome in eating disorders', *The Psychiatric Clinics of North America* 19: 843–59.

Karwautz, A., Rabe-Hesketh, S., Collier, D., Sham, P. and Treasure, J.L. (1999) 'Non-shared risk factors for anorexia nervosa: a study using a discordant sister-pair design', paper submitted for publication.

Keel, P.K. and Mitchell, J.E. (1997) 'Outcome in bulimia nervosa', *American Journal of Psychiatry* 154: 313–21.

Kendler, K.S., Walters, E.E., Neale, M.C., Kessler, R.C., Heath, A.C. and Eaves, L.J. (1995) 'The structure of the genetic and environmental risk factors for six major psychiatric disorders in women', *Archives of General Psychiatry* 52: 374–83.

Lacey, J.H. (1993) 'Self-damaging and addictive behaviour in bulimia nervosa', *British Journal of Psychiatry* 163: 190–4.

Levine, M.D. and Marcus, M.D. (1998) 'The treatment of binge eating disorder', in: H.W. Hoek, J.L. Treasure and M.A. Katzman (eds) *Neurobiology in the Treatment of Eating Disorders*, Chichester: John Wiley & Sons.

Lilenfeld, L.R., Kaye, W.H., Greeno, C.G., Merikangas, K.R., Plotnicov, K., Pollice, C., Rao, R., Strober, M., Bulik, C.M. and Nagy, L. (1998) 'A controlled family study of anorexia nervosa and bulimia nervosa: psychiatric disorders in first-degree relatives and effects of proband comorbidity', *Archives of General Psychiatry* 55: 603–10.

Mayer, L.E.S. and Walsh, B.T. (1998) 'Pharmacotherapy of eating disorders', in: H.W. Hoek, J.L. Treasure and M.A. Katzman (eds) *Neurobiology in the Treatment of Eating Disorders*, Chichester: John Wiley & Sons.

Meyer, C., Waller, G. and Water, S. (1998) 'Emotional states and bulimic psychopathology', in: H.W. Hoek, M.A. Katzman and J.L. Treasure (eds) *Neurobiology in the Treatment of Eating Disorders*, Chichester: John Wiley & Sons Ltd.

Minuchin, S., Rosman, B.L. and Baker, L. (1978) *Psychosomatic Families*, Cambridge, MA: Harvard University Press.

Nielsen, S. (1990) 'The epidemiology of anorexia nervosa in Denmark from 1973–1987: a nationwide register study of psychiatric admission', *Acta Psychiatrica Scandinavica* 81: 507–14.

Patton, G.D., Johnson-Sabine, E., Wood, K., Mann, A.H. and Wakeling, A. (1990) 'Abnormal eating attitudes in London schoolgirls – a prospective epidemiological study', *Psychological Medicine* 20: 282–394.

Robinson, P. (1999) 'The 1998 UK Survey of Specialist Eating Disorder Services', paper given at the Eating Disorders Special Interest Group. Grovelands Priory Hospital, London, February.

Royal College of Psychiatrists (1992) *Eating Disorders*, Council Report, CR14, London.

Russell, G.F.M., Szmukler, G., Dare, C. and Eisler, I. (1987) 'An evaluation of family therapy in anorexia nervosa and bulimia nervosa', *Archives of General Psychiatry* 44: 1047–56.

Russell, G.F.M. (1979) 'Bulimia nervosa an ominous variant of anorexia nervosa', *Psychological Medicine* 9: 429–48.

Schmidt, U. (1998) 'Treatment of bulimia nervosa', in: H.W. Hoek, J.L. Treasure and M.A. Katzman (eds) *The Integration of Neurobiology in the Treatment of Eating Disorders*, in the press.

Schmidt, U., Tiller, J., Blanchard, M., Andrews, B. and Treasure, J. (1997) 'Is there a specific trauma precipitating the onset of anorexia nervosa?', *Psychological Medicine* 27: 523–30.

Schmidt, U., Tiller, J. and Treasure, J. (1993) 'Setting the scene for eating disorders: childhood care, classification and course of illness', *Psychological Medicine* 23: 663–72.

Sharpe, C.W. and Freeman, C.P.L. (1993) 'The medical complications of anorexia nervosa', *British Journal of Psychiatry* 153: 452–62.

Sullivan, P.F., Bulik, C.M. and Kendler, K.S. (1998) 'Genetic epidemiology of bingeing and vomiting', *British Journal of Psychiatry* 173: 75–9.

Sullivan, P.F. (1995) 'Mortality in anorexia nervosa', *American Journal of Psychiatry* 152: 1073–4.

Thiels, C., Schmidt, U., Treasure, J., Garthe, R. and Troop, N. (1998) 'Guided self-change for bulimia nervosa incorporating a self-treatment manual', *American Journal of Psychiatry* 155: 947–53.

Treasure, J., Collier, D. and Campbell, I.C. (1997) 'Ill-fitting genes: the biology of weight and shape control in relation to body composition and eating disorders', *Psychological Medicine* 27: 505–8.

Treasure, J.L. and Holland, A.J. (1995) 'Genetic factors in eating disorders', in: G. Szmukler, C. Dare and J. Treasure (eds) *Handbook of Eating Disorders. Theory, Treatment and Research*, Chichester: John Wiley and Sons.

Treasure, J.L., Katzman, M., Schmidt, U., Troop, N., Todd, G. and De Silva, P. (1999) 'Engagement and outcome in the treatment of bulimia nervosa: first phase of a sequential design comparing motivation enhancement therapy and cognitive behavioural therapy', *Behavior Research and Therapy*, in press.

Treasure, J. and Schmidt, U. (1999) 'Beyond effectiveness and efficiency lies quality in services for eating disorders', *European Eating Disorders Review* 7: 162–78.

Troop, N.A. and Treasure, J.L. (1997) 'Setting the scene for eating disorders, II: Childhood helplessness and mastery', *Psychological Medicine* 27: 531–8.

Turnbull, S., Ward, A., Treasure, J., Jick, H. and Derby, L. (1996) 'The demand for eating disorder care: an epidemiological study using the general practice research data base', *British Journal of Psychiatry* 169: 705–12.

Van Hoeken, D., Lucas, A.R. and Hoek, H.W. (1998) 'Epidemiology', in: H.W. Hoek, J.L. Treasure and M.A. Katzman (eds) *Neurobiology in the Treatment of Eating Disorders*, Chichester: John Wiley and Sons.

Welch, S.L. and Fairburn, C.G. (1994) 'Sexual abuse and bulimia nervosa: three integrated case control comparisons', *American Journal of Psychiatry* 151: 402–7.

Welch, S.L. and Fairburn, C.G. (1996b) 'Impulsivity or comorbidity in bulimia nervosa. A controlled study of deliberate self harm and alcohol and drug misuse in a community sample', *British Journal of Psychiatry* 169: 451–8.

Wilson, T.G. (1996) 'Treatment of bulimia nervosa: when CBT fails', *Behaviour Research and Therapy* 34: 197–212.

WHO (1992) ICD-10. *Clinical Descriptions and Diagnostic Guidelines*, Geneva: WHO.

Chapter 9

Alcohol and drug misuse in women

Jane Marshall

INTRODUCTION

Social and cultural attitudes exert a profound influence on drinking and drug use behaviour in women. As a result women are less likely to drink and to use illegal drugs than men and are less likely to develop alcohol and drug problems. However, these attitudes have also given rise to the negative stereotype of the deviant, 'hard to treat addicted woman'. This stigma acts as a barrier to treatment (Blume, 1992) and prevents such women from attaining 'the highest standard of physical and mental health', a right enshrined in the Beijing Platform for Action, adopted at the Fourth World Conference on Women in 1995 (Haslegrave, 1997).

In this chapter the following issues will be discussed:

1 Epidemiology of substance misuse and dependence in women, with a focus on alcohol and illicit drugs;
2 Factors influencing the development of substance misuse and dependence in women;
3 Clinical features of substance misuse and dependence in women;
4 Treatment services and treatment outcome.

The chapter will focus mainly on alcohol misuse and dependence because, to date, the alcohol literature is richer and more methodologically robust than the drug literature.

EPIDEMIOLOGY OF SUBSTANCE MISUSE AND DEPENDENCE IN WOMEN

General population surveys of alcohol consumption and drug use typically find that women drink and use illicit drugs less frequently than men. Recent studies suggest that the gap is closing. Over the past fifty years women's alcohol consumption has increased. This has been facilitated in part by a change in social role allowing women more opportunities to drink (Wilsnack and Wilsnack, 1995; Plant, 1997). Younger cohorts of women are drinking more heavily than older women, and this may put them at particularly high risk of developing alcohol-related problems (Wilsnack et al., 1994).

Information from the 1996 British Household Survey indicates that there has been a gradual increase in alcohol consumption among British women between 1984 and 1996. In 1996 the proportion of women drinking over fourteen units per week was 14 per cent, compared with 9 per cent in 1984 (see Table 9.1). Single women were more likely to be drinking heavily when compared with married, widowed, separated or divorced women. Most of the heavy drinking women were in full time employment (Thomas et al., 1998). In contrast, alcohol consumption among men has remained fairly constant over the same period, with 27 per cent of men drinking over twenty-one units per week (Thomas et al., 1998).

In the United States the Epidemiologic Catchment Area study reported a 4.6 per cent lifetime prevalence of DSM-III alcohol abuse or dependence in women (Helzer et al., 1991). The corresponding figure for men was 23.8 per cent. Rates were highest in the 18–29 year and 30–44 year groups in both sexes. Another American survey, the National Comorbidity Survey (NCS), carried out on a population aged 15–54 years, reported a lifetime prevalence of alcohol dependence among women of 8.2 per cent (Anthony et al., 1994). This study confirmed higher rates of dependence in younger drinkers. The male : female ratio for alcohol dependence in the ECA study was 5.2 : 1 (Helzer et al., 1991) compared to 2.8 : 1 in the NCS study (Anthony et al., 1994) which was carried out ten years later.

The Psychiatric Morbidity Survey carried out in Great Britain from August 1993 to August 1994 found that the overall rate of dependence on illicit drugs in the general population was 2.2 per cent (Meltzer et al., 1995; Jenkins et al., 1998). Men had a higher prevalence (2.9 per cent) compared with women (1.4 per cent) (see Table 9.2). Drug dependence was commonest in the 16–24-year age group (10 per cent) and again men were twice as likely to be drug dependent as women.

In the United States the ECA study reported a 4.8 per cent lifetime prevalence of a DSM-III abuse/dependence syndrome

Table 9.1 General household surveys, 1984–1996: alcohol consumption level by sex

Great Britain

Persons aged 18 and over

Alcohol consumption level (units per week)	1984 %	1986 %	1988 %	1990 %	1992 %	1994 %	1996 %
MEN							
Non-drinker	7	6	7	6	6	7	7
Under 1	10	9	10	9	10	9	8
1 to 10	37	36	35	36	36	35	35
11 to 21	21	22	22	22	22	22	23
22 to 35	12	14	13	13	14	15	15
36 to 50	6 } 25	6 } 27	7 } 27	7 } 28	7 } 27	6 } 27	6 } 27
51 and over	6	7	7	7	6	6	6
Base = 100%	8044	8415	8371	7844	8150	7411	6920
WOMEN							
Non-drinker	13	11	12	12	12	14	13
Under 1	24	24	23	23	23	21	19
1 to 7	41	41	40	40	39	37	37
8 to 14	14	14	14	14	15	15	16
15 to 25	6	7	7	7	8	9	9
26 to 35	2 } 9	2 } 10	2 } 10	2 } 11	2 } 11	2 } 13	2 } 14
36 and over	1	2	2	2	2	2	2
Base = 100%	9399	9845	9814	9150	9490	8906	8298

Source: Office for National Statistics (1996). Living in Britain. Preliminary results from the 1996 General Household Survey, p. 18.

Table 9.2 Prevalence of psychiatric disorders per 1000 population in adults aged 16–64 years in Great Britain: 1993

	Women	Men	All adults
Rate per thousand in past week (S.E.)			
Mixed anxiety and depressive disorder	94 (5)	54 (4)	77 (3)
Generalised anxiety disorder	34 (3)	28 (2)	31 (2)
Depressive episode	25 (2)	17 (2)	21 (1)
Phobias	14 (2)	7 (1)	11 (1)
Obsessive-compulsive disorder	15 (2)	9 (2)	12 (1)
Panic disorder	9 (1)	8 (2)	8 (1)
Any neurotic disorder	195 (7)	123 (5)	160 (5)
Rate per thousand in past 12 months (S.E.)			
Functional psychosis	4 (1)	4 (1)	4 (1)
Alcohol dependence	21 (2)	75 (5)	47 (3)
Drug dependence	14 (2)	29 (3)	22 (2)

Source: Jenkins et al. (1998)

involving illicit drugs in women, concentrated in the 18–29-year age group (Anthony and Helzer, 1991).

Historically cigarette smoking has been more prevalent among males, but recent evidence suggests that the proportion of men and women in Great Britain who smoke is similar (29 per cent and 28 per cent respectively) (ONS, 1997). In contrast, women are more likely to use prescribed psychoactive drugs than are men.

FACTORS INFLUENCING THE DEVELOPMENT OF SUBSTANCE MISUSE AND DEPENDENCE IN WOMEN

Drinking and drug-using behaviour in women is influenced by a range of demographic factors such as age, marital status, employment and ethnicity. These factors interact with other risk factors such as genetic predisposition, psychological and socio-cultural factors to determine the onset and course of drinking and drug use. Although it is likely that the addictive process itself is similar in both men and women, its pattern and course in women is determined by the following factors.

Genetic factors

Family, twin and adoption studies strongly suggest a genetic predisposition to alcohol dependence (Merikangas, 1990). Kendler et al. (1992), using a population-based sample of female twins, showed that 40–60 per cent of the variance in 'alcoholism' among women is attributable to genetically mediated factors. Many factors may contribute to this variance including personality characteristics and parental psychopathology (Prescott et al., 1997). In another study using a similar population of female twins, Kendler and Prescott (1998) found that the vulnerability to cocaine abuse and dependence in women is substantially influenced by genetic factors.

Psychological factors

The role of psychological factors in the aetiology of addictive disease is generally still poorly understood. Studies using clinical populations demonstrate high levels of psychopathology. Women patients have higher rates of anxiety disorder, psychosexual dysfunction, bulimia (Ross *et al.*, 1988), depressive symptoms and lower self-esteem (Beckman, 1978; Walitzer and Sher, 1996), and borderline personality disorder (Nace *et al.*, 1986; Vaglum and Vaglum, 1985; Walitzer and Sher, 1996), whereas male patients have higher rates of antisocial personality disorder (Ross *et al.*, 1988). There is a modest relationship between substance misuse and eating disorder (Schuckit *et al.*, 1996). While this degree of comorbidity is accepted, it has proved more difficult to separate out whether the psychopathology preceded the substance misuse or arose as a consequence of it. Longitudinal studies have helped to explore this issue. Jones (1971) found that women who reported feelings of low self-esteem and impaired ability to cope at junior high and high school later became problem drinkers. This study was limited by the low numbers of female drinkers. In another longitudinal study female college students, who later developed drinking problems, were more likely than their male counterparts to report that they drank to relieve social anxiety and to elevate their mood in social situations (Fillmore *et al.*, 1979).

Retrospective studies have explored the occurrence of traumatic events that might have predisposed to later problems with alcohol. The ECA data show that a history of sexual abuse increased the lifetime prevalence of later alcohol problems by a factor of 3 and drug problems by a factor of 4 (Winfield *et al.*, 1990).

Further understanding of the relationship between substance misuse and psychopathology in women has emerged from studying comorbidity. The ECA survey reported that 19 per cent of women who met criteria for lifetime alcohol abuse/dependence also met criteria for a lifetime diagnosis of major depression (compared with 7 per cent of non-alcoholic women and 5 per cent of alcoholic men).

When Helzer and Pryzbeck (1988) compared men and women with alcohol abuse/dependence and major depression, they found that depression was the primary problem in 66 per cent of women but in only 22 per cent of men.

Socio-cultural factors

Increased alcohol consumption is associated with younger age, higher educational levels, higher socio-economic status and being single or divorced (Wilsnack *et al.*, 1994). Cohabitation is strongly associated with problem drinking, possibly because it is an 'ambiguous and stressful' state, or because it involves heavy drinking partners (Wilsnack and Wilsnack, 1995). Likewise heavy or problem drinking is common amongst divorced and separated women. Divorce appears to put women without a drinking problem at greater risk for increased drinking. On the other hand many heavy drinking women reduced their alcohol consumption following divorce.

In the United States white women are most likely to drink, African-American the least and Hispanic are intermediate. Little is known about the cultural and ethnic differences amongst women in the United Kingdom.

Women are influenced by the drinking habits of their partners (Wilsnack and Wilsnack, 1995). Further risk factors include sexual dysfunction, physical and sexual abuse during childhood, childhood parental loss through separation (Kendler *et al.*, 1996), having an unstable family of origin, being in a violent relationship, stressful life events and poly drug use (Edwards *et al.*, 1997: 149; Davison and Marshall, 1996). Women are also more likely to date the onset of their problem to a stressful life event, and to say that they started to misuse alcohol in order to forget family problems and to increase their social confidence (Copeland and Hall, 1992).

Risk factors across the life course

Although these risk factors are relevant across all age groups, some are more specific to certain stages in the life cycle. Peer influence is the dominant factor amongst female adolescents. Young, single working women, particularly those under 25 years, drink heavily, possibly for a variety of reasons, including a relaxation in attitudes to women drinking, greater opportunities to drink and financial independence. Many women alter their drinking habits during their 20s and 30s. Infertility, postnatal depression, marital or relationship breakdown, bereavement or physical illness are all possible risk factors at this stage. Different stresses influence drinking behaviour during the 40s and 50s. The departure of children from the family home, unemployment, bereavement (partner, family, friends), marital or relationship breakdown, loss of attractiveness and physical slowing down are all important factors. Elderly women with alcohol problems are more likely to be widows, living alone and to be depressed.

Women are 'late bloomers' when it comes to developing drinking patterns which put them at risk for serious problems. Men typically manifest such patterns in their 20s, but women do so a decade later, in their 30s. On the other hand serious alcohol problems in women also peak in the 30s whereas they peak at least a decade later in men (Fillmore, 1987). This means that the emergence and persistence of frequent and heavy drinking and alcohol problems occupies a smaller 'temporal space' in the life course of women (Fillmore et al., 1987), and that they are at greater risk of developing alcohol-related problems than are men.

Women are often introduced to and supplied with drugs by their male partners. Their pattern of use is also influenced by the pattern of use of their partners.

The intense social stigma associated with substance misuse in women leads to feelings of guilt and shame and to a tendency for women to drink and take illicit drugs alone. The extent of the problem is therefore often hidden until it is well advanced. Women typically do not see alcohol and drugs as their primary problem and may seek medical help repeatedly because of physical problems, depression and insomnia. The failure to recognize substance misuse in women early in its development may have serious and catastrophic consequences. They tend to present late in pregnancy and not to avail of antenatal care. They are at higher risk of obstetric complications. Foetal Alcohol Syndrome (FAS) and Foetal Alcohol Effects (FAE) are the devastating consequences of heavy drinking during pregnancy. Alcohol-dependent women are also at high risk of developing alcohol-related physical complications than are men. This complicates the whole treatment process and inevitably has a profound effect on treatment outcome.

CLINICAL FEATURES OF SUBSTANCE MISUSE AND DEPENDENCE IN WOMEN

Women with alcohol and drug problems are a heterogenous population. In this section the physical, psychological and social complications of substance misuse in women will be discussed. Pregnancy and childbirth will then be considered separately and this will be followed by a series of case vignettes.

Physical complications

Women start drinking at a later age than men, but present for treatment at approximately the same age. This suggests a rapid development of dependence, sometimes referred to as 'telescoping' (Blume, 1992), which may be particularly associated with depression (Smith *et al.*, 1983).

Women are at greater risk of certain physical complications associated with heavy drinking than are men, and such complications develop earlier in their drinking careers. These include liver disease, cardiomyopathy and brain damage (Edwards *et al.*, 1997). Unfortunately alcoholic hepatitis almost always progresses to cirrhosis in women, even following abstinence (Edwards *et al.*, 1997: 128). Moderate alcohol consumption (24g per day) has been consistently associated with a slight increase in risk of breast cancer (Longnecker *et al.*, 1988). Chronic heavy drinking is also associated with inhibition of ovulation, decrease in gonadal mass, infertility and a wide variety of gynaecological and obstetric complications (Blume, 1992).

Why do women develop alcohol problems at lower levels of alcohol consumption than men? This may be due, in part, to the fact that women metabolize alcohol differently from men. First, they have a lower average content of body water, which means that a standard dose of alcohol will give rise to higher blood and tissue alcohol concentrations in a woman compared with a man of the same weight. Higher blood and tissue alcohol levels mean a longer elimination time in women for a given dose of alcohol. Second, alcohol undergoes a first-pass metabolism in the stomach, through oxidation by gastric alcohol dehydrogenase (ADH). Women have lower levels of gastric ADH and therefore absorb significantly more of the alcohol they consume. Furthermore women with drinking problems have been shown to have extremely low levels of gastric ADH, and virtually no first-pass metabolism (Frezza *et al.*, 1990). Third, women also show increased blood alcohol concentration (BAC) variability, faster alcohol metabolism and less alcohol tolerance compared with men (Blume, 1992).

Alcohol-dependent women have a greatly shortened life expectancy, and an increased risk of premature death compared with alcohol dependent men (Lindberg and Agren, 1988). The causes of premature death include alcohol intoxication, cirrhosis of the liver, suicide, violent death and breast cancer (Lindberg and Agner,

1988). In a more recent sample of 'alcoholic' women predictors of mortality included 'benders' or *delirium tremens* (Lewis *et al.*, 1995).

Drug misuse and dependency in women is also associated with high rates of physical morbidity. Women who drink heavily and misuse drugs are at risk of unprotected sex. Many believe that they are infertile due to the effect of alcohol and opiates on their menstrual cycle. Consequently there is a risk of unwanted pregnancies. There is also a 25–40 per cent risk of transmission of HIV from an infected mother to her unborn child. Women who inject drugs, particularly those who share needles and have unprotected sex with drug-using partners, put themselves at substantial risk of contracting HIV, hepatitis B and hepatitis C. This is aggravated by the fact that male to female sexual transmission occurs more easily than the reverse. Klee (1993) found that many amphetamine and heroin users have regular sexual partners, of whom about 90 per cent also inject. Women injecting amphetamines and cocaine may be at particular risk, due to the increase in sexual behaviour associated with these drugs (Klee, 1993).

Psychological/psychiatric complications

Clinical populations of opiate addicts have significant rates of affective disorder, which are higher in women compared with men (Khantzian, 1985; Rounsaville and Kleber, 1985).

A recent Australian national survey of 267 women in treatment for alcohol and other drug problems (Swift *et al.*, 1996) found that poly drug use and substance dependence was the norm. More than half the sample were mothers, of whom one-third had lost custody of their children. Almost three-quarters had a history of sexual or physical abuse. More than one-quarter of the sample had been hospitalized for psychological problems and about half (48 per cent) had received counselling for anxiety or depression. Many (26 per cent) of these women had attempted self harm by cutting or burning their skin, and 44 per cent had attempted suicide.

A recent community study carried out in Ontario found that psychiatric comorbidity was associated with a greater severity of problem drinking. This has implications for treatment services (Ross and Shirley, 1997). Certainly substance misuse services for women should be in a position to evaluate and treat both substance misuse and comorbid psychiatric disorders.

Substance misuse and post-traumatic stress disorder (PTSD) commonly occur together and the course of the combined disorder appears to be more severe than the course of either disorder alone (Brown *et al.*, 1995).

Social complications

Women with alcohol problems have high levels of marital instability. They are more likely than their male counterparts to be divorced or living with partners who also have problems when they enter treatment. They are also more likely to have childcare responsibilities and to experience opposition from family and friends with respect to treatment.

More female drug misusers have a regular sexual partner, particularly a drug-using partner, than do male drug users (Gossop *et al.*, 1994). Women are more likely to be dependent on a partner for obtaining their supply of drugs. More women have children and more are single parents with responsibility of childcare (Gossop *et al.*, 1994). This may be severely stressful for women who are fully stretched just coping with basic issues of day-to-day living; unsurprisingly children in these circumstances have emotional and educational difficulties and there is always the risk of family breakdown. Women are less likely than men to be involved in criminal activities or to be imprisoned as a result of their drug use (Gossop *et al.*, 1994). However, more women are involved in prostitution.

Substance-misusing women are at increased risk of violence, even during pregnancy (Amaro *et al.*, 1990). In a study of pregnant women in North Carolina, victims of violence were more likely to have used multiple substances before pregnancy and to be continuing their substance use during pregnancy (Martin *et al.*, 1996).

Pregnancy and childbirth

Women who drink and use drugs during pregnancy risk causing significant harm to their offspring. They are at high risk of developing obstetric complications for general reasons, such as smoking, poor nutrition, poor antenatal clinic attendance, poor physical health, adverse life events and violence, as well as for alcohol and drug-specific reasons.

Eighty per cent of female drug users are of childbearing age. Opiate-dependent mothers are at increased risk of premature deliveries, intrauterine growth retardation, and perinatal death. Rates of perinatal mortality range from 2.7–10.7 per cent (see Dawkins et al., 1997). Babies may be born with opiate withdrawal symptoms and a sub-acute withdrawal syndrome may last several months. They book late (or not at all) and generally receive poor antenatal care. There is increasing evidence that cocaine adversely affects the foetus, causing high rates of premature delivery, low birth weight and psychomotor impairment.

The opiate withdrawal syndrome affects alertness and sleep regulation in neonates. These babies are difficult to handle and feed, and this in turn may lead to early attachment problems (Dawkins et al., 1997). The severity of the withdrawal syndrome depends on maternal methadone dose at delivery (Dawe et al., 1992). A retrospective case study comparing fifty-seven pregnant drug users (intravenous opiate users) with case-matched controls did not find significantly increased rates of obstetric and neonatal problems in the drug-using group (Dawkins et al., 1997). Twenty-two women (39 per cent) had discontinued their opiate use at the time of delivery. The babies born to these mothers had higher birth weights, were of greater gestational age and had shorter hospital stays when compared with the babies born to the women who were still using at least one substance. Thirty-two (56 per cent) of the infants had withdrawal symptoms, of whom twenty-seven required drug treatment. The mean duration of treatment was 48 days (range 2–181 days). The study showed that pregnant drug users are generally concerned for their unborn children and thus are motivated to comply with treatment which improves the outcome of pregnancy (Dawkins et al., 1997).

The Foetal Alcohol Syndrome (FAS) is almost always seen in the offspring of seriously alcohol-dependent women. It has an estimated incidence of between 0.3 and 3 cases per 1000 live births (Abel and Sokol, 1991), and is thought to be the third most common cause of mental retardation in North America, after Downs Syndrome and spina bifida (Blume, 1992). Other foetal alcohol effects (FAE) such as spontaneous abortion, reduced birth weight and behaviour changes are associated with lesser degrees of drinking. The greatest risk to the foetus from the mother's drinking is probably within the first few weeks of conception, before she even knows that she is pregnant. In the UK, the advice is to drink no more than one or two 'units' (or standard drinks) once or twice a week during pregnancy. In the United States abstinence from alcohol during pregnancy is recommended.

Case vignettes

Mary was a 23-year-old student who had been depressed for one year and had dropped out of college. Her GP referred her to her local community psychiatric service where she was started on paroxetine (an antidepressant of the Selective Serotonin Reuptake Inhibitor variety). Despite taking her medication regularly, support from a Community Psychiatric Nurse and a course of ten cognitive behaviour sessions with a psychologist, she did not improve. The psychologist then became concerned about her alcohol consumption and referred her to the community alcohol team for assessment. She admitted to a long history of heavy alcohol consumption dating back to the age of 17. Alcohol had helped her to overcome her shyness in social situations and she had come to rely on it 'like a friend'. She drank secretly at home and at the time of referral to the community alcohol team she was drinking one bottle of vodka per day and was severely alcohol-dependent. Following a failed community detox she was referred for inpatient treatment in a specialist unit. She decided on a period of residential rehabilitation and remained abstinent. Her depression resolved without recourse to medication and she returned to college.

Joan was a 35-year-old, married teacher with a family history of alcohol problems. Her childhood, marked by her father's heavy alcohol consumption and violence, had been extremely unhappy. She was intelligent and 'escaped' from the situation by reading and being studious. She did well at school, but was lonely when she went away to university. Here she began to drink an occasional glass of wine which helped her to become animated and the life and soul of the party. She trained as a teacher and went to work in an inner-city comprehensive, where she met her husband, also a teacher. They regularly drank in a local pub with colleagues after school. She gave up alcohol during her first pregnancy, when she was 28 years old. During her maternity leave she became lonely, isolated and depressed. The baby was difficult, her friends were working and she knew very few neighbours or women of her own age with children. Most days she managed to get the baby to sleep for a little while in the afternoon. She would watch the TV and have a glass of white wine. Within three months she was drinking a bottle of wine per day on her own and sharing another bottle with her husband in the evenings. Her drinking continued surreptitiously when she resumed her teaching post and only came to light when she was charged with drinking and driving two years later.

Pauline was a 23-year-old secretary. She met Clive through friends. He was older, 30, and very charming. Not knowing that he had a long history of intravenous opiate use, and was on methadone maintenance, she moved in with him. Friends frequently called to the house offering drugs. Clive continued to attend the methadone maintenance clinic but occasionally used heroin intravenously 'on top'. Pauline injected heroin once or twice to see what it was like. She had no intention of 'ending up like Clive' and always used clean needles. Within one month she was injecting daily and using methadone when she couldn't get heroin (Clive shared his maintenance supply with her). This pattern of use continued for eighteen months. She didn't seek any help because Clive was always able to find a supply. Much to her surprise she then found out that she was five months' pregnant. Her periods had been irregular since she started heroin and she hadn't noticed that they had stopped. She went to her GP who put her on a reducing methadone script and referred her to the antenatal clinic. She was reluctant to attend the local drug dependence clinic for fear of incriminating Clive. The antenatal clinic put her in touch with a drug service specializing in pregnant women. She benefited greatly from the extra support, and was able to stop methadone. Her daughter was born at 38 weeks' gestation and weighed 5lbs. She remained abstinent from heroin and other opiates, but began to drink in a problematic manner. Neighbours reported her to Social Services because of concerns about the welfare of the baby. She was referred to her local community alcohol team and managed to cut back her alcohol consumption to sensible levels. Social Services put her in touch with a local mother–infant network, which offered support.

TREATMENT SERVICES AND TREATMENT OUTCOME

Women are at risk of developing substance misuse problems about half as much as men. However, the number of women attending treatment services is between one-third and one-tenth the number of men, indicating that they are unrepresented in traditional services and are not availing of the treatment that they so obviously need (see Swift and Copeland, 1996).

Existing treatment services have, by and large, been set up to serve men who are the majority of treatment users. The psychological and physical differences between men and women in the development, pattern and course of their substance misuse have not been taken into account. Beckman (1994) has described the internal and external barriers perceived by women needing treatment for alcohol problems. Internal barriers include denial of the severity of the drinking problem (Thom, 1986), fear of stigmatization (Copeland and Hall, 1992; Reed, 1987), concern about leaving or losing their children and guilt and shame. The external barriers were concerned with interpersonal issues including opposition by family and friends and the social costs of family disruption. Other 'structural' barriers were also important. These included differential referral patterns, inadequate training of health professionals and lack of resources (see Beckman, 1994 for references). One of the most potent barriers to treatment for women is the social stigma attached to substance misuse. This is magnified in alcohol and drug-using mothers who genuinely fear that they will lose their children if they come forward for treatment. Women with small children may not have access to support and childcare if they decide to tackle their problem. For many women the traumatic memory of childhood sexual abuse and physical abuse at the hands of men are so great that they cannot bring themselves to attend traditional mixed-gender services. Women seek help in a more roundabout way, often presenting to their GP with problems such as irregular periods, diarrhoea, abdominal pain, tiredness, anxiety and depression. They may even get as far as their local psychiatric services without their problem being recognized.

Women are underrepresented in outcome studies for treatment of alcohol problems (Vannicelli and Nash, 1984), but seem to do as well as men. They may do better during the first year after treatment, whereas men have better results at follow-up after 12 months (Jarvis, 1992). Women may be better than men at using self-help material to reduce heavy or problem drinking (Sanchez-Craig et al., 1989). The presence of comorbid psychopathology is an important factor. Paradoxically the treatment of depression associated with 'alcoholism' was also associated with better outcomes among women compared with men in Rounsaville *et al.*'s study (1987). This was thought to be related to the fact that women were using alcohol to self-medicate their depression.

There is considerable debate as to whether women are better served in a women-only or 'mixed' treatment programme. Dahlgren and Willander (1989) showed superior 2-year outcomes for a specialized female unit versus a mixed male/female facility. An Australian study compared the profiles of women seeking drug and alcohol treatment in a specialist women's service with two traditional mixed-sex services (Copeland and Hall, 1992; Copeland *et al.*, 1993). There were no differences in outcomes, but women attending the women-only service were more likely to have dependent children, to be lesbian, to have a maternal history of drug or alcohol problems, and to have suffered sexual abuse in childhood. Gender-sensitive services may have a role in attracting women who would not otherwise engage in treatment.

Fewer studies have compared men and women in treatment for drug dependence. In a study of opiate addicts, Rounsaville *et al.* (1982) found that women had higher treatment retention rate and experienced fewer legal problems at follow-up compared with men.

The Australian study mentioned earlier (Swift *et al.*, 1996; Swift and Copeland, 1996) suggested that the main social stigma and labelling barriers to treatment included lack of childcare and support, lack of awareness of treatment options, and concerns about confrontational models used by some services. Women are not readily attracted into specialist alcohol and drug services and tend to approach more generalist services. It is therefore vital that primary care workers and general psychiatrists, physicians, para-suicide teams and A&E workers, should be aware of the special needs of women and help to bridge the gap between generalist and specialist services. Links between generalist and specialist services are fundamental to early intervention in cases of women with substance misuse problems. Women should also be given some choice in their treatment and be matched to appropriate levels and types of intervention.

Recommendations for service planning have been described previously (Davison and Marshall, 1996). If treatment services are to attract women they must be accessible and safe, use a non-confrontational style and be prepared to meet the specific and wide-ranging needs of women clients.

REFERENCES

Abel, E.L. and Sokol, R.J. (1991) 'A revised conservative estimate of the incidence of FAS and its economic impact', *Alcoholism: Clinical and Experimental Research* 15: 512–24.

Amaro, H., Fried, L.E., Cabral, H. and Zuckerman, B. (1990) 'Violence during pregnancy and substance use', *American Journal of Public Health* 80: 575–9.

Anthony, J.C., Warner, L.A. and Kessler, R.C. (1994) 'Comparative epidemiology of dependence on tobacco, alcohol, controlled substances and inhalants: basic findings from the National Comorbidity Survey', *Experimental and Clinical Psychopharmacology* 2: 244–68.

Anthony, J.C. and Helzer, J.E. (1991) 'Syndromes of drug abuse and dependence', in *Psychiatric Disorders in America: The Epidemiologic Catchment Area Study*, edited by L.N. Robins and D.A. Regier, New York: Free Press, pp. 116–54.

Beckman, L.J. (1978) 'Self esteem of women alcoholics', *Journal of Studies on Alcohol* 39: 491–8.

Beckman, J.L. (1994) 'Treatment needs of women with alcohol problems', *Alcohol Health and Research World* 18: 206–11.

Blume, S.B. (1992) 'Alcohol and other drug problems in women', in: J.H. Lowinson, P. Ruiz and R.B. Millman (eds) *Substance Abuse, a Comprehensive Textbook*, 2nd ed., Baltimore: Williams and Wilkins, pp. 794–807.

Brown, P.J., Recupero, P.R. and Stout, R. (1995) 'PTSD substance use comorbidity and treatment utilization', *Addictive Behaviours* 20: 251–4.

Copeland, J., Hall, W. and Didcott, P. (1993) 'A comparison of a specialist women's service and other drug treatment service with two traditional mixed-sex services: client characteristics and treatment outcome', *Drug and Alcohol Dependence* 32: 81–92.

Copeland, J. and Hall, W. (1992) 'A comparison of women seeking drug and alcohol treatment in a specialist women's and two traditional mixed-sex treatment services', *British Journal of Addiction* 87: 1293–302.

Dahlgren, L. and Willander, A. (1989) 'Are special treatment facilities for female alcoholics needed? A controlled 2-year follow-up study from a specialised female unit (EWA) versus a mixed male/female treatment facility', *Alcoholism: Clinical and Experimental Research* 13: 499–505.

Davison, S. and Marshall, E.J. (1996) 'Women who abuse alcohol and drugs', in: K. Abel *et al.* (eds) *Women and Mental Health*, London: Routledge, pp. 128–44.

Dawe, S., Gerada, C. and Strang, J. (1992) 'Establishment of a liaison service for pregnant opiate-dependent women', *British Journal of Addiction* 87: 867–71.

Dawkins, J.L., Tylden, E., Colley, N. and Evans, C. (1997) 'Drug abuse in

214 Jane Marshall

pregnancy: obstetric and neonatal problems. Ten years' experience', *Drug and Alcohol Review* 16: 25–31.

Edwards, G., Marshall, E.J. and Cook, C.C.H. (1997) *The Treatment of Drinking Problems*, 3rd ed., Cambridge: Cambridge University Press.

Fillmore, K.M. (1987) 'Women's drinking across the life course as compared to men's', *British Journal of Addiction* 82: 801–11.

Fillmore, K.M., Bacon, S.D. and Hyman, M. (1979) *The 27-year Longitudinal Panel Study of Drinking by Students in College*, 1979 Report to National Institute of Alcoholism and Alcohol Abuse, Contract no. ADM 281-76-0015, Washington DC.

Frezza, M., di Padova, C., Pozzato, G., Terpin, M., Baraona, E. and Lieber, C.S. (1990) 'High blood alcohol levels in women. The role of decreased gastric alcohol dehydrogenase activity and fuse-pass metabolism', *New England Journal of Medicine* 322: 95–9.

Gossop, M., Griffiths, P. and Strang, J. (1994) 'Sex differences in patterns of drug taking behaviour', *British Journal of Psychiatry* 164: 101–4.

Haslegrave, M. (1997) 'What she wants', *Lancet* 349: (sI): 1–2.

Helzer, J.E., Burnam, A. and McEvoy, L. (1991) 'Alcohol abuse and dependence', in: L.N. Robins and D.A. Regier (eds) *Psychiatric Disorders in America: The Epidemiological Catchment Area Study*, New York: Free Press, pp. 81–115.

Helzer, J.E. and Pryzbeck, T.R. (1988) 'The co-occurrence of alcoholism with other psychiatric disorders in the general population and its impact on treatment', *Journal of Studies on Alcohol* 49: 219–24.

Jarvis, T.J. (1992) 'Implications of gender for alcohol treatment research: a quantitative and qualitative review', *British Journal of Addiction* 87: 1249–61.

Jenkins, R., Bebbington, P., Brugha, T.S., Farrell, M., Lewis, G. and Meltzer, H. (1998) 'British Psychiatric Morbidity Survey', *British Journal of Psychiatry* 173: 4–7.

Jones, M.C. (1971) 'Personality antecedents and correlates of drinking patterns in women', *Journal of Consulting and Clinical Psychology* 36: 61–9.

Kendler, K.S. and Prescott, L.A. (1998) 'Cocaine use, abuse and dependence in a population-based sample of female twins', *British Journal of Psychiatry* 173: 345–50.

Kendler, K.S., Neale, M.C., Prescott, C.A., Kessler, R.C., Heath, A.C., Corey, L.A. and Eaves, L.J. (1996) 'Childhood parental loss and alcoholism in women: a causal analysis using a twin-family design. *Psychological Medicine* 26: 79–95.

Kendler, K.S., Heath, A.C., Neale, M.C., Kessler, R.C. and Eaves, L.J. (1992) 'A population based twin study of alcoholism in women', *JAMA* 268: 1877–82.

Khantzian, E.J. and Treece, C. (1988) 'DSM-III psychiatric diagnosis of narcotic addicts', *Archives of General Psychiatry* 42: 1067–71.

Khantzian, E.J. (1985) 'The self-medication hypothesis of addictive disorders: focus on heroin and cocaine dependence', *American Journal of Psychiatry* 142: 1259–64.

Klee, H. (1993) 'HIV risks for women drug injectors: heroin and amphetamine users compared', *Addiction* 88: 1055–62.

Lewis, C.E., Smith, E., Kercher, C. and Spitznagel, E. (1995) Assessing gender interactions in the prediction of mortality in alcoholic men and women: a 20 year follow-up study', *Alcoholism: Clinical and Experimental Research* 19: 1162–72.

Lindberg, S. and Agren, G. (1988) 'Mortality among male and female hospitalised alcoholics in Stockholm 1962–1983', *British Journal of Addiction* 83: 1193–200.

Longnecker, M.P., Berlin, J.A., Orza, M.J. and Chalmers, T.C. (1988) 'A meta-analysis of alcohol consumption in relation to risk of breast cancer', *JAMA* 260: 652–6.

Martin, S.L., English, K.T., Andersen Clark K., Cilenti, D. and Kupper, L.L. (1996) 'Violence and substance use among North Carolina pregnant women', *American Journal of Public Health* 86: 991–8.

Meltzer, H., Gill, B., Petticrew, M. and Hinds, K. (1995) OPCS Surveys of Psychiatric Morbidity in Great Britain – Report I: *The Prevalence of Psychiatric Morbidity Among Adults Living in Private Households*, London: HMSO.

Merikangas, K.R. (1990) 'The genetic epidemiology of alcoholism', *Psychological Medicine* 20: 11–22.

Nace, E.P., Saxon, J.J. and Shore, N. *et al.* (1986) 'Borderline personality disorder and alcoholism treatment: a one-year follow-up study', *Journal of Studies on Alcohol* 47: 196–200.

Office for National Statistics (1997) *Living in Britain. Preliminary Results from the 1996 General Household Survey*, London: Office for National Statistics.

Plant, M. (1997) *Women and Alcohol: Contemporary and Historical Perspectives*, London: Free Association Books.

Prescott, C., Neale, M.C., Corey, L.A. and Kendler, K.S. (1997) 'Predictors of problem drinking and alcohol dependence in a population-based sample of female twins', *Journal of Studies on Alcohol* 58: 167–81.

Reed, B.G. (1987) 'Developing women-sensitive drug dependence treatment services: why so difficult?', *Journal of Psychoactive Drugs* 19: 151–64.

Ross, H. and Shirley, M. (1997) 'Life-time problem drinking and psychiatric co-morbidity among Ontario women', *Addiction* 92: 183–96.

Ross, H.E., Glaser, F.B. and Stiasny, S. (1988) 'Sex differences in the prevalence of psychiatric disorders in patients with alcohol and drug problems', *British Journal of Addiction* 83: 1179–92.

Rounsaville, B.J., Dolinsky, Z.S., Babor, T.F. and Meyer, R.E. (1987) 'Psychopathology as a predictor of treatment outcome in alcoholics', *Archives of General Psychiatry* 44: 505–13.

Rounsaville, B.J. and Kleber, H.D. (1985) 'Untreated opiate addicts: how do they differ from those seeking treatment?', *Archives of General Psychiatry* 42: 1072–7.

Rounsaville, B.J., Tierney, T., Crits-Christoph, K., Weissman, M.M. and Kleber, H.D. (1982) 'Predictors of outcome in treatment of opiate addicts', *Comprehensive Psychiatry* 23: 462–78.

Sanchez-Craig, M., Leigh, G., Spivak, K. and Lei, H. (1989) 'Superior outcome of females over males after brief treatment for the reduction of heavy drinking', *British Journal of Addiction* 84: 395–404.

Schuckit, M.A., Jayson, E.T., Anthenelli, R.M., Bucholz, K.K., Hesselbrock, V.M. and Nurnberger, J.I. (1996) 'Anorexia nervosa and bulimia nervosa in alcohol dependent men and women and their relatives', *American Journal of Psychiatry* 153: 74–82.

Smith, E.M., Cloninger, C.R. and Bradford, S. (1983) 'Predictors of mortality in alcoholic women: a prospective follow-up study', *Alcoholism: Clinical and Experimental Research* 7: 237–43.

Swift, W. and Copeland, J. (1996) 'Treatment needs and experiences of Australian women with alcohol and other drug problems', *Drug and Alcohol Dependence* 40: 211–19.

Swift, W., Copeland, J. and Hall, W. (1996) 'Characteristics of women with alcohol and other drug problems: findings of an Australian national survey', *Addiction* 91(8): 1141–50.

Thom, B. (1986) 'Sex differences in help-seeking for alcohol problems. I: The barriers to help seeking', *British Journal of Addiction* 81: 777–88.

Thomas, M., Walker, A., Wilmot, A. and Bennett, B. (1998) *Living in Britain – Results from the 1996 General Household Survey*, London: Office for National Statistics.

Vaglum, S. and Vaglum, P. (1985) 'Borderline and other mental disorders in alcoholic female psychiatric patients: a case control study', *Psychopathology* 18: 50–60.

Vannicelli, M. and Nash, L. (1984) 'Effect of sex bias on women's studies on alcoholism', *Alcoholism: Clinical and Experimental Research* 8: 334–6.

Walitzer, K.S. and Sher, J.K. (1996) 'A perspective of self-esteem and alcohol use disorders in early adulthood: evidence for gender differences', *Alcoholism: Clinical and Experimental Research* 20: 1118–24.

Wilsnack, S.C. and Wilsnack, R.W. (1995) 'Drinking and problem drinking in US women', in: M. Galanter (ed.) *Recent Developments in Alcoholism*, vol 12, New York: Plenum Press.

Wilsnack, S.C., Wilsnack, R.W. and Hiller-Sturmhofel, S. (1994) 'How women drink. Epidemiology of women's drinking and problem drinking', *Alcohol Health and Research World* 18: 173–84.

Wilsnack, S.C., Klassen, A.D. and Schur, B.E. *et al.* (1991) 'Predicting onset and chronicity of women's problem drinking: a five year longitudinal analysis', *American Journal of Public Health* 81: 305–18.

Winfield, I., George, L.K., Swartz, M. and Blazer, D.G. (1990) 'Sexual assault and psychiatric disorders among a community sample of women', *American Journal of Psychiatry* 147: 335–41.

Chapter 10

Psychiatric services for women

Dora Kohen

In the last decades the National Health Service in the UK and the mental health system in the the whole world have undergone radical changes. The philosophy of psychiatric care has changed to embrace a more humane, democratic, flexible and indepth understanding of psychiatric problems. Several issues which were known to be taboo have come to the forefront of the ideological debate.

Changes in the philosophy of mental health have been mainly reflected in the provision of care. Care in the community generally has brought a better understanding of the problems, and more insightful solutions to individual patients' care. There has been a welcome expansion in the number of professionals and in non-professional voluntary bodies involved in the care of the individual. This expansion has brought non-statutory bodies as well as the media into the arguments and debates around health in general and mental health in particular and has served to improve the provision of care.

More recently mental illness has been in the forefront of the news and 'aggressive behaviour' and 'dangerousness' has gained immense attention from all. The media representation of the 'seriously mentally ill' and offending behaviour has led to the development of services targeting a predominantly male population. This has led to a different hierarchy of those deserving to receive specialist psychiatric interventions with the quiet 'non-dangerous' female psychiatric population partly left behind.

The era of 'Care in the community' has found a large number of neglected female psychiatric patients trying to fit into male-designated services.

It is in recent years that the debate about the specific needs of female psychiatric patients has been more directly addressed.

Although segregation of services and fragmentation of adult services is quite undesirable, it is now well accepted that there is a need for gender-specific services in every subspecialty of psychiatry. The model should be a community care model with primary care, and community systems backed up by inpatient psychiatric beds when necessary.

It has been accepted that comprehensive mental health services for women should be based on the collaboration of well integrated, tiered services ranging from local self-help and voluntary groups to community facilities attached to general practice surgeries. Community mental health teams or specialized rehabilitation teams should be closely linked to inpatient and outpatient statutory services, the different departments of social services and secondary and tertiary care providers. Mental health services are comprehensive when they can recognize the psychological and psychiatric problems of the members of the local community and can meet these needs with sensitivity before they become crisis.

With the growing input of local voluntary organizations, self-help groups, patients' councils and others, the system has become quite inclusive. Now the need is for the NHS to plan and guide in a responsive manner.

The voluntary sector has been sensitive to women's needs. It has offered treatment by communication and support in the form of listening, encouraging and helping to resolve conflicts. While it will be more difficult and sometimes impossible for the voluntary sector to offer services for the acutely ill, it can offer formal and informal community support and social and psychological input for women with personal, social and psychological problems. It can increase personal sensitivity to respond to specific local needs.

There has been a large number of official or non-governmental publications and reports on local, regional and nationwide services introducing their novel views, successful practices and sometimes sharing their concerns. One of them is the Joseph Rowntree Foundation which has published Findings on Social Care Research in 1994. They found that services usually ignored particular needs of women users. The report identified innovative projects and characteristics of good practice; 250 projects have been included in their database. The findings show that the services which were nominated were small, voluntary projects with limited mainstream funding. The majority of services dealt with child-related needs such as mother-and-baby groups, and help with postnatal depression. They have noted crisis services that respond to the needs of women in emotional distress. Some of them focus on specific problems such as self-injury, eating disorders such as bulimia, sexual abuse, physical abuse and domestic violence. They described individual one-to-one and support groups including informal self-awareness groups and information and practical help.

There are a large number of such local groups all over the UK, but it is difficult to keep an updated directory. There is very little centralization or uniformity of services. It would be very useful to have inclusive and comprehensive information on the functioning of local groups and to allow for the experiences to be shared and problems resolved.

SERVICES FOR WOMEN WITH SEVERE, ENDURING MENTAL ILLNESS

These provide services for women with a diagnosis of severe mental illness who have had several admissions to acute psychiatric wards with a long list of social problems, including isolation, neglect, homelessness and inability to cope with the demands of daily routine. This group includes women who are patients with long-term illness, and who have problems around social competence and overdependence on services.

Specific service provision for older women, young adults and ethnic minority women is limited and is in need of improvement. Perkins and Rowland (1991) have highlighted the limitations in research concerning female patients and their service usage, and found services unresponsive to older women. Patel et al. (1994) in their opinion survey found that the majority of women did not feel they were admitted to facilities appropriate to their needs. Ideally these services should include gender-specific inpatient facilities, treatment options tailored for women's needs, including pharmacotherapy, family assessment, parenting groups, women's groups and cognitive behavioural interventions. Motherhood and schizophrenia, pregnancy, breastfeeding while on neuroleptics, old age issues are all contentious and need to be highlighted (Seeman and Cohen, 1998).

The acute psychiatric ward and the mentally ill woman

With the civil liberties movement of the 1960s and community care as a progressive philosophy, long-stay hospitals were closed and patients from the community were admitted to mixed acute psychiatric wards in district general hospitals. Mixed ward environment was found to be distressful and demanding for women. On the one side there was the woman sexually, physically and emotionally abused by fellow inpatients. On the other side there were the constant verbal threats, noise and demands that can put quite a lot of pressure on severely ill women under the effects of sedating neuroleptic treatment. Lack of privacy and lack of sensitivity to women's needs added to the distress of female inpatients.

These problems have found several platforms of discussion in the last decade. The NHS has been looking into the feasibility of single-sex inpatient facilities for women. In 1999 hospitals have been instructed to take the gender issue into account and to organize female-only facilities at every level of inpatient treatment. One such facility has been running since the beginning of 1996 in East London. It is an acute psychiatric service for women and it has been shown to be one of the ways forward (Kohen, 1997; Kohen, 1999). This acute psychiatric ward that only admits women patients with severe mental illness has been popular with ethnic minorities, pregnant women and first-episode psychosis where a lot of adjustment needs to take place in the family. The over-50 psychiatric patient who finds it hard to cope with the demands of young psychotic men has used this single-sex ward successfully. An audit of quality of life and patient satisfaction has shown that patients and voluntary organizations have given overwhelming support to the service. This service has generated discussion around gender and manpower, ward environment and therapies for female inpatients. Advantages of mixed wards, including the understanding that they reflect the real world, have been put forward as an argument in their favour. The discussions have been important in further raising awareness of the issues around gender and acute psychiatric admissions.

The single-sex ward in East London has been a starting model for many districts who are now in the process of establishing similar acute wards. It is hoped that the severely mentally ill woman will be able to have the choice between a single-sex and mixed-admission ward and longitudinal practice will give a better idea of further specific needs.

Psychiatric intensive care units (PICU) and women

It is well known that only 20–30 per cent of all patients in PICU are women and there are instances where there may be only one or two female patients in a PICU of 10–15 males. This situation is known to cause a lot of distress to the heavily sedated psychiatric female patient who remains almost defenceless in a demanding environment. Now there are several changes being brought to this service, including more female nurses, women-only areas and women's groups addressing specific day-to-day issues in male-dominated services.

Rehabilitation services for severely mentally ill women

Rehabilitation provisions in the community have been established to look into the social, behavioural and psychiatric needs of the patient body without specific gender sensitivity. But now community services have been able to adjust themselves to local requirements and have followed the trend to offer gender specific services. It is quite rewarding to see that those services now have regular women's groups looking into female issues and setting the pace for future need-oriented provisions.

Specific inpatient and community services for women with learning disabilities and psychiatric problems are vital for this vulnerable group. Although the numbers are decreasing by the day, there are still some single-sex long-term wards in mental handicap hospitals established at the turn of the century and now earmarked for closure. For some patients, these old-fashioned, segregated and institutional wards still serve the desirable purpose of privacy.

Residential services for people with learning disabilities in the community are relatively new. Most of them do take into consideration recent guidelines and provide for women-only activities, appropriate single-sex facilities and mixed provisions as necessary.

PERINATAL PSYCHIATRIC SERVICES

Pregnancy related psychiatric services have not had the high profile they deserve although the prevalence of patients with postnatal depression and puerperal psychosis that need psychiatric input is well established. It is known that all women with postnatal depression and postpartum psychosis will need specialist services in the community and a small percentage will need admission facilities into acute psychiatric services.

The spectrum of psychiatric disorders during pregnancy and after delivery shows that we need a multitude of services to provide for this very specific population with an increased need for psychiatric input. Although the term postpartum depression is well established, it is an undisputed fact that depression may start in the early weeks of pregnancy and the woman may need input from community services to support her throughout the pregnancy and the postpartum period. Established specialist multidisciplinary teams and community psychiatric nurses with an interest in perinatal psychiatry attached to CMHT (community mental health teams), the perinatal psychiatric services or outreach perinatal provisions serve this purpose.

Community services should be there to assess prenatal and postnatal depression and to review the woman with a previous diagnosis of severe mental illness who has become pregnant. Staff should be trained and sensitive to the needs of the woman and should have the support of more specialized teams if necessary. General practice surgeries and health visitors should be able to recognize, assess and refer psychiatric problems to the necessary agencies when appropriate.

A wide spectrum of organizations including voluntary bodies, self-help groups, local women's groups and ethnic minority women's agencies should be included in the list. Community organizations should have access to locality mental health teams and CPN services to refer women who may need additional professional psychiatric input. A further step should be specialized outpatient services where general practitioners can refer their patients for assessment and treatment. General practitioners together with their health visitor teams and other professional groups involved in the system always appreciate information on the novel treatment and management of perinatal psychiatric disorders.

Self-help and voluntary organizations are a valid way of supporting women with perinatal psychological problems and their
benefits increase immensely when they have close links with the
statutory services and are able to link with health service facilities
when necessary.

Obstetric liaison services

Antenatal clinics are services where prenatal psychiatric problems
can be recognized. Brockington (1996) has an up-to-date summary
of liaison work with antenatal obstetric clinics where antenatal
psychological problems were detected, assessed and referred to
relevant agencies.

MOTHER–BABY ADMISSION UNITS

Mother-and-baby units (MBU) are appropriate psychiatric admission facilities for women with psychiatric problems and their babies
up to 6 months to one year of age. The first national survey conducted in 1985–6 by Aston and Thomas in an unpublished report
showed that there were 294 MBU beds which amounted to 6 bed/
million. In the report by Prettyman and Friedman in 1991, there
was a reduction of beds by almost half to 133 which amounted to 2
bed/million population. This represents a reduction by half of the
beds within 5 years. This real reduction was due to the closure of
MBU beds in the Midlands. We now know that most probably
there has been a small increase in beds in some inner city districts
such as East London and in Wales but it is difficult to state the exact
number of MBU beds today.

In 1991 the above survey showed that of 201 districts 19 per cent
had dedicated facilities for mentally ill mothers and their babies; 48
per cent reported that mothers with babies were admitted to acute
psychiatric wards while 27 per cent used facilities in other districts;
10 per cent of all the districts reported that they had no facilities.
At the time there was a general acknowledgement of the importance of providing a psychiatric mother-and-baby facility of some
sort. (Prettyman and Friedman, 1991).

Today the importance of inpatient mother-and-baby facilities for
the severely mentally ill women who are ready to look after the

newborn is well recognized. But it is also the case that the majority of women with perinatal psychiatric problems are supported in the community. It is well understood that a pregnant or postpartum woman would very much benefit from being at home and therefore community services should be co-ordinated in such a way that the mother with her baby can be cared for at home. There is no doubt that perinatal psychiatric services are invaluable in identifying, and addressing the specific needs of women at this sensitive period of their lives. Both in North America and Western Europe there is a movement toward specialized services looking at the needs of mothers and the ways of improving their mental health, wellbeing and interaction with their infants (Murray and Cooper, 1997). Now community facilities such as assessment, outreach and domiciliary services and a small number of mother-and-baby beds are well-accepted components of a comprehensive service.

SERVICES FOR WOMEN WITH EATING DISORDERS

The great majority of patients with eating disorders are women and at present eating disorder services are mainly designated for women and their families. There are reliable epidemiological data on levels of morbidity and the needs and treatment responses of the population with eating disorders (Turnbull et al., 1996) but optimal services have not yet been planned. There are models ranging from community-oriented district services to more centralized and specialized services for patients at the extreme end of the spectrum.

The Royal College of Psychiatrists Council Report (1992) recommends consultant-led local services together with appropriate non-medical support to be established across the country. A multidimensional assessment should include input from therapists, dietitians and physical and psychiatric assessment by medical staff. There has been an escalation in the number of referrals over the years into the eating disorder services and most of these patients have had additional psychiatric problems requiring active intervention (Surgenor and Fear, 1996).

There has been an increase in eating disorder services in the UK in the last decade. Today registrations show that there are 38 NHS centres and 24 private facilities specializing in eating disorders. Millar (1998) describes his specialist out-patient-based eating disorder services as a model for future assessment and treatment units.

Despite the severity and the cost of treatment for eating disorders, especially anorexia nervosa, there are no guidelines to steer service planning and purchasing activities. Up to very recently, issues around core services have not been negotiated in detail. Evidence on efficacy and cost effectiveness of eating disorder services should be taken into consideration when planning future services.

ALCOHOL AND DRUG REHABILITATION PROGRAMMES FOR WOMEN

There are fewer women than men in the alcohol and drug abuse scene and therefore fewer, if any, services are specifically oriented to women users. There is evidence to demonstrate that, while there is a continuing underrepresentation of women in alcohol treatment services, if the appropriate climate and environment were created, the percentage of women using the services would increase. Copeland and Hall (1992) have discussed that women-only facilities may help women who might not otherwise have agreed to treatment in substance abuse.

Current services for alcohol and drug abuse include primary care, inpatient care such as general, specialist and private care, outpatient care, community-based teams, voluntary agencies and self-help organizations. Multidisciplinary community drug and alcohol teams are intended to work with general practitioners but now they are involved in the delivery of care in the form of advice, information and outpatient detoxification (Davison and Marshall, 1991).

Women drugs users have been surveyed in London (Hunter and Judd, 1998). This survey shows that in London there seems to be a good understanding of community-based drug services, drug dependency units, community drug teams, residential rehabilitation centres and residential detoxification groups and needle exchange programmes. A number of women injectors in London seem to have regular contact with generic services. Primary care services and drug agencies alike have been successful in attracting female injectors. It is also known that some residential services for women with drug and alcohol problems and their children have responded to specific needs and have resulted in successful outcomes.

Addicted women who become pregnant and go into labour have caused an increase in the number of legal and medical problems for the maternity services. The follow-up of addicted mothers with their newborn babies has been resolved by the collaboration of social services and drug and alcohol services. Now residential care for drug addicts and their children and substance rehabilitation programmes are valid models used around the UK.

In the US there have been many programmes assessing the treatment utilization or non-utilization of substance abuse services by pregnant women. Pregnant women who utilized services were found to have had past treatment for substance abuse and to have experienced physical and/or sexual violence during pregnancy (Messer et al., 1996).

Dawe et al. (1992) describe a service for pregnant opiate addicts where a key worker from the community drug team identifies needs and facilitates collaboration between the woman's social, medical, psychiatric and paediatric workers. But the need for services for perinatal women with substance abuse and severe mental health disorders is still unmet. The interaction of pregnancy, addiction and mental illness creates complex needs that often go unrecognized by treatment providers. Services currently available for the dually diagnosed are typically fragmented and unco-ordinated, and provision of those services is often hampered by philosophical differences, difficulties in funding and lack of central administration. Integration of different levels of treatment and different services are necessary for the dually diagnosed women (Grella, 1997).

The most important approach in managing pregnant substance-abusing women is to provide a multidimensional, objective and nonjudgemental service. Detoxification, rehabilitation and ongoing treatments of various intensity are necessary to treat the patient during pregnancy and to maximize the opportunity of success in the postnatal period. The treatment team should include child care, health visitors, community psychiatric workers, social services and specialists in substance abuse and family members.

For any form of programme to be effective, the substance abusing woman should develop full insight into her abuse and should be ready to address her problems. Referrals to self-help and voluntary groups are important steps in initiating recognition and treatment. Substance misuse often appears to be influenced by the family structure and especially by the partner's habits. Therefore partners should be included in all treatment programmes to ensure support and success.

Stigmatization of female drug and alcohol abusers and fear of losing custody of the children may cause women to hide their addiction. Group and individual therapies are helpful in addressing issues of low self-esteem, shame and stigmatization.

FORENSIC PSYCHIATRIC SERVICES FOR WOMEN

Women are known to have much less involvement with the criminal justice system than men. This well established fact together with some epidemiological and psychiatric data have contributed to the understanding that female offenders often have medical and psychiatric problems rather than being hardened criminals (Smith, 1984). A monitoring and screening procedure has been established to divert these mentally disordered offenders from the criminal justice system into the health system. But this procedure has faced at times insurmountable difficulties at the level of implementation. Recent work shows that 14 per cent of women on remand and 14 per cent of sentenced women have been assessed as having a psychotic illness (Home Office, 1977; Fryers et al., 1998). Within the same assessment 75 per cent of women on remand have been shown to have neurotic symptomatology of differing severity (Fryers, 1998). Of these women, 40 per cent have attempted deliberate self-harm at least once prior to being arrested. This suggests that these symptoms have been present before the current situation arose. Of women on remand or sentenced, 31 per cent warranted the diagnosis of antisocial personality disorder (Fryers, 1998). In their case notes and interview study of women serving a prison sentence, Maden et al. (1994) have shown that, as compared to men, women prisoners had higher rates of mental handicap (6 per cent versus 2 per cent), substance abuse (26 per cent versus 12 per cent) and personality disorder (18 per cent versus 10 per cent).

The numbers today show that a high proportion of the female population in prison is psychiatrically very unwell. There may be at least 400 women in prison with recent or current psychotic disorders. There may be several folds of women with neurotic symptoms and personality disorders in the prison system. Mentally disordered offenders have often been rejected by psychiatric services

(Maden, 1996) because they have been perceived as aggressive, violent and difficult to place. They have often been associated with substance abuse, learning difficulties or irreversible organic disorders. Many of these offenders have challenging behaviours which are unacceptable in open ward and hospital conditions. Success in treatment of behavioural problems relies heavily on compliance and collaboration, and most of those offenders do not offer either of them.

Although hospital transfer is reasonably well established for women with psychotic disorders, female inmates with personality disorders, recidivism and substance abuse remain difficult to place and are rejected by the services. Prison managements have tried to establish some quite successful psychological, psychotherapeutic and psychiatric services to serve their female population, but the truth is that the majority of the inmate population remains frustrated and ill-prepared for the demands of the community to which they will return sooner or later.

The psychiatric services for female prisoners should be planned jointly between the prison psychiatric and social services, so that prisoners should spend the shortest possible time in the prison. The prison service will be more effective if it recognizes the expertise of the NHS and works jointly to provide high quality health care (Reed and Lyne, 1997). The needs of female prisoners should not be separated from those of mentally disordered patients in the community.

The Reed Report (1992) addresses the service needs of mentally disordered offenders. It describes the need for specific facilities for female offenders and underlines their special requirements, such as treatment in secure psychiatric units, distances to the local community and the disruption of family ties. Because of the smaller number of female offenders, centralization of services is necessary. The report shows the importance of local medium- or low-security units. Also, facilities should be appropriately designed for women where safety, security and trained staff are provided. It recommends close links between prison medical services and the NHS.

The central principle of the report is that mentally disordered offenders are the responsibility of NHS and social services rather than the criminal justice system. Mentally disordered offenders will benefit from transfer into appropriate NHS facilities if they have a diagnosis of severe enduring mental illness such as schizophrenia. Even when there are close links with the services women with personality disorders, substance abuse and minor psychiatric morbidity tend to remain within the prison population. Therefore the development of appropriate and specific services for this population within the prison system is essential.

Rehabilitation treatment programmes for drug users and alcohol treatment groups are important. Therapeutic communities within the prison system, social help including help to facilitate visits with their children, mother and baby units could improve mentally disordered offenders' conditions in prison.

Diversion schemes from the prison system to psychiatric services and court diversion schemes which assess offenders before sentencing have been quite effective in the appropriate placement of the offender. But the numbers of mentally disordered offenders in prisons are still unacceptably large. There is a need for further local and regional medium secure units and more secure NHS accommodation and community programmes. Whether prison-based or community-based, services that combine the security of the prisons with the mental health care will be the next step in future planning. There is also a need for a central professional team to replace the present local and sometimes fragmented arrangements. The rehabilitation and reintegration services offered women on their discharge into the community should be reviewed regularly to decrease the risk of reoffending.

CONCLUSION

There is a growing need for specific psychiatric services for women. In many areas of psychiatry this need is now recognized and is being addressed quite successfully. But there are some areas that will need further input, discussion and financial support from all agencies involved. The aim is to help women recognize their problems at an early stage and offer relevant, acceptable, accessible and cost-effective treatment and rehabilitation.

Services for women should be sensitive to cultural aspects, ethnic backgrounds, individual orientation and specific local needs. All service planning should involve consultation with service users.

As psychiatric patients, women should feel safe and respected. There should be sufficient female staff involved at all levels of service planning, managing and delivery.

Providing women-only services will have considerable resource implication in terms of staff training and environmental facilities. Systematic evaluation of services and audit of patient satisfaction and of local requirements should help the development of the necessary gender-specific services.

REFERENCES

Aston, A. and Thomas, L. (1986) 'Survey of mother and baby units in England and Wales in 1986', unpublished report.

Brockington, I. (1996) *Motherhood and Mental Health*, Oxford: Oxford University Press.

Copeland, J. and Hall, W. (1992) 'A comparison of women seeking drug and alcohol treatment in a specialist women's and two traditional mixed-sex treatment service', *British Journal of Addiction* 87: 1293–302.

Davison, S. and Marshall, J. (1991) 'Women with drug and alcohol problems', in K. Abel, M. Buszewicz, S. Davison, S. Johnson and E. Staples (eds) *Planning Community Mental Health Services for Women: A Multiprofessional Handbook*, London: Routledge.

Dawe, S., Gerada, C. and Strang, J. (1992) 'Establishment of a liaison service for pregnant opiate-dependent women', *British Journal of Addiction* 87: 867–71.

Dell, S., Robertson, G., James, K. and Grounds, A. (1993a) Remands and Psychiatric Assessment in Holloway Prison 1: The psychotic population, *British Journal of Psychiatry*, 163: 634–40.

Dell, S., Robertson, G., James, K. and Grounds, A. (1993b) 2: The non-psychotic population, *British Journal of Psychiatry* 163: 640–4.

Department of Health and Home Office (1992) *Review of Health and Social Services for Mentally Disordered Offenders and Others Requiring Similar Services*, Final Summary Report Cmnd 2088.

Fryers, T., Brugha, T., Grounds, A. and Melzer, D. (1998) 'Severe mental illness in prisoners', *British Medical Journal* 317: 1025–6.

Grella, C.E. (1997) 'Services for perinatal women with substance abuse and mental health disorders: the unmet need', *Journal of Psychoactive Drugs* 29: 67–78.

HO Statistics of mentally disordered offenders, England and Wales (1996) *Statistical Bulletin 20/97*, London: Home Office, 1997.

Hunter, G. and Judd, A. (1998) 'Women injecting drug users in London: use and views of health services', *Executive Summary* 60: 1–4.

Joseph Rowntree Foundation, Mental Health (1994) Findings, Social Care Research 51.

Kohen, D. (1999) 'Specialised in-patient psychiatric services for women', *Psychiatric Bulletin* 23: 31–3.

Kohen, D. (1997) 'An inner city district with specialized mental health services for women', *Marce Society Bulletin* 9–10.

Maden, T. (1996) *Women, Prisons and Psychiatry: Mental Disorder Behind Bars*, Oxford: Butterworth-Heinemann Ltd.

Maden, T., Swinton, M. and Gunn, J. (1994) 'Psychiatric disorder in women serving a prison sentence', *British Journal of Psychiatry* 164: 44–54.

Messer, K., Clark, K.A. and Martin, S.L. (1996) 'Characteristics associated with pregnant women's utilization of substance abuse treatment services', *American Journal of Drug and Alcohol Abuse* 22: 403–22.

Millar, H.R. (1998) 'New eating disorders service', *Psychiatric Bulletin* 22: 751–4.

Murray, L. and Cooper, P.J. (1997) 'The role of infant and maternal factors, in postpartum depression, mother–infant interactions, and infant outcome', ch. 5, 111–35, in L. Murray and P.J. Cooper (eds) *Postpartum Depression and Child Development*, New York, London: The Guilford Press.

Patel, A., Doshi, M. and Oyebode, F. (1994) 'Mixed sex wards', *Psychiatric Bulletin* 18: 577.

Perkins, R.E. and Rowland, L.A. (1991) 'Sex differences in service usage in long term psychiatric care: are women adequately served?', *British Journal of Psychiatry* 158 (suppl. 10): 75–9.

Prettyman, R.J. and Friedman, T. (1991) 'Care of women with puerperal psychiatric disorders in England and Wales', *British Medical Journal* 302: 1245–6.

Reed, J. and Lyne, M. (1997) 'The quality of health care in prison: results of a year's programme of semistructured inspections', *British Medical Journal* 315: 1420–4.

The Royal College of Psychiatrists (1992) Council Report 14, *Eating Disorders*, CR 14: 1–47.

Seeman, M.V. and Cohen, R. (1998) 'A service for women with schizophrenia', *Psychiatric Services* 49: 674–7.

Smith, R. (1984) *Prison Health Care*, London: British Medical Association.

Surgenor, L.J. and Fear, J.L. (1996) 'Referrals to a comprehensive eating disorders service', *New Zealand Medical Journal* 109: 74–6.

Turnbull, S., Ward, A., Treasure, J., Jick, H. and Derby, L. (1996) 'The demand for eating disorder care: an epidemiological study using the general practice research database', *British Journal of Psychiatry* 169: 705–12.

Index